TWENTIETH CENTURY VIEWS

The aim of this series is to present the best in contemporary critical opinion on major authors, providing a twentieth century perspective on their changing status in an era of profound revaluation.

Maynard Mack, *Series Editor*
Yale University

MILTON

MILTON

A COLLECTION OF CRITICAL ESSAYS

Edited by
Louis L. Martz

Prentice-Hall, Inc. *Englewood Cliffs, N. J.*
A SPECTRUM BOOK

Contents

MILTON

Introduction

by Louis L. Martz

I

The essays in this volume have been chosen and arranged with two aims in mind: first, to represent the basic points of controversy that have troubled and stimulated a huge outpouring of Miltonic criticism during the past thirty or forty years—controversy that has engaged the talents of many of our finest poets, critics, and scholars; and secondly, to provide a commentary from different points of view upon the entire course of Milton's poem. The selections open with two essays that sum up the main aspects of Milton's style and theme that have come under question in our time. T. S. Eliot's urbane piece of iconoclasm touches upon nearly every quality of Milton, man and poet. As a man he is "unsatisfactory" from any point of view, says Eliot; as a poet he is satisfying only because he is the greatest master of "sound" in the language. William Empson's subtler and much more genial essay uses the puzzled rationality of two eighteenth century critics as a guide to the difficulties of the poem, while his witty insight, friendly to Milton's genius, proposes bold solutions to most of the critical problems under discussion. With the studies by Lewis, Rajan, and Prince, we turn to concentrate upon the problems of style dealt with by Eliot and Empson, and long ago discerned by Samuel Johnson in a famous passage quoted by Eliot in his later, more moderate essay on Milton (1947):

Through all his greater works there prevails an uniform peculiarity of *Diction,* a mode and cast of expression which bears little resemblance to that of any former writer, and which is so far removed from common use, that an unlearned reader, when he first opens his book, finds himself surprised by a new language.

This novelty has been, by those who can find nothing wrong in Milton, imputed to his laborious endeavours after words suitable to the grandeur of his ideas. *Our language,* says Addison, *sunk under him.* But the truth is, that, both in prose and verse, he had formed his style by a perverse and pedantick principle. He was desirous to use English words with a foreign idiom. This in all his prose is discovered and condemned; for there judgement operates freely, neither softened by the beauty, nor awed by the dignity of his thoughts; but such is the power of his poetry, that his call is obeyed

1

without resistance, the reader feels himself in captivity to a higher and a nobler mind, and criticism sinks in admiration.

Milton's style was not modified by his subject: what is shown with greater extent in *Paradise Lost,* may be found in *Comus.* One source of his peculiarity was his familiarity with the Tuscan poets: the disposition of his words is, I think, frequently Italian; perhaps sometimes combined with other tongues. Of him, at last, may be said what Jonson says of Spenser, that *he wrote no language,* but has formed what Butler calls a *Babylonish Dialect,* in itself harsh and barbarous, but made by exalted genius and extensive learning, the vehicle of so much instruction and so much pleasure, that, like other lovers, we find grace in its deformity.[1]

Here is the center of the modern controversy over Milton's style, for what Johnson's admiration could excuse, the modern writer has often found impossible to accept. The reasons for this modern dissatisfaction are implied in Eliot's "Note" of 1936, in which his attack is focussed on the "deterioration" of the language to which Milton has allegedly contributed through his "bad influence" upon poetry—"an influence against which we still have to struggle." In his essay of 1947, Eliot made plain the sources of his discontent, which lay in the efforts of Eliot and his contemporaries to effect a revolution in English poetry. As Eliot says, the trouble arose from the fact that Milton seemed to represent "poetry at the extreme limit from prose;"

and it was one of our tenets that verse should have the virtues of prose, that diction should become assimilated to cultivated contemporary speech, before aspiring to the elevation of poetry. Another tenet was that the subject-matter and the imagery of poetry should be extended to topics and objects related to the life of a modern man or woman; that we were to seek the non-poetic, to seek even material refractory to transmutation into poetry, and words and phrases which had not been used in poetry before.

"And the study of Milton," Eliot concludes, "could be of no help: it was only a hindrance" [2]—to the ends that Eliot, Pound, and others had in mind in their revolt against what Edith Sitwell has called "the silvery tintinnabulations of teaspoons left over from the tea-parties of the Victorian Aunts of Poetry." [3]

Part of the trouble, of course, came from the frequent idolatry of Milton among the great Victorians, a viewpoint admirably summed up by Matthew Arnold: ". . . if the discipline of respect for a high and

---

[1] Samuel Johnson, *Lives of the English Poets,* World's Classics ed. (2 vols., London, 1952), I, 131-32.

[2] T. S. Eliot, *On Poetry and Poets* (London: Faber, 1957), p. 160; the version of the 1947 essay in this 1957 volume omits some important pages and notes in the original lecture, which may be found complete in *Proceedings of the British Academy,* vol. 33; in *Sewanee Review,* LVI (1948), 185-209; and in *Milton Criticism,* ed. James Thorpe, New York: Rinehart, 1950.

[3] See her essay in *An Examination of Ezra Pound,* ed. Peter Russell (Norfolk, Conn.: New Directions, 1950), p. 37.

flawless excellence is peculiarly needed by us, Milton is of all our gifted men the best lesson, the most salutary influence. In the sure and flawless perfection of his rhythm and diction he is as admirable as Virgil or Dante. . . . That Milton, of all our English race, is by his diction and rhythm the one artist of the highest rank in the great style whom we have; this I take as requiring no discussion, this I take as certain." [4] In questioning this certainty, in requiring discussion, Eliot's tactic was to make that very "perfection" into a sign of Milton's grave limitations: he was a master of rhythm and diction, yes, but that very mastery seems to have led to "the hypertrophy of the auditory imagination at the expense of the visual and tactile, so that the inner meaning is separated from the surface. . . . I cannot feel," says Eliot, "that my appreciation of Milton leads anywhere outside the mazes of sound," and sometimes, he adds in a devastating aside, "I feel that this is not serious poetry, not poetry fully occupied about its business, but rather a solemn game." [5]

This was a point of view bound to find some sympathy in writers attuned to the poetry of the 1920s and the 1930s, with its use of colloquial idiom, its "sense of particularity," its inclusion of imagery from the common and the local. F. R. Leavis, for example, picked up the attack in a vigorous essay of 1933—three years before the appearance of Eliot's summary "Note," but stimulated by some of Eliot's scattered remarks in earlier essays. The core of Leavis's dissatisfaction lies in what he calls "the hieratic stylization, the swaying ritual movement" in the verse of *Paradise Lost*. Too often, he feels, "the pattern, the stylized gesture and movement, has no particular expressive work to do, but functions by rote, of its own momentum, in the manner of a ritual." The result is "a certain sensuous poverty," a medium of writing "that is incompatible with sharp, concrete realization . . . incompatible with an interest in sensuous particularity." Thus, "cultivating so complete and systematic a callousness to the intrinsic nature of English, Milton forfeits all possibility of subtle or delicate life in his verse." [6]

C. S. Lewis's defense is to accept this description of the style as "ritual" and to see that manner as essential to the poem's epic achievement: the reader "must be made to feel that he is assisting at an august ritual." Sensuous particularity would only break the grand sweep of this movement; generality of image is indispensable to the poem's greatness; a "calculated pomp and grandiosity" is exactly right, for effects of spontaneity and colloquialism would break the essential grandeur and remoteness of the action. The manner of Vergilian and Miltonic epic must

---

[4] Matthew Arnold, *Essays in Criticism, Second Series* (London, 1888), pp. 61-63. See *Milton Criticism,* ed. Thorpe, pp. 373-74.

[5] From the essay reprinted below. In this Introduction quotations from the critics are taken from the essays following, unless otherwise documented.

[6] See Leavis's essay on Milton in *Revaluation* (London: Chatto and Windus, 1936), pp. 45-47, 50, 53; the essay originally appeared in *Scrutiny*, II (September 1933), 123-36.

be "something stylized, remote from conversation, hierophantic." Such a poet "makes his epic a rite so that we may share it; the more ritual it becomes, the more we are elevated to the rank of participants." It is a brilliant defense, full of an essential truth about Milton's epic mode. And yet it may leave us uneasy, with a sense that one aspect of the poem has been polemically exaggerated to the point of making discussion impossible: as Lewis says elsewhere in his book, "Dr. Leavis does not differ from me about the properties of Milton's epic verse. . . . He sees and hates the very same that I see and love." [7] This puts the problem beyond the realm of criticism, into the immeasurable realms of "taste," belief, and unreasoning affection.

But the issues are not so clearly divided. Leavis does not hate Milton, but only disapproves vehemently of certain aspects of his work, and Lewis himself in the pages here reprinted shows his subtle awareness of aspects of Milton's style that cannot be properly comprehended under the term "ritual." For ritual implies a set, unvarying form of words; yet Lewis is willing to praise Milton's use of Latin constructions because they "enable the poet to depart, in some degree," from the "fixed order" of words required by normal English usage, "and thus to drop the ideas into his sentence in any order he chooses." He notes the "subterranean virtue" of the Miltonic simile and describes the way in which Milton frequently works through a "melting down of the ordinary units of speech, this plunge back into something more like the indivisible, flowing quality of immediate experience." He concedes that Milton in his poem speaks of his verse as "unpremeditated," and near the end of this selection Lewis recognizes a degree of overemphasis in his argument: "Thus far of Milton's style on the assumption that it is in fact as remote and artificial as is thought. No part of my defence depends on questioning that assumption, for I think it ought to be remote and artificial. But it would not be honest to suppress my conviction that the degree to which it possesses these qualities has been exaggerated."

One should, then, qualify this emphasis on ritual stylization, the mighty onward impulse of the grand style, by stressing also the intimate, sensuous, "particular" qualities that are inseparably involved with the dominant, characteristic mode of Milton's epic sweep. As Empson says, in one of those remarks that open a volume of possibilities: "Milton aims both at a compact and weighty style, which requires short clauses, and a sustained style with the weight of momentum, which requires long clauses." In dealing with Milton's "fluid grammar," Empson notes the "sliding, sideways, broadening movement, normal to Milton"; and we might also see this movement in the "dissolving-view method of characterization" that he finds in Milton's presentation of Satan, and especially

[7] C. S. Lewis, *A Preface to Paradise Lost* (London: Oxford University Press, 1942), p. 130.

in the "ambivalence of feeling," the subtle, incalculable, far-reaching implications of Milton's epic similes and other images.

Milton's "main business," as Empson says, "was to convey the whole range of feeling inherent in the myth." Thus Milton's imagery conveys "very complex feelings about Paradise," and, we might add, about every other issue and scene in the poem. If his God seems harsh and arbitrary in places, that effect is mitigated by the bounty and goodness of God displayed in his gift of Creation to man, as Watkins argues in his splendid account of Milton's vision of the divine plenitude. If at first Satan seems heroic and admirable as a character, he is at the same time surrounded by the "counterplot" which Hartman explores in his fine commentary on the imagery of the opening books. So it is with the style: the poem is not consistently remote and artificial in its language; it frequently descends to common speech and normal idiom, even in the opening book, where the grand style appears at its grandest:

> O how unlike the place from whence they fell!

> Awake, arise, or be for ever fall'n.
>   They heard, and were abasht, and up they sprung
> Upon the wing, as when men wont to watch
> On duty, sleeping found by whom they dread,
> Rouse and bestir themselves ere well awake.

> Next came one
> Who mourn'd in earnest, when the Captive Ark
> Maim'd his brute Image, head and hands lopt off
> In his own Temple, on the grunsel edge,
> Where he fell flat, and sham'd his Worshipers:

> Soon had his crew
> Op'nd into the Hill a spacious wound
> And dig'd out ribs of Gold. Let none admire
> That riches grow in Hell; that soyle may best
> Deserve the pretious bane.

Such passages, in their relative directness, moderate the remoteness and strangeness of the language elsewhere and serve to keep the poem in contact with the roots of daily English speech in Milton's day and our own. As Rajan notes, the variety of Milton's style in *Paradise Lost* was long ago pointed out by Alexander Pope, in a passage that helps to resolve the modern controversy:

> it should have been observed of Milton, that he is not lavish of his exotic words and phrases every where alike, but employs them much more where the subject is marvellous, vast, and strange, as in the scenes of Heaven, Hell, Chaos, &c., than where it is turned to the natural or agreeable, as in the pictures of paradise, the loves of our first parents, the entertainments of angels,

and the like. In general, this unusual style better serves to awaken our ideas in the descriptions and in the imaging and picturesque parts, than it agrees with the lower sort of narrations, the character of which is simplicity and purity. Milton has several of the latter, where we find not an antiquated, affected, or uncouth word, for some hundred lines together; as in his fifth book, the latter part of the eighth, the former of the tenth and eleventh books, and in the narration of Michael in the twelfth.[8]

Finally, to conclude this discussion of Miltonic style, one should note how the study by F. T. Prince suggests a further significance in Milton's verbal arrangements by showing that Milton's style was not the work of a great and willful "eccentric," but was rather part of a great European tradition in Vergilian imitation, based directly upon Milton's intimate knowledge of Italian poetry. His epic style, in short, is a skillful effort to accomplish in English what the Italians had shown to be possible: to re-create the effects of Vergil in the vernacular tongue. Thus, the very contours of the Miltonic idiom come to have an allusive and metaphorical function: they continually remind us, along with constant allusions to Latin roots and Vergilian phrases, that one of Milton's primary aims is to "translate" the mode of ancient epic into the celebration of a Christian theme. As Prince well says, "Miltonic diction is thus but one aspect of a form of poetry in which everything is unified: matter, meaning, emotion, method. What might appear superficially a mere complexity of ornament, in fact contributes essentially to the structure of the verse, and corresponds to the strength of the 'inspiration,' the poetic emotion."

II

A. J. A. Waldock's chapter introduces, in a modern and very persuasive form, the view of Milton's Satan which has formed the center of a second great area of controversy, already touched upon in Empson's strong sympathy for Satan, and in his statement, "People are by now agreed that Milton partly identified Satan with part of his own mind, and that the result though excellent was a little unintentional." The view that Satan is the real hero of the poem, or that Milton permitted Satan to develop into a character far more appealing than his overt theology could have allowed, arose during the Romantic era, with its rebellion against all established forms of authority and its emphasis upon the cultivation of personality, whether in the author or in one of his characters. It was Blake who made the most extreme and celebrated enunciation of this view, when in *The Marriage of Heaven and Hell* (1793), he declared: "The reason Milton wrote in fetters when he wrote of Angels & God, and at liberty when of Devils & Hell, is because he was a true

---

[8] From the Postscript to the translation of the *Odyssey* (1723) issued under Pope's supervision and in part translated by him; see *Milton Criticism*, ed. Thorpe, p. 349.

Poet and of the Devil's party without knowing it." Then Shelley carried on the paradox in his *Defence of Poetry* (1821):

> Nothing can exceed the energy and magnificence of the character of Satan as expressed in *Paradise Lost*. It is a mistake to suppose that he could ever have been intended for the popular personification of evil. . . . Milton's Devil as a moral being is as far superior to his God, as one who perseveres in some purpose which he has conceived to be excellent in spite of adversity and torture, is to one who in the cold security of undoubted triumph inflicts the most horrible revenge upon his enemy, not from any mistaken notion of inducing him to repent of a perseverance in enmity, but with the alleged design of exasperating him to deserve new torments. Milton has so far violated the popular creed (if this shall be judged to be a violation) as to have alleged no superiority of moral virtue to his god over his devil. And this bold neglect of a direct moral purpose is the most decisive proof of the supremacy of Milton's genius.

That this argument is still very much alive, Empson shows in his latest study, *Milton's God*,[9] which expands this paradox in great detail.

Perhaps the most eloquent and balanced utterance of the Romantic view has been given by William Hazlitt, whose words deserve to be quoted at length, for they reveal both the strength and the limitations of this view:

> Satan is the most heroic subject that was ever chosen for a poem; and the execution is as perfect as the design is lofty. He was the first of created beings, who, for endeavouring to be equal with the highest, and to divide the empire of heaven with the Almighty, was hurled down to hell. His aim was no less than the throne of the universe; his means, myriads of angelic armies bright, the third part of the heavens, whom he lured after him with his countenance, and who durst defy the Omnipotent in arms. His ambition was the greatest, and his punishment was the greatest; but not so his despair, for his fortitude was as great as his sufferings. His strength of mind was matchless as his strength of body; the vastness of his designs did not surpass the firm, inflexible determination with which he submitted to his irreversible doom, and final loss of all hope. His power of action and of suffering was equal. He was the greatest power that was ever overthrown, with the strongest will left to resist or to endure. He was baffled, not confounded. He still stood like a tower; or

>   . . . As when Heaven's fire
> Hath scathed the forest oaks or mountain pines:

> He was still surrounded with hosts of rebel angels, armed warriors, who own him as their sovereign leader, and with whose fate he sympathises as he views them round, far as the eye can reach; though he keeps aloof from them in his own mind, and holds supreme counsel only with his own breast. An outcast from Heaven, Hell trembles beneath his feet, Sin and Death are at his heels, and mankind are his easy prey.

[9] London, Chatto and Windus, 1961.

> All is not lost; th' unconquerable will,
> And study of revenge, immortal hate,
> And courage never to submit or yield,
> And what else is not to be overcome,

are still his. The sense of his punishment seems lost in the magnitude of it; the fierceness of tormenting flames is qualified and made innoxious by the greater fierceness of his pride; the loss of infinite happiness to himself is compensated in thought, by the power of inflicting infinite misery on others. Yet Satan is not the principle of malignity, or of the abstract love of evil— but of the abstract love of power, of pride, of self-will personified, to which last principle all other good and evil, and even his own, are subordinate. From this principle he never once flinches. His love of power and contempt for suffering are never once relaxed from the highest pitch of intensity. His thoughts burn like a hell within him; but the power of thought holds dominion in his mind over every other consideration. The consciousness of a determined purpose, of "that intellectual being, those thoughts that wander through eternity," though accompanied with endless pain, he prefers to nonentity, to "being swallowed up and lost in the wide womb of uncreated night." He expresses the sum and substance of all ambition in one line. "Fallen cherub, to be weak is miserable, doing or suffering!" After such a conflict as his, and such a defeat, to retreat in order, to rally, to make terms, to exist at all, is something; but he does more than this—he founds a new empire in hell, and from it conquers this new world, whither he bends his undaunted flight, forcing his way through nether and surrounding fires. The poet has not in all this given us a mere shadowy outline; the strength is equal to the magnitude of the conception. The Achilles of Homer is not more distinct; the Titans were not more vast; Prometheus chained to his rock was not a more terrific example of suffering and of crime. Wherever the figure of Satan is introduced, whether he walks or flies, "rising aloft incumbent on the dusky air," it is illustrated with the most striking and appropriate images: so that we see it always before us, gigantic, irregular, portentous, uneasy, and disturbed—but dazzling in its faded splendour, the clouded ruins of a god. The deformity of Satan is only in the depravity of his will; he has no bodily deformity to excite our loathing or disgust. The horns and tail are not there, poor emblems of the unbending, unconquered spirit, of the writhing agonies within. Milton was too magnanimous and open an antagonist to support his argument by the bye-tricks of a hump and cloven foot. . . . He relied on the justice of his cause, and did not scruple to give the devil his due. Some persons may think that he has carried his liberality too far, and injured the cause he professed to espouse by making him the chief person in his poem. Considering the nature of his subject, he would be equally in danger of running into this fault, from his faith in religion, and his love of rebellion; and perhaps each of these motives had its full share in determining the choice of his subject.[10]

Hazlitt and Waldock together, I think, suggest that this interpretation arises from reading with an excessive emphasis upon Satan as actor and

[10] William Hazlitt, "On Shakspeare and Milton," in *Lectures on the English Poets* (London, 1818), pp. 124-28. See *Milton Criticism*, ed. Thorpe, pp. 107-9.

speaker—as dramatic or novelistic "character" read without the compensations and qualifications provided by other aspects of the poetry. Waldock, to be sure, is aware that the poet's voice in the opening books frequently warns the reader not to take Satan at face value. But Waldock regards these warnings simply as unfair treatment of a character that has fortunately developed beyond the range of Milton's strict theological intentions: the poet's voice, for Waldock, is a kind of censor, trying to blot out these attractive indecencies that have escaped from the uncontrollable subconscious of the unwilling author.

Geoffrey Hartman's essay shows a fallacy in this point of view, by reminding us that it is not only the poet's overt voice that condemns Satan, but also an extensive range of image and allusion that accompanies Satan throughout the first four books. Satan does not stand alone: as he speaks we are reminded of the abominations of Moloch and Chemos and the other pagan deities, devils in disguise; and at the same time the fresh and radiant imagery of Creation suggests that more is at work in the universe than Satan's will. The creative, redemptive power of God is suggested in the similes, preparing the way for the greater manifestation of God's creative power that occurs in the middle books. Douglas Bush, taking another standpoint, argues effectively that the Satanist view stems in large part from our loss of the world of value that Milton inhabited; without an understanding of what reason meant to Milton, the entire poem is thrown out of focus and irreparably damaged. And finally, W. B. C. Watkins offers what is perhaps the most effective of all answers to the Satanist heresy by directing attention to the middle books, with their vital manifestation of divine creativity and fertility, a power against which the efforts of Satan come to appear barren and futile, however much they may have appealed to readers in the opening books. The loss of that earlier appeal is perceptively studied by Arnold Stein, in his lively view of the War in Heaven as deliberate parody and comedy.

In these middle books of the poem (4-8), as I have argued in *The Paradise Within*[11] Milton may be said to have reached an essential goal of his poem's journey; for his theme is not simply the loss of Paradise: it is also, as his opening prologue implies, the potential recovery of Paradise, the restoration of Eden by which the ways of God to men may be found just:

> Of Mans First Disobedience, and the Fruit
> Of that Forbidden Tree, whose mortal tast
> Brought Death into the World, and all our woe,
> With loss of *Eden,* till one greater Man
> Restore us, and regain the blissful Seat,
> Sing Heav'nly Muse, that on the secret top
> Of *Oreb,* or of *Sinai,* didst inspire
> That Shepherd, who first taught the chosen Seed,
> In the Beginning how the Heav'ns and the Earth
> Rose out of *Chaos* . . .

[11] New Haven, Yale University Press, 1964.

". . . loss of *Eden, till one greater* Man/Restore us:" these words do not refer only to the ultimate resurrection of the good; that recovery, in some measure, is even now witnessed by the poet, as he prays for the same inspiration of the Spirit that was given to the shepherd who *first* taught the chosen seed. We shall, as the poem proceeds, see heaven and earth once again rise out of chaos, through the imagination of the poet who has been granted this gift of interior recovery.

It is curious that Milton, in the prose argument "procured" by the printer after the first issue of the poem had appeared, should say: "The first Book proposes first in brief the whole Subject, *Mans disobedience, and the loss thereupon of Paradise wherein he was plac't . . .* ," for the whole poem makes it plain that "loss" is not by any means the "whole Subject." Tillyard's account of the action of recovery in Books 9 and 10 shows that the process of man's restoration through grace is an indispensable part of Milton's subject. As the vision of the poet recovers the meaning of Paradise in the middle books, so Adam and Eve at the close of Book 10 recover that inward Paradise in their humility, their penitence, their gratitude, and, above all, in their restored love of each other and of God. A further demonstration of this principle of restoration is, as Joseph Summers shows, the expressed aim of the last two books; and Summers makes out a nearly convincing case for Milton's success in this final aim. But something goes wrong, I believe, in these closing books: the poetry flags, the vision of redemption wanes, a harsh and bitter tone gradually replaces the buoyant voice of the bard who has guided us through most of the poem: Michael's narration in Book 12 does not provide the evidence of God's bounty that Raphael had demonstrated in his beautiful account of the Six Days of Creation. Milton seems somehow to have lost touch with the creative center of his design.

It is probably fruitless to conjecture why this failure of poetic energy (as it seems to me) should have occurred at the poem's close. But perhaps a reason may be discerned in Samuel Johnson's account of Milton's genius:

> The appearances of nature, and the occurrences of life, did not satiate his appetite of greatness. To paint things as they are, requires a minute attention, and employs the memory rather than the fancy. Milton's delight was to sport in the wide regions of possibility; reality was a scene too narrow for his mind. He sent his faculties out upon discovery, into worlds where only imagination can travel, and delighted to form new modes of existence, and furnish sentiment and action to superior beings, to trace the counsels of hell, or accompany the choirs of heaven.[12]

That is to say, Milton's imagination flourished in the realm of the ideal —when his powers were working to represent the principle of proud rebellion, the essential attributes of unfallen humanity, the pristine har-

[12] *Lives of the English Poets,* World's Classics ed. (1952), I, 123.

mony and purity of the newly created universe, or the motions of penitence and love in the recovery of our first parents after the Fall. But when struggling with the fierce contradictions of contemporary theological debate, he produced the harsh tone of his unattractive Deity; and when faced in the closing books with the lamentable history of mankind, his hope found refuge in austere assertions of providence. That man could be redeemed, could show to a fit audience, however few, the power of redemption at work; that the divine power of creation in man and God remained vital, for all the destructive acts of evil—these are the regions of possibility toward which his great poem bends its flight. His finest powers sought new modes of existence, or, as Hart Crane said of his own poetic hopes, "New thresholds, new anatomies!"

> to travel in a tear
> Sparkling alone, within another's will.

A Note on the Verse
of John Milton

by *T. S. Eliot*

While it must be admitted that Milton is a very great poet indeed, it is something of a puzzle to decide in what his greatness consists. On analysis, the marks against him appear both more numerous and more significant than the marks to his credit. As a man, he is antipathetic. Either from the moralist's point of view, or from the theologian's point of view, or from the psychologist's point of view, or from that of the political philosopher, or judging by the ordinary standards of likeableness in human beings, Milton is unsatisfactory. The doubts which I have to express about him are more serious than these. His greatness as a poet has been sufficiently celebrated, though I think largely for the wrong reasons, and without the proper reservations. His misdeeds as a poet have been called attention to, as by Mr. Ezra Pound, but usually in passing. What seems to me necessary is to assert at the same time his greatness—in that what he could do well he did better than any one else has ever done—and the serious charges to be made against him, in respect of the deterioration—the peculiar kind of deterioration—to which he subjected the language.

Many people will agree that a man may be a great artist, and yet have a bad influence. There is more of Milton's influence in the badness of the bad verse of the eighteenth century than of anybody's else: he certainly did more harm than Dryden and Pope, and perhaps a good deal of the obloquy which has fallen on these two poets, especially the latter, because of their influence, ought to be transferred to Milton. But to put the matter simply in terms of 'bad influence' is not necessarily to bring a serious charge: because a good deal of the responsibility, when we state the problem in these terms, may devolve on the eighteenth-century poets themselves for being such bad poets that they were incapable of being influenced except for ill. There is a good deal more to the charge against Milton than this; and it appears a good deal more serious if we affirm

"A Note on the Verse of John Milton." Originally published in *Essays and Studies by Members of the English Association*, XXI (1936), 32-40. Reprinted as "Milton I" in *On Poetry and Poets* by T. S. Eliot, New York, London. Copyright © 1957 by T. S. Eliot. Reprinted by permission of Farrar, Straus & Giroux, Inc. and Faber and Faber Ltd.

that Milton's poetry could *only* be an influence for the worse, upon any poet whatever. It is more serious, also, if we affirm that Milton's bad influence may be traced much farther than the eighteenth century, and much farther than upon bad poets: if we say that it was an influence against which we still have to struggle.

There is a large class of persons, including some who appear in print as critics, who regard any censure upon a 'great' poet as a breach of the peace, as an act of wanton iconoclasm, or even hoodlumism. The kind of derogatory criticism that I have to make upon Milton is not intended for such persons, who cannot understand that it is more important, in some vital respects, to be a *good* poet than to be a *great* poet; and of what I have to say I consider that the only jury of judgment is that of the ablest poetical practitioners of my own time.

The most important fact about Milton, for my purpose, is his blindness. I do not mean that to go blind in middle life is itself enough to determine the whole nature of a man's poetry. Blindness must be considered in conjunction with Milton's personality and character, and the peculiar education which he received. It must also be considered in connexion with his devotion to, and expertness in, the art of music. Had Milton been a man of very keen senses—I mean of *all* the five senses—his blindness would not have mattered so much. But for a man whose sensuousness, such as it was, had been withered early by book-learning, and whose gifts were naturally aural, it mattered a great deal. It would seem, indeed, to have helped him to concentrate on what he could do best.

At no period is the visual imagination conspicuous in Milton's poetry. It would be as well to have a few illustrations of what I mean by visual imagination. From *Macbeth*:

> *This guest of summer,*
> *The temple-haunting martlet, does approve*
> *By his loved mansionry that the heaven's breath*
> *Smells wooingly here: no jutty, frieze,*
> *Buttress, nor coign of vantage, but this bird*
> *Hath made his pendent bed and procreant cradle:*
> *Where they most breed and haunt, I have observed*
> *The air is delicate.*

It may be observed that such an image, as well as another familiar quotation from a little later in the same play,

> *Light thickens, and the crow*
> *Makes wing to the rooky wood,*

not only offer something to the eye, but, so to speak, to the common sense. I mean that they convey the feeling of being in a particular place at a particular time. The comparison with Shakespeare offers another indication of the peculiarity of Milton. With Shakespeare, far more than with any other poet in English, the combinations of words offer perpetual

novelty; they enlarge the meaning of the individual words joined: thus
'procreant cradle', 'rooky wood'. In comparison, Milton's images do not
give this sense of particularity, nor are the separate words developed in
significance. His language is, if one may use the term without disparage-
ment, *artificial* and *conventional*.

> *O'er the smooth enamel'd green* . . .

> . . . *paths of this drear wood*
> *The nodding horror of whose shady brows*
> *Threats the forlorn and wandering passenger.*

('Shady brow' here is a diminution of the value of the two words from
their use in the line from *Dr. Faustus*

> *Shadowing more beauty in their airy brows.*)

The imagery in *L'Allegro* and *Il Penseroso* is all general:

> *While the ploughman near at hand,*
> *Whistles o'er the furrowed land,*
> *And the milkmaid singeth blithe,*
> *And the mower whets his scythe,*
> *And every shepherd tells his tale,*
> *Under the hawthorn in the dale.*

It is not a particular ploughman, milkmaid, and shepherd that Milton
sees (as Wordsworth might see them); the sensuous effect of these verses is
entirely on the ear, and is joined to the concepts of ploughman, milkmaid,
and shepherd. Even in his most mature work, Milton does not infuse new
life into the word, as Shakespeare does.

> *The sun to me is dark*
> *And silent as the moon,*
> *When she deserts the night*
> *Hid in her vacant interlunar cave.*

Here *interlunar* is certainly a stroke of genius, but is merely combined
with 'vacant' and 'cave', rather than giving and receiving life from them.
Thus it is not so unfair, as it might at first appear, to say that Milton
writes English like a dead language. The criticism has been made with
regard to his involved syntax. But a tortuous style, when its peculiarity
is aimed at precision (as with Henry James), is not necessarily a dead one;
only when the complication is dictated by a demand of verbal music, instead of by any demand of sense.

> *Thrones, dominations, princedoms, virtues, powers,*
> *If these magnific titles yet remain*
> *Not merely titular, since by decree*
> *Another now hath to himself engrossed*
> *All power, and us eclipsed under the name*
> *Of King anointed, for whom all this haste*

> *Of midnight march, and hurried meeting here,*
> *This only to consult how we may best*
> *With what may be devised of honours new*
> *Receive him coming to receive from us*
> *Knee-tribute yet unpaid, prostration vile,*
> *Too much to one, but double how endured,*
> *To one and to his image now proclaimed?*

With which compare:

'However, he didn't mind thinking that if Cissy should prove all that was likely enough their having a subject in common couldn't but practically conduce; though the moral of it all amounted rather to a portent, the one that Haughty, by the same token, had done least to reassure him against, of the extent to which the native jungle harboured the female specimen and to which its ostensible cover, the vast level of mixed growths stirred wavingly in whatever breeze, was apt to be identifiable but as an agitation of the latest redundant thing in ladies' hats.'

This quotation, taken almost at random from *The Ivory Tower,* is not intended to represent Henry James at any hypothetical 'best', any more than the noble passage from *Paradise Lost* is meant to be Milton's hypothetical worst. The question is the difference of intention, in the elaboration of styles both of which depart so far from lucid simplicity. The sound, of course, is never irrelevant, and the style of James certainly depends for its effect a good deal on the sound of a voice, James's own, painfully explaining. But the complication, with James, is due to a determination not to simplify, and in that simplification lose any of the real intricacies and by-paths of mental movement; whereas the complication of a Miltonic sentence is an active complication, a complication deliberately introduced into what was a previously simplified and abstract thought. The dark angel here is not *thinking* or conversing, but making a speech carefully prepared for him; and the arrangement is for the sake of musical value, not for significance. A straightforward utterance, as of a Homeric or Dantesque character, would make the speaker very much more real to us; but reality is no part of the intention. We have in fact to read such a passage not analytically, to get the poetic impression. I am not suggesting that Milton has no idea to convey which he regards as important: only that the syntax is determined by the musical significance, by the auditory imagination, rather than by the attempt to follow actual speech or thought. It is at least more nearly possible to distinguish the pleasure which arises from the *noise,* from the pleasure due to other elements, than with the verse of Shakespeare, in which the auditory imagination and the imagination of the other senses are more nearly fused, and fused together with the thought. The result with Milton is, in one sense of the word, *rhetoric.* That term is not intended to be derogatory. This kind of 'rhetoric' is not necessarily bad in its influence; but it may be considered bad in relation to the historical life of a language as a whole. I have said elsewhere that the living English which was Shakespeare's became split up into two components one of which was exploited by Milton and the other by Dryden. Of the two, I still think Dryden's development the healthier, because it was Dryden who preserved, so far as it was preserved at all, the tradition of conversational language in poetry: and I might add that it seems to me easier to get back to healthy language from Dryden than it is to get back to it from Milton. For what such a generalization is worth, Milton's influence on the eighteenth century was much more deplorable than Dryden's.

If several very important reservations and exceptions are made, I think that it is not unprofitable to compare Milton's development with that of James Joyce. The initial similarities are musical taste and abilities, followed by musical training, wide and curious knowledge, gift for acquiring languages, and remarkable powers of memory perhaps fortified by defective vision. The important difference is that Joyce's imagination is not naturally of so purely auditory a type as Milton's. In his early work, and at least in part of *Ulysses,* there is visual and other imagination of the highest kind; and I may be mistaken in thinking that the later part of *Ulysses* shows a turning from the visible world to draw rather on the resources of phantasmagoria. In any case, one may suppose that the replenishment of visual imagery during later years has been insufficient; so that what I find in *Work in Progress* is an auditory imagination abnormally sharpened at the expense of the visual. There is still a little to be seen, and what there is to see is worth looking at. And I would repeat that with Joyce this development seems to me largely due to circumstances: whereas Milton may be said never to have seen anything. For Milton, therefore, the concentration on sound was wholly a benefit. Indeed, I find, in reading *Paradise Lost,* that I am happiest where there is least to visualize. The eye is not shocked in his twilit Hell as it is in the Garden of Eden, where I for one can get pleasure from the verse only by the deliberate effort not to visualize Adam and Eve and their surroundings.

I am not suggesting any close parallel between the 'rhetoric' of Milton and the later style of Joyce. It is a different music; and Joyce always maintains some contact with the conversational tone. But it may prove to be equally a blind alley for the future development of the language.

A disadvantage of the rhetorical style appears to be, that a dislocation takes place, through the hypertrophy of the auditory imagination at the expense of the visual and tactile, so that the inner meaning is separated from the surface, and tends to become something occult, or at least without effect upon the reader until fully understood. To extract everything possible from *Paradise Lost,* it would seem necessary to read it in two different ways, first solely for the sound, and second for the sense. The full beauty of his long periods can hardly be enjoyed while we are wrestling with the meaning as well; and for the pleasure of the ear the meaning is hardly necessary, except in so far as certain key-words indicate the emotional tone of the passage. Now Shakespeare, or Dante, will bear innumerable readings, but at each reading all the elements of appreciation can be present. There is no interruption between the surface that these poets present to you and the core. While therefore, I cannot pretend to have penetrated to any 'secret' of these poets, I feel that such appreciation of their work as I am capable of points in the right direction; whereas I cannot feel that my appreciation of Milton leads anywhere outside of the mazes of sound. That, I feel, would be the matter for a separate study, like that of Blake's prophetic books; it might be well worth the trouble, but would have little to do with my interest in the poetry. So far as I perceive anything, it is a glimpse of a theology that I find in large part repellent, expressed through a mythology which would have better been left in the Book of *Genesis,* upon which Milton has not improved. There seems to me to be a division, in Milton, between the philosopher or theologian and the poet; and, for the latter, I suspect also that this concentration upon the auditory imagination leads to at least an occasional levity. I can enjoy the roll of

> . . . *Cambalu, seat of Cathaian Can*
> *And Samarchand by Oxus, Temir's throne,*
> *To Paquin of Sinaean kings, and thence*
> *To Agra and Lahor of great Mogul*
> *Down to the golden Chersonese, or where*
> *The Persian in Ecbatan sate, or since*
> *In Hispahan, or where the Russian Ksar*
> *In Mosco, or the Sultan in Bizance,*
> *Turchestan-born* . . . ,

and the rest of it, but I feel that this is not serious poetry, not poetry fully occupied about its business, but rather a solemn game. More often, admittedly, Milton uses proper names in moderation, to obtain the same effect of magnificence with them as does Marlowe—nowhere perhaps better than in the passage from *Lycidas*:

> *Whether beyond the stormy Hebrides,*
> *Where thou perhaps under the whelming tide*
> *Visit'st the bottom of the monstrous world;*
> *Or whether thou to our moist vows deny'd*
> *Sleep'st by the fable of Bellerus old,*
> *Where the great vision of the guarded Mount*
> *Looks toward Namancos and Bayona's hold* . . .

than which for the single effect of grandeur of sound, there is nothing finer in poetry.

I make no attempt to appraise the 'greatness' of Milton in relation to poets who seem to me more comprehensive and better balanced; it has seemed to me more fruitful for the present to press the parallel between *Paradise Lost* and *Work in Progress*; and both Milton and Joyce are so exalted in their own kinds, in the whole of literature, that the only writers with whom to compare them are writers who have attempted something very different. Our views about Joyce, in any case, must remain at the present time tentative. But there are two attitudes both of which are necessary and right to adopt in considering the work of any poet. One is when we isolate him, when we try to understand the rules of his own game, adopt his own point of view: the other, perhaps less usual, is when we measure him by outside standards, most pertinently by the standards of language and of something called Poetry, in our own language and in the whole history of European literature. It is from the second point of view that my objections to Milton are made: it is from this point of view that we can go so far as to say that, although his work realizes superbly one important element in poetry, he may still be considered as having done damage to the English language from which it has not wholly recovered.

Milton and Bentley:
The Pastoral of the Innocence
of Man and Nature

by William Empson

Bentley's escapade has remained something of a scandal; if he was really incapable of understanding Milton, said Mrs. Woolf, how far can we credit these eminent classicists on their own ground? [1] Or is it Milton, after all, whose language must not be taken seriously, as if he was a real classic? English critics adopt a curious air of social superiority to Bentley; he is the Man who said the Tactless Thing. There seems no doubt that he raised several important questions about Milton's use of language, that no one could answer them at the time, and that it is still worth while to look for the answer.

So far as I know, Zachary Pearce, later a bishop, only, of the many contemporary opponents of Bentley (his first notes on the edition were rushed out the same year), did not take refuge in being rude. The result

"Milton and Bentley." From *Some Versions of Pastoral* by William Empson, London, 1935. All rights reserved. Reprinted by permission of the author, New Directions, and Chatto & Windus Ltd. Mr. Empson has suggested that we note the essay "Empson and Bentley" in *Ikon: John Milton and the Modern Critics* by Robert Martin Adams (Cornell University Press, 1955), where a number of points are raised concerning inaccuracies in the present essay. Some of these are not mistakes, but differences in the texts used; others are debatable; a few clear slips (none of them affecting the argument) have been corrected in the present reprinting. Some abridgment (as indicated by ellipsis marks) has been made necessary by requirements of space. Mr. Empson has asked us to add that the author considers that many of the questions raised in his essay have been answered in his later book *Milton's God* (1961).

[1] In 1732 Richard Bentley, an eminent scholar of the classics, issued an edition of *Paradise Lost* in which he undertook to "correct" Milton's text on the grounds that the blind poet was at the mercy of an "Amanuensis" and also of some "Friend or Acquaintance" who saw the book through the press. According to Bentley, the text of the poem contained "monstrous Faults" and even some spurious verses which this "suppos'd Friend" saw fit "to foist into the Book." In 1733 Zachary Pearce issued a much more sensible publication in which he presented "A Review of the Text of the Twelve Books of Milton's *Paradise Lost*: In which the Chief of Dr. Bentley's Emendations Are Consider'd; And several other Emendations and Observations are offer'd to the Public." [ED.]

is that they seem very alike, both in their merits and their limitations;
Pearce often gave in to Bentley, or gave more plausible emendations (as
by altering punctuation) so as to accept Bentley's objections, when nowa-
days the original text seems normal and beautiful. Pearce often gives
valuable help, but for a serious answer he counts as on Bentley's side; he
is even more 'rational'; which may help to make Bentley seem less stupid. . . .

As a rule, then, I shall try to wipe the eye of both of them, and show
that though the question is real the answer justifies Milton. The 'psychological' manner, which their failure shows to be necessary, may easily be
offensive; it implies that Milton wrote in a muddle without knowing his
own mind. As a rule, if Milton's sympathies were divided, he understood
the conflict he was dramatising, and if the result is hard to explain it is
easy to feel. But I shall take first, to win sympathy for the Doctor, some
cases where I think he is right, where there is a muddle whose effect is
unsatisfying. In any case it is refreshing to see the irruption of his firm
sense into Milton's world of harsh and hypnotic, superb and crotchety
isolation; Sir Walter Raleigh said that there could not have been a child
in *Paradise Lost,* because one touch of common sense would have destroyed it; it was left for the great Doctor to take upon himself this
important rôle. Nearly all the critics have shown faint distress when
Raphael is entertained by our parents at a fruitarian meal with fruit bev-
erages, 'no fear lest dinner cool,' and 'holds discourse' about how

> food alike those pure
> Intelligential substances require
> As doth your Rational . . .
> . . . they hear, see, smell, touch, taste,
> Tasting concoct, digest, assimilate,
> And corporeal to incorporeal turn.

'If the Devils want feeding, our Author made poor provision for them in
his Second Book; where they have nothing to eat but Hell-fire; and no
danger of their dinner cooling.' This is adequate; it sends one back to
the text in a fit state to appreciate poetry when the author next grants
us some; it is a snort worthy of the nostrils of Milton himself.

Here Milton went on putting concrete for abstract till it became absurd; sometimes he uses vague poetic language which conflicts with concrete details already settled. The difficulty is that we are asked to believe
the scheme as a whole.

> Such Pleasure took the Serpent to behold
> This Flourie Plat, the sweet recess of Eve
> Thus earlie, thus alone; her Heav'nly Forme
> Angelic, but more soft, and Feminine,
> Her graceful Innocence, her every Aire
> Of gesture or least action overawd
> His malice.

Angelic. 'So we must suppose, that she has Six Wings, as Raphael had.' *More soft.* (In i. 423 the spirits can assume either sex, are uncompounded, and not manacled with joint or limb.) 'If Eve had been more soft . . . than such were, she had been no Fit Mate for her Husband.' Pearce replies 'Why may not Angelic be spoken metaphorically, as well as Heavenly, which certainly is so?' but we ought not to have to be fobbed off when there are live walking metaphors just round the corner.

A similar case, where they both shy rightly at Milton's evasive use of language, shows the process of finding concrete for abstract caught halfway; it has the squalid gelatinous effect of ectoplasm in a flashlight photograph.

> The aggregated Soyle
> Death with his Mace petrific, cold and dry,
> As with a Trident smote, and fix't as firm
> As *Delos* floating once; the rest his look
> Bound with Gorgonian rigor not to move
> And with Asphaltic slime; broad as the Gate,
> Deep to the Roots of Hell the gather'd beach
> They fasten'd.

'Bound with rigor and with slime. That could not, or at least must not, pass from Milton.' So he emends *and* to 'as,' and Pearce fights a rearguard action to change only the stops. It would be a grand clash in an Elizabethan; they can afford to confuse cause and effect, abstract and concrete, because there is no doubt that they mean something solid, but Milton will see us damned if we don't believe his story, and we expect him to believe it himself.

Pearce insists at one point, with an air of defending Milton against outrageous insult, that his scheme could not possibly be inconsistent if carefully enough considered. I cannot think it an Augustan stupidity to expect this; I too find it irritating when the sun suddenly takes to wheels (v. 140), when prayers are at last found to be as solid as angels (xi. 14), when Hell, in the twelfth book, is replanted inside the earth (41) and heaven placed in reach of Babel (50). There is a touch of the window-dressing of the *Sugar-Cane* about these muddles, which have no purpose, and about the following astronomical ones, whose purpose is disingenuous.

Satan at the top of the universe

> Looks down with wonder on the sudden view
> Of all this world at once . . . from pole to pole
> He views its breadth. . . .

Then he moves towards it

> Amongst innumerable stars, that shone
> Stars distant, but nearby seemed other worlds.

Raphael from the same place sees the world as

> Not unconform to other shining globes

but can see cedars on it. No doubt the angels have good eyesight, but
the purpose is clear. When the Earth is looked at fair and square it is
very large and well in the centre of things; only incidentally, to add
grandeur and seem up-to-date, is it a small planet attached to one of
innumerable stars. Copernicus is too strong to be ignored, so one must
show one is broadminded and then have him attacked by Raphael (viii.
73). These are trivial enough points, and Milton is wholly entitled to
muddles when serious forces are at work in them, when they carry the
complexity of his poetic material; as in some other muddles about stars
and perhaps in the many about the sex of the angels. But his mixture of
pomposity and evasiveness makes him fair game as soon as they are not
justified; he left a grim posterity of shoddy thinking in blank verse.

Given this fundamental sympathy with Bentley's outlook one can view
his worst efforts with affection and pleasure, and be properly charmed by
the note where Satan, disguised as a familiar toad, is whispering ill
dreams to the sleeping Eve. 'Why may I not add *one* Verse to *Milton,* as
well as his Editor add so *many?*' inquires Bentley with the innocent wil-
fulness of the great Victoria:

> Him thus intent Ithuriel with his spear,
> *Knowing no real Toad durst there intrude,*
> Touch'd lightly.

It is the Doctor who dare intrude anywhere and will never whisper any
harmful fancies. 'Here, you see, the Versification and Sentiment are quite
of a Piece. How naturally does the Movement of the Line imitate the
croaking of a Toad!' It is like dogs who cannot bear not to join in the
singing. Let me quote the funniest remark of Pearce at once, and have
done with this facetious tone.

> out from the ground uprose
> As from his Laire the Wilde Beast where he wonns
> In Forrest wilde

'*Lair* or *Layer* signifies *bed,* the use of which Word is still kept up among
us, when we say, that in potted Meats there is a *Lair* of one thing above a
Lair of another.' One had thought this horror peculiar to modern life.

The most obvious case where neither Bentley nor Pearce can approve
Milton's method is where he uses a serious secret pun.

> iv. 264.   The Birds thir quire apply; aires, vernal aires,
> Breathing the smell of field and grove, attune
> The trembling leaves.

'*Air,* when taken for the *Element,* has no Plural Number, in *Greek, Latin,*
or *English;* where Airs signify *Tunes.* . . . Therefore he must give it

here; *Air . . . attunes.'* Pearce gives tolerable authority for taking different airs for different breezes. But it is strange that Bentley should actually use the word *tunes,* and then quote the word *attunes,* and still not see there is a pun. The airs attune the leaves because the air itself is as enlivening as an air; the trees and wild flowers that are smelt on the air match, as if they caused, as if they were caused by, the birds and leaves that are heard on the air; nature, because of a pun, becomes a single organism. A critical theory is powerful indeed when it can blind its holders to so much beauty.

iv. 555.   Thither came Uriel, gliding through the Eev'n
           On a Sun beam.

'I never heard but here, that the *Evening* was a Place or Space to *glide* through. *Evening* implies Time, and he might with equal propriety say: Came gliding though Six a clock. But it's the Printer's Language: the Author gave it, *gliding through the* HEAVEN.' Pearce gives precedent for coming through the evening, and points out that the part of the earth occupied by evening *is* a place, especially to so astronomical a creature. I am glad not to have to tell them what was evidently in Milton's mind; that the angel is sliding, choosing a safe gradient, down a nearly *even* sunbeam; like the White Knight on the poker. But as so often when Milton is on the face of it indefensible the line seems to absorb the harshness of its absurdity; the pun gives both Uriel and the sunset a vast and impermanent equilibrium; it is because of the inevitable Fall of our night that he falls to earth, in the hush and openness of evening, himself in a heroic calm.

vi. 483.   These in their dark Nativitie the Deep
           Shall yield us, pregnant with infernal flame.

(Satan, while yet in Heaven, in the first triumph of his invention of artillery.) Pearce says 'we may suppose the Epithet *infernal* to have been added to *flame,* that it might stand oppos'd to Heav'n's ray mentioned in l. 480. . . . But (says the Dr.) it is too soon yet for Satan to mention INFERNAL *flame.* That is too hard to be proved: Hell had been mentioned in the speeches of the Combatants on the preceding Day, viz. in vi. 186, 276, 291.' Satan says, as a fact, that he will fetch fire 'from below' to answer the fire of God; he says, as a pun and a defiance, if we may suppose him to have understood the previous day's hints about hell, that he will use the fire of punishment as the material of victory, and the voice of Milton behind him assures us that they are *pregnant* with more fire than they have planned.

This horror will grow mild, this darkness light.

' 'Tis quite too much that the *Darkness* turn into *Light,* 'tis as if he had made *Horror* turn into *Joy.'* 'Surely this was no more than for *Horror* to turn to *Mild,* for both *Mild* and *Light* don't express the highest degree, but only something that, by comparison with what they then suffered, might be called *Mild* and *Light.'* I quote this as a very slight pun which yet has an effect, which Bentley is right in noticing. Both these senses are present, and the combination allows Belial to suggest high hopes without obvious absurdity.

As for the conscious puns of Satan's mockery, of course they both recognise those easily enough. Pearce can 'make no attempt to defend' the pun about infantry, but Bentley is willing to defend puns so long as they are funny.

> . . . the Passages of Satan and Belial's Jesting have been censured by an Ingenious Gentleman, who had a settled Aversion to all Puns, as they are call'd . . . if that Niceness be carry'd to Extremity, it will depretiate half the good sayings of the old Greek and Latin Wits. . . . He copied those Jocose Sayings from his great predecessor Homer.

Here, as often, Bentley is the more broad-minded of the two.

Another of the main points at issue concerns Milton's rhythm; there seems no doubt that Bentley didn't understand it, but there may be some question whether Pearce did or not. He defended the text, in any case where the rhythm seemed queer to Bentley, by pointing out that it was queer in many other cases as well; it might then, one would suppose, be queer on some system, if such a system could be conceived. 'Milton affected in many places to make such a Roughness as this at the beginning of his Verse.' If the text is frequently rough, and roughness is a fault, that only supports Bentley's view that the text has frequently been corrupted. And even when he attempts more positive approval it is hard to know what is in his mind.

> Half wheeling to the shield, half to the spear.
> Our minds, and teach us to cast off this yoke.

'The bad Measure may be assisted thus,' etc. 'But I see no bad Measure at all in the common Reading; the small stress laid in the pronunciation upon the word *to* does not in my opinion injure the Verse.' Is a stress, even when small, a long syllable, or a short stress a short syllable? The discussion comes to very little conclusion.

At the last moment, however, before his first edition was published, Pearce suddenly understood a Miltonic rhythm, and explained it at the end of the preface; a dramatic affair; it shows that Bentley was some use.

> No sooner had th' Almighty ceas't, but all
> The multitude of Angels with a shout
> Loud as from numbers without number, sweet
> As from blest voices, uttering joy, Heav'n rung
> With Jubilee, and loud Hosannas fill'd
> Th' eternal Regions.

To Bentley this was evidently not grammar, and he let in a couple of main verbs, like ferrets. Pearce could only save the text by putting brackets from *Heaven* to *Hosannas,* so that it is the angels who filled the regions, with a shout. In the preface *angels uttering joy* becomes an ablative absolute, so that the sentence encloses the hierarchy as if with effort and rises through four lines to the main verb.

But though a large-scale rhythm was in reach of discovery he never feels that the iambic beat could be seriously tampered with; both of them find

> Dropped from the Zenith, like a falling star

quite impossible; and it is Bentley who suspects that the line about the unwieldy elephant may actually be intended to be rough.

People are now agreed in approving Milton's rhythms, and accepting his subdued puns without looking at them closely. I don't know what is the normal view about his vague or apparently disordered grammar, which Bentley thought indefensible; especially the use of *and* or *or* when the sense needs more detailed logical structure. Pearce defended it very little. The chief reason for it is that Milton aims both at a compact and weighty style, which requires short clauses, and a sustained style with the weight of momentum, which requires long clauses.

> vii. 113.   to recount Almightie works
> What words or tongue of Seraph can suffice,
> Or heart of man suffice to comprehend?

Bentley emends to 'words from tongue,' but thereby loses the completeness of the statement; 'How can any stage in the production of the speech of seraphs be adequate; how can they find words, and if they could how could their tongues pronounce them?' But besides this, the merit of *or* is its fluidity; the way it allows 'words from tongue' to be suggested without pausing for analysis, without holding up the single movement of the line.

> xi. 273-285.   O flours,
> That never will in other Climate grow,
> My early visitation, and my last
> At Eev'n, which I bred up with tender hand
> From the first op'ning buds, and gave ye Names,
> Who now shall reare ye to the Sun, or ranke
> Your Tribes, and water from th' ambrosial Fount?
> Thee lastly, nuptial Bowre, by mee adornd
> With what to sight or smell was sweet; from thee
> How shall I part, and whither wander down
> Into a lower World, to this obscure
> And wilde, how shall we breathe in other Aire
> Less pure, acustomed to immortal Fruits?

I have quoted a whole passage to show the accumulation of its imagery. Bentley objects to the last lines: 'What do the *Fruits,* now to be parted

with, signify to her *Breathing* in other Air? There was to be a change of
Diet too, as well as of Air'; so he emends it to 'Air less pure? What
eat . . .' Pearce says, 'To eat (for the future) Fruits not immortal, and
to have Air less pure too, were Circumstances which might well justify
her sollicitous enquiry about her Breathing in the lower World'; indeed
the sense is plain enough. But the effect of Bentley's emendation is to
make Eve's pathos into a declamatory piece of argument. The sliding,
sideways, broadening movement, normal to Milton, is exaggerated into a
non sequitur to show a climax; on the other hand, in the tired repeated
rhythm of the last two lines, she leaves floating, as things already far off,
all that makes up for her the 'atmosphere' of Paradise. There is something like a pun in the way she is enabled at once to sum up her argument and trail away in the weakness of her appeal; it is a delicate piece
of brushwork such as seems blurred until you step back.

Pearce is clear about points of fluid grammar, as one sees from his fondness for brackets to bring out less obvious connections.

> Taste this, and be henceforth among the Gods
> Thyself a Goddess, not to Earth confin'd,
> But sometimes in the Air, as wee, sometimes
> Ascend to Heav'n, by merit thine, and see
> What life the Gods live there, and such live thou.

'The Words *as wee*,' remarks Pearce, 'are so plac'd between the Sentences
as equally to relate to both, and in the first Sentence the Verb *be* is understood. Dr. B. has altered the passage thus:

> But sometimes range in air, sometimes, as wee,

But in this reading of the Doctor's are not the Angels excluded from
ranging in the Air?' Surely there is a dramatic reason for the gawkiness
of the line here; the doubt implied as to whether he could go to Heaven
himself shows a natural embarrassment in the disguised Satan. But the
essential step is to notice, as Pearce does, the fluidity of the grammar.

He also recognises implied conceits of the straightforward kind that
would have made an antithesis for the Augustan couplet.

> ix. 631.   He leading swiftly rowld
> In tangles, and made intricate seem strait,
> To mischief swift.

Bentley dislikes the two *swifts,* but 'the Sense rises by repeating the same
word with a new Circumstance to it.'

> Tangled his coils, and tangled were his wiles,
> And swift he marches, who so swift beguiles.

It is rather pretty to see them fitting the thing into their more conscious
formula.

Bentley's merit as a critic of Milton is of a different kind; he may only produce a trivial piece of nagging, but he has a flair for choosing an important place to do it. Thus his complaint about the first words of Satan seem to me to draw attention to an unexpected dramatic subtlety.

> If thou beest he; But O how fall'n! how chang'd
> From him, who in the happy Realms of Light
> Cloth'd with transcendent brightness didst outshine
> Myriads though bright: If he whom mutual league,
> United thoughts and counsels, equal hope,
> And hazard in the Glorious Enterprise,
> Joyned with me once, now misery hath joynd
> In equal ruin: into what pit thou seest
> From what highth fal'n, so much the stronger provd
> He with his Thunder; and till then who knew
> The force of those dire Arms. . . .

Bentley emends *doth joyn And equal ruin*. 'See the series of the whole sentence: *Whom mutual league, united counsels, equal hope and hazard in our Revolt, joined with me* ONCE, viz. in close friendship; *Now Misery hath join'd;* in what? in closer friendship? no, in equal Ruin. Great Sense, and great Comfort in this great Calamity. *Equal Ruin,* in reddition to equal hope, now again joins us in a *stricter friendship.'* Pearce accepts *and,* 'very right and necessary, I think,' but exclaims 'how unpoetical is *doth join.'*

The main objection here is that the words claim to give a source of comfort, and do not. They claim to give what resolution may be gained from despair. But I think the shift Bentley describes is part of the thought, and explains what in such a speaker needs explanation even at such a moment, the reason why Satan breaks his sentence. He begins speaking to Beelzebub as an equal, and then, strengthened by his own rhetoric, feels that this would be excessive 'comfort' for a rival angel. If their *hope* (personal advantage hoped for) in the enterprise was equal they both hoped to rule; if their *ruin* (personal loss of glory) is equal they were once equal in glory. Satan breaks the sentence with *into what pit,* and their equal ruin (as in *ruining from heaven*), *in* being attracted by *into,* may now only be their equal physical fall. From then on, in his supreme expression of all but lunatic heroism, he speaks only of himself.

Milton's attitude to Satan is a great source of disagreement; Bentley rightly finds something suspicious about the generosity of the language used, and picks out some curious examples of it.

> **xi. 101.** Take to thee from among the Cherubim
> Thy choice of flaming Warriors, least the Fiend
> Or on behalf of Man, or to invade
> Vacant possession some new trouble raise.

Bentley emends *or on behalf of man* to 'or in despite to us'; 'Whence came this new Good-will to Man from the Arch-Enemy?' The view that there is a calculated progressive decay of Satan is not upheld by this passage; it comes very late and had to be striking for Bentley to bother about it; he is beginning to explain he is old and tired, and repeat his arguments.

> ix. 166.   O foul descent! that I who erst contended
>   With Gods to sit the highest, am now constrained
>   Into a Beast, and mixt with bestial slime,
>   This essence to incarnate and imbrute,
>   That to the hight of Deitie aspir'd.

'Milton would not use thus the word *Incarnate;* He knew a higher Essence, than Seraphical, was afterwards Incarnated'; indeed I think one may trace even here that curious parallel between Satan and the Christ, which makes the scenes in Heaven and Hell correspond to one another so closely. But perhaps it is rather Man than the Son of Man who complains in his words.

There is an odd phrase, or as Bentley puts it 'a shocking expression,' in one of these parallel passages, which seems to show a flash of contempt for the good angels. Satan in the second book chose to take the risk on his own shoulders, to go alone to the new world for the benefit of his party 'or on behalf of man.' God in the third book tries to make one of the good angels, as a similar act of public spirit, go to the world to redeem man; all of them refuse.

> Say Heav'nly Powers, where shall we find such love,
> Which of ye will be mortal to redeem
> Man's mortal crime, and just th' unjust to save,
> Dwels in all Heaven charity so deare?

'Lead a perfect human life to save those who are imperfect' is of course the sense from which this has diverged, but 'which of ye will be just' is a piercing question for the immaculate hierarchy.

> vii. 55.   things to thir thought
>   So unimaginable as hate in Heav'n,
>   And War so near the Peace of God in bliss
>   With such confusion;

Bentley emends *peace* to 'seat," because the text implies that the Peace of God was not incapable of being disturbed. It does indeed; Milton is at pains to give this impression, while denying that it is true; only so can Satan's heroism be saved from a taint of folly. Perhaps the strangest means adopted to make one feel this is the ironical speech which God, 'smiling,' makes to his Son when the attack is being prepared against them.

> v. 729.   Let us advise, and to this hazard draw
>   With speed what force is left, and all imploy

> In our defence, lest unawares we lose
> This our high place, our Sanctuarie, our Hill.

One accepts this in reading as the brutal mockery of a much superior force, but it does not seem that of an absolutely superior force, such as there would be no sense in attacking.

Indeed, Satan has a much more plausible defence on grounds of ignorance than Eve had (ix. 775); he does not know whether God is of like nature with the angels (v. 796) and sprang into existence at the same moment (v. 859; but there is a *young* cherub in iii. 637), or whether as he claims he is almighty, their creator, and of absolutely superior nature. Milton himself in ii. 108, God himself in iii. 341, speak of the angels as gods; Milton's language about the creation (vii. 227 and 505) implies, as Bentley pointed out, that they were not created; and Abdiel's official statement in v. 837, that God created them by the instrumentality of the Son, is in flat contradiction with v. 603, where the angels are shown the Son when he is newly begotten. Of course we are supposed to know about God, but there is no clear tradition to tell us how much Satan knows— so far as there is Milton is at pains to muddle it. If Satan believed God to be a usurping angel there is no romantic diabolism at all in giving him our heartiest admiration. I think this is a sharp issue; what the critic has to deal with is not a 'complex personality' but one plain character superimposed on another quite separate from it.

The most striking single example of this dissolving-view method of characterisation occurs when Satan is struck 'stupidly good' on his first view of Adam and Eve:

> whom my thoughts pursue   10
> With wonder, and could love . . .
> whom I could pity thus forlorn
> Though I unpitied. . . .

Milton himself is providing some pity here.

> League with you I seek
> And mutual amity so streight, so close,
> That I with you must dwell, or you with me
> Henceforth; my dwelling haply may not please
> Like this fair Paradise, your sense, yet such
> Accept your Maker's gift; he gave it me
> Which I as freely give; Hell shall unfold
> To entertain you two, her widest Gates,
> And send forth all her kings.

Bentley found the terms inaccurate but the tone natural—a brutal irony in the style of the address to the gunners. The gates of hell can no longer be either shut or opened 'nor need he lie and feign here, for he speaks to himself only,' and the emendation is arranged to give 'a Sarcasm rather bitterer.' This seems to be the accepted view, though a sort

of generosity, a sense of the grandeur of the situation, is admitted from
the parallel in Isaiah. Sir Walter Raleigh, with evasive humour, said it
was 'true hospitality.'

But Satan might mean it as a real offer. It is clear that the devils can
carry life on in hell, and apparently men can only suffer; Satan need not
know this; the irony is that of Milton's appalling God. The two views
of Satan seem actually to be separated to the two ends of the sentence.
The cuddling movement of *mutual amity*, with the flat mouth of the
worm, in *am-*, opening to feed on them, the insinuating hiss of *so streight*,
so close, full of the delicious softness of the tormentor, belong to the
Satan who will have his guests tortured by incongruous Furies (ii. 596);
so the voices whispered to Bunyan, and he thought his bowels would
burst within him. Then there is a patch of argufying, in which he seems
to feel nothing, as a connection (one might be sentimentally playful like
this before killing a young pig). And only the theory of ignorance provides a character for the last three lines; their melancholy and their
grandeur is that of Milton's direct statements; he does not use *all*, his
key word, for any but a wholesale and unquestioned emotion; what we
are to feel here is the ruined generosity of Satan and the greatness of the
fate of man. It seems to me obviously useless to try and fit the two into
a consistent character.

The subject of the poem is not a personal Satan but the Fall of Man;
the more life Milton could put into our feelings about Satan the better,
but his main business was to convey the whole range of feeling inherent
in the myth, and the myth clearly involves contradictions. Satan is both
a devil and a host who will receive man with honour, because the fall of
a man is terrible and yet just this shows that he is important (which
makes the belief tolerable). Satan is both the punisher of sin and the
supreme sinner (Milton did not invent this, and in neither capacity is
Satan 'Milton'); these are combined because 'sin punishes itself and turns
to hatred,' because 'it is hard to distinguish sin from independent judgment, courage, the force needed for a full life,' and I think because 'the
sinner becomes the judge.' Then perhaps, thirdly, Satan is Milton as
rebel and also the paganism Milton had renounced; from the first he
has bitterness, from the second the sadism of the Italianate stage villain.
Now of course no mere clash between these forces would be a substitute
for a conceivable Satan, but the fact that at this crucial point there is a
troubling of the surface of the coherent Satan somehow convinces us
that they are all at work. It acts not as a puzzle about the person Satan
but as a knot, a throttling irony, in the myth; it so sharply concentrates
the forces of the story that we are impressed at their not breaking their
frame. It looks like a dramatic irony; I think it is more; it is a dramatic
failure of character.

Bentley is always ruthless about the large ornamental comparisons,
where some incident in the story has a detail in common with, more or

less of some quality than, some otherwise irrelevant incident which is described in detail; he classes whole paragraphs of them as 'romantic, and inserted by the editor.' But it is here that Milton shows his attitude to the work as a whole; it is at best mere protection to reply as Pearce did by talking about 'imagination.' I shall take first two more examples about Satan. Satan flying up to the gates of hell

> Now shaves with level wing the Deep, then soares
> Up to the fiery concave touring high.
> As when far off at Sea a Fleet descri'd
> Hangs in the Clouds, by *Aequinoctial* Winds
> Close sailing from *Bengala,* or the Iles
> Of *Ternate* and *Tidore,* whence Merchants bring
> Thir spicie drugs; they on the trading flood
> Through the wide *Ethiopian* to the Cape
> Ply stemming nightly toward the Pole. So seem'd
> Far off the flying Fiend:

Bentley cuts out the whole passage. Pearce's defence amounts to claiming charity for poets who have classical authority for their licences.

> As to what he adds, *why is this all done nightly, to contradict the whole account, since at that time a sail cannot be descried?* It may be answered, that here is no Contradiction at all; for Milton in his Similitudes (as is the practice of Homer and Virgil too) after he has shown the common resemblance, often takes the liberty of wandering into some unresembling Circumstances: which have no other relation to the Comparison, than that it gave him the Hint, and (as it were) set fire to the Train of his Imagination.

The trouble is that this defends an irrelevant piece of description, one which is merely distracting, as well as one that satisfies the imagination through implied comparisons relevant to the main impulse of the poem.

The description here seems entirely of this second sort. The ships ply nightly because Satan was in the darkness visible of Hell; are far off so that they hang like a mirage and seem flying like Satan (the word *ply,* sounding like 'fly,' ekes this out); and are going towards the Pole because Satan (from inside) is going towards the top of the concave wall of Hell. They carry spices, like those of Paradise, because they stand for paganism and earthly glory, for all that Milton had retained contact with after renouncing and could pile up into the appeal of Satan; Satan is like a merchant because Eve is to exchange these goods for her innocence; and like a fleet rather than one ship because of the imaginative wealth of polytheism and the variety of the world. (It fits in with Satan as a symbol, not as a character.)

> iv. 977. While thus he spake, th' Angelic Squadron bright
> Turnd fierie red, sharpning in mooned hornes
> Thir Phalanx, and begann to hemm him round
> With ported Spears, as thick as when a field

> Of *Ceres* ripe for harvest waving bends
> Her bearded Grove of ears, which way the wind
> Swayes them; the careful Plowman doubting stands
> Least on the threshing floore his hopefull sheaves
> Prove chaff. On th' other side *Satan* allarm'd
> Collecting all his might dilated stood,
> Like *Teneriffe* or *Atlas* unremov'd:

Bentley omits the ploughman sentence.

> The Editor deserts the notion, and from a salutary Gale of Wind . . . he
> passes to a Tempest, and frightens the Husbandman with the loss of all his
> Grain. What an Injury is this to the Prior Comparison? What are Sheaves
> bound up in a Barn to the Phalanx, that hem'd Satan?

It certainly makes the angels look weak. If God the sower is the ploughman, then he is anxious; another hint that he is not omnipotent. If
the labouring Satan is the ploughman he is only anxious for a moment,
and he is the natural ruler or owner of the good angels. The main effect
is less logical; the homely idea is put before the description of Satan to
make him grander by contrast, an effect denied to the other angels.

> Besides, to suppose a Storm in the Fields of Corn, implies that the Angels
> were in a ruffle and hurry about Satan, not in regular and military Order.

More than that; first the angels lean forward, calm and eager, in rows,
seeming strong; then as the description approaches Satan, who is stronger,
they are in a ruffle and hurry.

People are by now agreed that Milton partly identified Satan with part
of his own mind, and that the result though excellent was a little unintentional. But to say this is to agree with many of Bentley's points;
you can hardly blame him for not admiring what nobody in his time
was prepared to defend; certainly you cannot blame his methods, as apart
from his tone, for they were surprisingly successful.

A whole series of a particular sort of ornamental comparison, that
which relates a detail of the Biblical myth to one of a classical myth, is
used to convey very complex feelings about Paradise and also for the
vilification of Eve. Bentley is sharp at picking out these implications, but
I think one can carry it further than he does.

> iv. 268.   Not that faire field
> Of *Enna,* where *Proserpin* gathring flours
> Herself a fairer Floure by gloomie *Dis*
> Was gatherd, which cost *Ceres* all that pain
> To seek her through the world; nor that sweet Grove
> Of *Daphne* by *Orontes,* and the inspir'd
> *Castalian* Spring might with this Paradise
> Of *Eden* strive; nor that *Nyseian* Ile
> Girt with the River *Triton,* where old *Cham,*
> Whom Gentiles *Ammon* call and *Libyan Jove,*

> Hid *Amalthea* and her Florid Son
> Young *Bacchus* from his Stepdame *Rhea's* eye;
> Nor where *Abassin* Kings thir issue Guard,
> Mount *Amara*, though this by som suppos'd
> True Paradise under the *Ethiop* Line
> By *Nilus* head, enclos'd with shining Rock,
> A whole dayes journey high, but wide remote
> From this *Assyrian* Garden, where the Fiend
> Saw undelighted all delight . . .

. . . with a silly thought in the middle, and as sillily conducted in its several parts. *Not Enna, says he, not Daphne, nor Fons Castalus, nor Nysa, nor Mount Amara, could compare with Paradise.* Why who, Sir, would suspect they could; though you had never told us it?

A man who had given his life to the classics might easily have suspected it; it is to Milton that the pagan beauty of these gardens has appealed more richly than the perfection of the garden of God. But I want here to play Bentley's trick and bring out the implications against Eve.

Proserpina, like Eve, was captured by the king of Hell, but she then became queen of it, became Sin, then, on Milton's scheme; Eve, we are to remember, becomes an ally of Satan when she tempts Adam to eat with her. Daphne was not seduced by Apollo as Eve was by Satan (both affairs involve desire, a devil, and a tree); Eve might really have done better than a mere pagan nymph; one must class her with the consenting Amalthea. And all the references to guarding children remind us that children were the result of the fall.

In the third comparison Milton takes an unusual version of the myth, on the authority (the sole authority, according to Masson) of Diodorus Siculus, who says that he got it from Dionysius, and that Dionysius got it from a tutor of Hercules. He follows that version of the story, out of his list of versions, with a very fine description of the gardens of the Nyseian isle, but I think one can give a more interesting reason why Milton adopted Bacchus in such a way as to make us confuse him with Jupiter. He wanted a mixed notion for demigod of the glory and fertility of the earth, because of his pagan feelings about Paradise, and yet for a sky-god, because Adam in spite of this stood for celestial virtue. And the fourth garden was like Eden because the issue of the Abassin kings were kept secluded there like Adam and Eve, but the appeal of the lines is to an idea opposite to that of seclusion. They fling into the scale against Paradise, only still to be outweighed, what many beside Milton would have thought worthy to be put to such a use; the Elizabethan excitement about distant travel and trading, about the discovery of luxury and the sources of the Nile.

Another odd case of Eve-baiting forms a disputed passage.

> ix. 503.   Pleasing was his shape,
> And lovely, never since of Serpent kind

> Lovelier, not those that in Illyria chang'd
> Hermione and Cadmus, or the God
> In Epidaurus; nor to which transform'd
> Ammonian Jove, or Capitoline was seen,
> Hee with Olympias, this with her who bore
> Scipio the highth of Rome.

Satan is as beautiful as his creator can make him; you are not to think there is anything low about him even in disguise. Probably he made a very fine toad. But it is remarkable, surely, that the first comparison, as always interpreted, implies that Eve turned into a snake and became Satan's consort, just as the other devils turn into snakes after the fall. *Those,* indeed, may be not the couple named but some serpent gods; Ovid gives the cause (revenge for a killed snake) but no causers of the metamorphosis (from the *Bacchae* they might be the snakes of Bacchus); and this would give *changed* its normal sense. Even so the last two comparisons treat the Fall as a sexual act after which Eve produced children by Satan, as in the Talmud, which makes her a regular seventeenth-century witch. And again, after the devils have been turned into serpents (an incident which seems to have been invented by Milton to drive these suggestions home) we hear that they

> **x. 580.**   fabled how the Serpent, whom they call'd
> Ophion with Eurynome, the wide-
> Encroaching Eve perhaps, had first the rule
> Of high Olympus, thence by Saturn driven
> And Ops, ere yet Dictaean Jove was born.

'*Ophion* the *Serpent* is *Eve's* Husband, and so all Mankind are descended from *Satan,*' remarks Bentley, and no less reasonably 'Where did she encroch, unless to bear children is wide encroching?' Pearce's only sensible reply is that in any case it was the spiteful invention of devils. But it was Milton who did the inventing. Pearce indeed catches the infection at one point and uses this trick to defend the text.

> Soon had his crew
> Op'nd into the Hill a spacious wound
> And dig'd out ribs of Gold.

Bentley wanted to read 'seeds of gold,' but the words here, said Pearce, 'allude to the formation of Eve in viii. 463.' I call this a profound piece of criticism; 'Let none admire that riches grow in Hell; that soil may best Deserve the precious bane.' It is not specially unkind to Eve; to connect her with the architecture of Pandemonium makes her stand for the pride and loyalty that won grandeur even from the fall. The following passage goes so far as to suggest that it was she who tempted Satan and turned him into a serpent. She was not afraid of him when she saw him in Eden, because she was

> ix. 519.   . . . us'd
> To such disport before her through the Field,
> From every Beast, more duteous at her call,
> Than at Circean call the Herd disguis'd.

Samson, too, calls Delilah a sorceress; no doubt he would have added Circe if he had heard of her.

Even the following comparison, as from the ranging and pouncing imagination of Dante, shows the same idea at the back of his mind. The devils when turned to serpents saw a multitude of trees laden with fruit;

> x. 556.   Parcht with scalding thurst and hunger fierce,
> Though to delude them sent, could not abstain,
> But on they rould in heaps, and up the Trees
> Climbing, sat thicker than the snakie locks
> That curld Megaera; greedily they pluck'd
> The Frutage fair to sight, like that which grew
> Neer that bituminous Lake where Sodom flamed.

Eve too, in iv. 307, has curled hair, modest but 'requiring,' that clutches at Adam like the tendrils of a vine. Eve now then is herself the forbidden tree; the whole face of Hell has become identical with her face; it is filled, as by the mockery of the temptress, with her hair that entangled him; all the beauty of nature, through her, is a covering, like hers, for moral deformity. But at least now we have exposed her; her hair is corpse worms; she is the bitter apple of her own crime, kind as the Eumenides. It is a relief to find Bentley snorting at the editor who 'unjudiciously diverts us from the Scene in View, to the snaky curls of a fictitious Fury.'

That Eve was Delilah, the more specious for her innocence, is only one end of Milton's feeling about her; in many of these examples the broad melancholy from the clash of paganism with Paradise is more striking than the snarl at Eve. But the Doctor thought no better of them for that; the snarls were only stupid, the melancholy was infidel; Milton's use of the pagan seemed to him to imply a doubt of the Christian mythology; and for myself I think, not only that he was right, but that the reverberations of this doubt are the real subject of the descriptions of the Garden. . . .

Bentley is very suspicious of the editor's irreligion, and finds evidence of it continually.

> a creature who, not prone
> And brute as other creatures, but endued
> With sanctity of reason, might erect
> His stature, and upright with front serene
> Govern the rest, self-knowing.

'As if his Erection were superadded to his Form by his own Contrivance; not originally made so by his Creator. I remember this senseless Notion spred about, that Man at first was a Quadruped, with a Kentish Tail.' (Kentish men were given tails by Thomas à Becket.) Coleridge makes a similar complaint about the *Essay on Man;* one does not easily realise that a sense of danger from this quarter has been in the air for so long. It is only very faintly hinted by Milton, if at all, but the hint was readily picked up.

The other examples are all classical comparisons. The angels sing to God, at the return of Christ from the Creation, that he is

> greater now in thy return
> Than from the Giant Angels.

This must be altered; it is an indiscreet hint at the Titans. (It seems anyway to show that the good angels admitted the bad ones to be greatly superior.) On the occasion to which they refer he pursued the bad angels

> With terrors and with furies to the bounds
> And Chrystall wall of Heav'n

'This must not pass by any means. We cannot allow *Furies* in Heaven; especially in the Messiah's party.' Pearce agrees but finds furies in Vergil who are only 'inward frights.' The following queer smack at Eve is a more serious piece of comparative mythology.

> the genial Angel to our Sire
> Brought her in naked beauty more adorn'd
> More lovely than Pandora, whom the Gods
> Endowd with all thir gifts, and O too like
> In sad event, when to the unwiser son
> Of Japhet brought by Hermes, she ensnar'd
> Mankind with her fair looks, to be aveng'd
> On him who had stole Jove's authentic fire.

Not only was Eve not trying to avenge Satan but Pandora was not trying to avenge Prometheus; 'to be revenged on Prometheus—that must be Pandora's revenge, and yet she had no Thought or Hand in it.' Iapetus is spelt Japhet, and Epimetheus might well be remembered as the first man if he lived in the first generation after the Flood; there is a neat piece of dovetailing in the manner of Ralegh's history. Yet Ralegh is a fearful name in this connection; Marlowe himself was among the wild gang of comparative anthropologists he collected round him in his great days.

Adam and Eve pray together after the fall; humbly enough,

> yet thir port
> Not of mean suitors, nor important less
> Seem'd thir Petition, then when th' ancient Pair
> In Fables old, less ancient yet then these,
> Deucalion and chaste Pyrrha to restore

> The race of Mankind drowned, before the Shrine
> Of Themis stood devout.

But was the Man bewitch'd, with his *Old Fables, but not as old as these?* Is *Adam* and *Eve's* History an *Old Fable* too, by this Editor's own Insinuation?

Pearce makes a case for a grammatical licence, but it seems clear that they were right to be surprised; Milton intends no unorthodoxy, but feels the poetic or symbolical meaning of the stories to be more important than their truth. The effect is that he compares Christian and pagan views of life as equally solid and possible. . . .

> To Pales, or Pomona, thus adornd,
> Likest she seemed, Pomona when she fled
> Vertumnus, or to Ceres in her Prime,
> Yet Virgin of Proserpina from Jove.

Why was she virgin, and from whom was she flying, Bentley would like to know; and as for *prime:* 'What? have Goddesses the decays of Old Age?' Pearce makes a good case for the façade of the comparison, but the questions deserve an answer that admits their importance. Ceres will decay like the other pagan gods when Christianity comes; the fall from paganism is like the fall from paradise. Eve has insisted on going off alone with her gardening tools to the Temptation; she is flying from the society of Adam and will not fly (it is a reproach against her) from Vertumnus, the god of autumn, of the Fall; the very richness of the garden makes it heavy with autumn. Ceres when virgin of the queen of Hell was already in her full fruitfulness upon the world; Eve is virgin of sin from Satan and of Cain, who in the Talmud was his child. Walking in 'virgin majesty' though not 'ignorant of nuptial rites' she seems at once strong because on Milton's theory freedom does not expose her to sensuality (so Elizabeth might appear, goddess of a paganism now extinguished), hence the more dangerously entitled to the forbidden knowledge, and weak because ignorant of it—she does not know what is at stake, and will fall through triviality. It seems to be ignorance that puts her into the ideal state that is fitted to receive all knowledge. Her lack of shame is felt as a pathetic degree of virginity, and yet it places her with the satyrs outside the Christian world. She and her husband seem great people socially—ambassadors of mankind—and yet savages in a low stage of development. And though she resolves all these opposites, which proves that she is in a state of perfection, the term suggests that there is still something lacking for a full human life. If Milton had been in the Garden, it has been brightly said, he would have eaten the apple at once and written a pamphlet to prove that that was his duty. Another view of the doctrine of the Fall is, I think, somewhere in his mind; that the human creature is essentially out of place in the world and needed no fall in time to make him so.

This very complete ambivalence of feeling is then thrown out and attached to Nature in the garden.

> Thus was this place
> A happy rural seat of various view:
> Groves whose rich Trees wept odorous Gumms and Balme,
> Others whose fruit burnished with Golden Rinde
> Hung amiable, Hesperian fables true,
> If true, here only, and of delicious taste.

Bentley emends *fables* to 'apples,' which makes the idea more obvious. The whole beauty of the thing is a rich nostalgia, but not simply for a lost Eden; sorrow is inherent in Eden itself, as Johnson found it in *L'Allegro,* and that the trees are weeping seems to follow directly from the happiness of the rural seat. The trees that glitter with unheeding beauty and the trees that weep with prescience are alike associated with the tree of knowledge; the same Nature produced the *balm* of healing and the fatal *fruit*; they cannot convey to Adam either its knowledge or the knowledge that it is to be avoided, and by their own nature foretell the necessity of the Fall. The melancholy of our feeling that Eden must be lost so soon, once attached to its vegetation, makes us feel that it is inherently melancholy. These are the same puzzles about the knowledge, freedom, happiness, and strength of the state of innocence, but applied to the original innocence of Nature. . . .

We first see Paradise through the eyes of the entering Satan, seated jealously like a cormorant on the Tree of Life. Like him we are made to feel aliens with a larger purpose; our sense of its pathos and perfection seems, as he does, to look down on it from above; the fall has now happened, and we must avoid this sort of thing in our own lives. Like so many characters in history our first parents may be viewed with admiration so long as they do not impose on us their system of values; it has become safe to admit that in spite of what is now known to be the wickedness of such people they had a perfection which we no longer deserve. Without any reason for it in Milton's official view of the story this feeling is concentrated onto their sexual situation, and the bower where Eve decks their nuptial bed (let not the reader dare think there is any loss of innocence in its pleasures) has the most firmly 'pagan' and I think the most beautiful of the comparisons.

> In shadier Bower,
> More sacred and sequestered, though but feigned,
> Pan or Sylvanus never slept, nor Nymph
> Nor Faunus haunted.

'*Pan, Sylvanus,* and *Faunus,* savage and beastly Deities, and acknowledg'd *feign'd,* are brought here in Comparison, and their wild Grottos forsooth are Sacred.' 'These three Verses, after all his objections, were certainly Milton's, and may be justified though not perhaps admired.'

Surely Bentley was right to be surprised at finding Faunus haunting the bower, a ghost crying in the cold of Paradise, and the lusts of Pan sacred even in comparison to Eden. There is a Vergilian quality in the lines, haunting indeed, a pathos not mentioned because it is the whole of the story. I suppose that in Satan determining to destroy the innocent happiness of Eden, for the highest political motives, without hatred, not without tears, we may find some echo of the Elizabethan fulness of life that Milton as a poet abandoned, and as a Puritan helped to destroy.

The Style of Secondary Epic

by C. S. Lewis

Forms and figures of speech originally the offspring of passion, but now the adopted children of power.

COLERIDGE

The style of Virgil and Milton arises as the solution of a very definite problem. The Secondary epic aims at an even higher solemnity than the Primary; but it has lost all those external aids to solemnity which the Primary enjoyed. There is no robed and garlanded *aoidos,* no altar, not even a feast in a hall—only a private person reading a book in an arm-chair. Yet somehow or other, that private person must be made to feel that he is assisting at an august ritual, for if he does not, he will not be receptive of the true epic exhilaration. The sheer writing of the poem, therefore, must now do, of itself, what the whole occasion helped to do for Homer. The Virgilian and Miltonic style is there to compensate for —to counteract—the privacy and informality of silent reading in a man's own study. Every judgment on it which does not realize this will be in-ept. To blame it for being ritualistic or incantatory, for lacking intimacy or the speaking voice, is to blame it for being just what it intends to be and ought to be. It is like damning an opera or an oratorio because the personages sing instead of speaking.

In a general and obvious sense this effect is achieved by what is called the 'grandeur' or 'elevation' of the style. As far as Milton is concerned (for I am not scholar enough to analyse Virgil) this grandeur is produced mainly by three things: (1) the use of slightly unfamiliar words and con-structions, including archaisms; (2) the use of proper names, not solely nor chiefly for their sound, but because they are the names of splendid, remote, terrible, voluptuous, or celebrated things; they are there to en-courage a sweep of the reader's eye over the richness and variety of the world—to supply that *largior aether* which we breathe as long as the poem lasts; (3) continued allusion to all the sources of heightened interest in our sense experience (light, darkness, storm, flowers, jewels, sexual love, and the like), but all over-topped and 'managed' with an air of magnanimous

"The Style of Secondary Epic," "Defence of This Style." From *A Preface to Paradise Lost* by C. S. Lewis, London, 1942. Reprinted by permission of the Oxford University Press.

austerity. Hence comes the feeling of sensual excitement *without* surrender or relaxation, the extremely tonic, yet also extremely rich, quality of our experience while we read. But all this you might have in great poems which were not epic. What I chiefly want to point out is something else —the poet's unremitting *manipulation* of his readers—how he sweeps us along as though we were attending an actual recitation and nowhere allows us to settle down and luxuriate on any one line or paragraph. It is common to speak of Milton's style as organ music. It might be more helpful to regard the reader as the organ and Milton as the organist. It is on us he plays, if we will let him.

Consider the opening paragraph. The ostensible philosophical purpose of the poem (to justify the ways of God to Man) is here of quite secondary importance. The real function of these twenty-six lines is to give us the sensation *that some great thing is now about to begin.* If the poet succeeds in doing that sufficiently, we shall be clay in his hands for the rest of Book 1 and perhaps longer; for be it noted that in this kind of poetry most of the poet's battles are won in advance. And as far as I am concerned, he succeeds completely, and I think I see something of how he does it. Firstly, there is the quality of weight, produced by the fact that nearly all the lines end in long, heavy monosyllables. Secondly, there is the direct suggestion of deep spiritual preparation at two points—*O spirit who dost prefer* and *What in me is dark.* But notice how cunningly this direct suggestion of great beginnings is reinforced by allusion to the creation of the world itself (*Dove-like sat'st brooding*), and then by images of rising and lifting (*With no middle flight intends to soar . . . raise and support—Highth of this great argument*) and then again how creation and rising come potently together when we are reminded that Heaven and Earth *rose out of Chaos,* and how in addition to this we have that brisk, morning promise of good things to come, borrowed from Ariosto (*things unattempted yet*), and how *till one greater Man* makes us feel we are about to read an epic that spans over the whole of history with its arch. All images that can suggest a great thing beginning have been brought together and our very muscles respond as we read. But look again and you will see that the ostensible and logical connexion between these images is not exactly the same as the emotional connexion which I have been tracing. The point is important. In one respect, Milton's technique is very like that of some moderns. He throws ideas together because of those emotional relations which they have in the very recesses of our consciousness. But unlike the moderns he always provides a façade of logical connexions as well. The virtue of this is that it lulls our logical faculty to sleep and enables us to accept what we are given without question.

This distinction between the logical connexions which the poet puts on the surface and the emotional connexions whereby he really manipulates our imagination is the key to many of his similes. The Miltonic simile does not always serve to illustrate what it pretends to be illustrating.

The likeness between the two things compared is often trivial, and is, indeed, required only to save the face of the logical censor. At the end of
Book I the fiends are compared to elves. Smallness is the only point of
resemblance. The first use of the simile is to provide contrast and relief,
to refresh us by a transition from Hell to a moonlit English lane. Its second use becomes apparent when we suddenly return to where

> far within
> And in thir own dimensions like themselves
> The great Seraphic Lords and Cherubim
> In close recess and secret conclave sat,
> A thousand Demy-Gods on golden seats.

                                                                    (I, 796.)

It is by contrast with the fairies that these councillors have grown so huge,
and by contrast with the fanciful simile that the hush before their debate
becomes so intense, and it is by that intensity that we are so well prepared
for the opening of Book II. It would be possible to go further and to say
that this simile is simply the point at which the whole purpose of trans-
forming the fiends to dwarfish stature is achieved, and that this transformation itself has a retrospective effect on the hugeness of Pandemonium.
For the logician it may appear as something 'dragged in by the heels',
but in poetry it turns out to be so bound up with the whole close of the
first Book and the opening of the second that if it were omitted the
wound would spread over about a hundred lines. Nearly every sentence
in Milton has that power which physicists sometimes think we shall have
to attribute to matter—the power of action at a distance.

Examples of this subterranean virtue (so to call it) in the Miltonic simile will easily occur to every one's memory. Paradise is compared to the
field of Enna—one beautiful landscape to another (IV, 268). But, of
course, the deeper value of the simile lies in the resemblance which is
not explicitly noted as a resemblance at all, the fact that in both these
places the young and the beautiful while gathering flowers was ravished
by a dark power risen up from the underworld. A moment later Eden is
compared to the *Nysician isle* and to *Mount Amara*. Unlearned readers
may reassure themselves. In order to get the good out of this simile it is
not at all necessary to look up these places in the notes, nor has pedantry
any share in the poet's motives for selecting them. All that we need to
know the poet tells us. The one was a river island and the other a high
mountain, and both were *hiding places.* If only we will read on, asking
no questions, the sense of Eden's secrecy, of things infinitely precious,
guarded, locked up, and put away, will come out of that simile and enrich what Milton is all the time trying to evoke in each reader—the consciousness of Paradise. Sometimes, I admit, the poet goes too far and the
feint of logical connexion is too outrageous to be accepted. In IV, 160-71
Milton wants to make us feel the full obscenity of Satan's presence in
Eden by bringing a sudden stink of fish across the sweet smell of the flow-

ers, and alluding to one of the most unpleasant Hebrew stories. But the
pretence of logical connexion (that Satan liked the flowers of Paradise
better than Asmodeus liked the smell of burning fish) is too strained. We
feel its absurdity.

This power of manipulation is not, of course, confined to the similes.
Towards the end of Book III Milton takes Satan to visit the sun. To
keep on harping on heat and brightness would be no use; it would end
only in that bog of superlatives which is the destination of many bad
poets. But Milton makes the next hundred lines as Solar as they could
possibly be. We have first (583) the picture of the sun *gently warming* the
universe, and a hint of the enormous distances to which this *virtue* penetrates. Then at line 588, by means of what is not much more than a pun
on the word *spot* we have Galileo's recent discovery of the sun-spots.
After that we plunge into alchemy because the almost limitless powers
attributed to gold in that science and the connexion of gold with the
solar influence make a kind of mirror in which we can view the regal, the
vivifying, the *archchemic* properties of the sun. Then, still working indirectly, Milton makes us realize the marvel of a shadowless world (614-20).
After that we meet Uriel (*Fire of God*), and because the sun (as every child
knew from Spenser and Ovid, if not from Pliny and Bernardus) is the
world's eye, we are told that Uriel is one of those spirits who are God's
eyes (650) and is even, in a special sense, God's singular *eye* in this material world (660) and 'the sharpest-sighted Spirit of all in Heav'n' (691).
This is not, of course, the sun of modern science; but almost everything
which the sun had meant to man up till Milton's day has been gathered
together and the whole passage in his own phrase, 'runs potable gold'.

A great deal of what is mistaken for pedantry in Milton (we hear too
often of his 'immense learning') is in reality evocation. If Heaven and
Earth are ransacked for simile and allusion, this is not done for display,
but in order to guide our imaginations with unobtrusive pressure into
the channels where the poet wishes them to flow; and as we have already
seen, the learning which a reader requires in responding to a given allusion does not equal the learning Milton needed to find it. When we have
understood this it will perhaps be possible to approach that feature of
Milton's style which has been most severely criticized—the Latinism of
his constructions.

Continuity is an essential of the epic style. If the mere printed page is
to affect us like the voice of a bard chanting in a hall, then the chant must
go on—smoothly, irresistibly, 'upborne with indefatigable wings'. We
must not be allowed to settle down at the end of each sentence. Even
the fuller pause at the end of a paragraph must be felt as we feel the pause
in a piece of music, where the silence is part of the music, and not as we
feel the pause between one item of a concert and the next. Even between
one Book and the next we must not wholly wake from the enchantment
nor quite put off our festal clothes. A boat will not answer to the rudder

unless it is in motion; the poet can work upon us only as long as we are kept on the move.

Roughly speaking, Milton avoids discontinuity by an avoidance of what grammarians call the simple sentence. Now, if the sort of things he was saying were at all like the things that Donne or Shakespeare say, this would be intolerably tiring. He therefore compensates for the complexity of his syntax by the simplicity of the broad imaginative effects beneath it and the perfect rightness of their sequence. For us readers, this means in fact that our receptivity can be mainly laid open to the underlying simplicity, while we have only to *play* at the complex syntax. It is not in the least necessary to go to the very bottom of these verse sentences as you go to the bottom of Hooker's sentences in prose. The general feeling (which will usually be found to be correct if you insist on analysing it) that something highly concatenated is before you, that the flow of speech does not fall apart into separate lumps, that you are following a great unflagging voice—this is enough to keep the 'weigh' on you by means of which the poet steers. Let us take an example:

> If thou beest he—but O how fall'n! how chang'd
> From him who in the happy Realms of Light
> Cloth'd with transcendent brightness didst outshine
> Myriads though bright: If he whom mutual league,
> United thoughts and counsels, equal hope
> And hazard in the Glorious Enterprise,
> Joynd with me once, now misery hath joynd
> In equal ruin: into what Pit thou seest
> From what highth fal'n.

(I, 84.)

This is a pretty complicated sentence. On the other hand, if you read it (and let the ghost of a chanting, not a talking, voice be in your ear) without bothering about the syntax, you receive in their most natural order all the required impressions—the lost glories of heaven, the first plotting and planning, the hopes and hazards of the actual war, and then the misery, the ruin, and the pit. But the complex syntax has not been useless. It has preserved the *cantabile,* it has enabled you to feel, even within these few lines, the enormous onward pressure of the great stream on which you are embarked. And almost any sentence in the poem will illustrate the same point.

The extremely Latin connexions between the sentences serve the same purposes, and involve, like the similes, a fair amount of illusion. A good example is *nor sometimes forget,* in III, 32. In this passage Milton is directly calling up what he indirectly suggests throughout, the figure of the great blind bard. It will, of course, be greatly enriched if the mythical blind bards of antiquity are brought to bear on us. A poet like Spenser would simply begin a new stanza with *Likewise dan Homer* or something of the sort. But that will not quite serve Milton's purpose: it is a little too like rambling, it might suggest the garrulity of an old gentleman in his chair. *Nor sometimes forget* gets him across from *Sion and the flowery brooks* to *Blind Thamyris* with an appearance of continuity, like the stylized movement by which a dancer passes from one position to another. *Yet not the more* in line 26 is another example. So are *sad task Yet argument* (IX, 13) and *Since first this subject* (IX, 25). These expressions do not represent real connexions of thought, any more than the prolonged syllables in Handel represent real pronunciation.

It must also be noticed that while Milton's Latin constructions in one way tighten up our language, in another way they make it more fluid. A fixed order of words is the price—an all but ruinous price—which English pays for being uninflected. The Miltonic constructions enable the poet to depart, in some degree, from this fixed order and thus to drop the ideas into his sentence in any order he chooses. Thus, for example,

> soft oppression seis'd
> My droused sense, untroubl'd, though I thought
> I then was passing to my former state
> Insensible, and forthwith to dissolve.

> (VIII, 291.)

The syntax is so artificial that it is ambiguous. I do not know whether *untroubled* qualifies *me* understood, or *sense,* and similar doubts arise about *insensible* and the construction of *to dissolve.* But then I don't need to know. The sequence *droused—untroubled—my former state—insensible—dissolve* is exactly right; the very crumbling of consciousness is before us and the fringe of syntactical mystery helps rather than hinders the effect. Thus, in another passage, I read

> Heav'n op'nd wide
> Her ever-during Gates, Harmonious sound
> On golden Hinges moving.

> (VII, 205.)

Moving might be a transitive participle agreeing with *gates* and governing *sound;* or again the whole phrase from *harmonious* to *moving* might be an ablative absolute. The effect of the passage, however, is the same whichever we choose. An extreme modern might have attempted to reach it with

> Gates open wide. Glide
> On golden hinges . . .
> Moving . . .
> Harmonious sound.

This melting down of the ordinary units of speech, this plunge back into something more like the indivisible, flowing quality of immediate expe-

rience, Milton also achieves. But by his appearance of an extremely car-
pentered structure he avoids the suggestion of fever, preserves the sense
of dignity, and does not irritate the mind to ask questions.

Finally, it remains to judge this style not merely as an epic style, but
as a style for that particular story which Milton has chosen. I must ask
the reader to bear with me while I examine it at its actual work of narration. Milton's theme leads him to deal with certain very basic images
in the human mind—with the archetypal patterns, as Miss Bodkin would
call them, of Heaven, Hell, Paradise, God, Devil, the Winged Warrior,
the Naked Bride, the Outer Void. Whether these images come to us from
real spiritual perception or from pre-natal and infantile experience con-
fusedly remembered, is not here in question; how the poet arouses them,
perfects them, and then makes them re-act on one another in our minds
is the critic's concern. I use the word 'arouses' advisedly. The naif reader
thinks Milton is going to *describe* Paradise as Milton imagines it; in reality the poet knows (or behaves as if he knew) that this is useless. His own
private image of the happy garden, like yours and mine, is full of irrelevant particularities—notably, of memories from the first garden he ever
played in as a child. And the more thoroughly he describes those particularities the further we are getting away from the Paradisal idea as it exists
in our minds, or even in his own. For it is something coming *through* the
particularities, some light which transfigures them, that really counts, and
if you concentrate on them you will find them turning dead and cold
under your hands. The more elaborately, in *that* way, we build the temple, the more certainly we shall find, on completing it, that the god has
flown. Yet Milton must *seem* to describe—you cannot just say nothing
about Paradise in *Paradise Lost*. While seeming to describe his own imagination he must actually arouse ours, and arouse it not to make definite
pictures, but to find again in our own depth the Paradisal light of which
all explicit images are only the momentary reflection. We are his organ:
when he appears to be describing Paradise he is in fact drawing out the
Paradisal Stop in us. The place where he chiefly does so (IV, 131-286) is
worth examination in detail.

It begins (131) *so on he fares. On* is the operative word. He is going on
and on. Paradise is a long way off. At present we are approaching only
its *border*. Distance means gradualness of approach. It is *now nearer*
(133). Then come the obstacles; a *steep wilderness* with *hairy sides* (135).
Do not overlook *hairy*. The Freudian idea that the happy garden is an
image of the human body would not have frightened Milton in the least,
though, of course, the main point is that the ascent was *grotesque and
wild* (136) and *access denied* (137). But we want something more than
obstacle. Remember that in this kind of poetry the poet's battles are
mainly won in advance. If he can give us the idea of increasing expec-
tancy, the idea of the Paradisal light coming but not yet come, then, when
at last he has to make a show of describing the garden itself, we shall be

already conquered. He is doing his work *now* so that when the climax comes we shall actually do the work for ourselves. Therefore, at line 137, he begins playing on the note of progression—upward progression, a vertical serialism. *Overhead* is *insuperable height* of trees (138). But that is not enough. The trees are ladder-like or serial trees (cedar, pine, and fir) with one traditionally eastern and triumphal tree (the palm) thrown in (139). They stand up like a stage set (140) where Milton is thinking of *silvis scaena coruscis*. They go up in tiers like a theatre (140-2). Already, while I read, I feel as if my neck ached with looking higher and higher. Then quite unexpectedly, as in dream landscapes, we find that what seemed the top is not the top. Above all these trees, *yet higher* (142) springs up the green, living wall of Paradise. And now a moment's rest from our looking upward; at a wave of the wand we are seeing the whole thing reversed—we are Adam, King of Earth, looking *down* from that green rampart into this lower world (144-5)—and, of course, when we return it seems loftier still. For even that wall was not the real top. Above the wall—yes, at last, almost beyond belief, we see for once with mortal eyes the trees of Paradise itself. In lines 147-9 we get the first bit of direct description. *Of course*, the trees have golden fruit. We always knew they would. Every myth has told us so; to ask for 'originality' at this point is stark insensibility. But we are not allowed to go on looking at them. The simile of the rainbow (150-2) is introduced, and at once our glimpse of Paradise recedes to the rainbow's end. Then the theme of serialism is picked up again—the air is growing purer every minute (153); and this idea (*Quan la douss aura venta*) at once passes into a nineteen-line exploitation of the most evocative of the senses, suddenly countered by the stench of Satan (167). Then a pause, as if after a crashing piece of orchestration, and we go back to the images of gradual approach, Satan still journeying *on* (172). Now the obstacles grow more formidable and it presently turns out (as the Trojans had found on sighting Italy) that the real entrance is *on the other side* (179). What follows is concerned with the main theme of the story and may be omitted here. We return to Paradise at 205. We are in at last, and now the poet has to do something in the way of description; well for him that the Paradise-complex in us is now thoroughly awake and that almost any particular image he gives us will be caught up and assimilated. But he does not begin with a particular image, rather with an idea—*in narrow room Nature's whole wealth.* The 'narrow room', the sense of a small guarded place, of sweetness rolled into a ball, is essential. God had *planted* it all (210). Not created it, but planted it—an anthropomorphic God out of Ezekiel xxxi, the God of our childhood and man's, making a toy garden as *we* made them when we were children. The earliest and lowest levels are being uncovered. And all this realm was studded once with rich and ancient cities; a *pleasant soil* (214), but the mountain of Paradise, like a jewel set in gold, *far more pleasant* (215) so that an emotion stolen from the splendour of the cities now flows into our feeling of Paradise. Then come the trees, the mythical and numinous trees, and *vegetable gold* from the garden of Hesperus (217-22). Then the rivers, which like Alph plunge into darkness and rise from it through *pores* at the bidding of *kindly thirst* (228), and Paradise again reminds us of a human body; and in contrast with this organic dark we have *crisped brooks* above (237) and the hard, bright suggestions of *pearl* and *gold* (238). Finally, from line 246 to 265, we get actual description. It is all, most rightly, generalized, and it is short. A reader who dislikes this kind of poetry would possibly express his objection to Milton's Paradise by saying it contained 'all the right things'—odorous gums, golden fruit, thornless roses, murmuring falls—and would prefer something he had not expected. But the unexpected has here no place. These references to the obvious and the immemorial are there not to give us new ideas about the lost garden but to make us know that the garden is found, that we have come home at last and reached the centre of the maze—our centre, humanity's centre, not some private centre of the poet's. And they last only long enough to do so. The representation begins swelling and trembling at 264 with the nervous reiteration of *airs* in order that it may *burst* in the following lines—may flow over into a riot of mythology where we are so to speak, drenched. That is the real climax; and then, having been emparadised, we are ready at line 288 to meet at last the white, erect, severe, voluptuous forms of our first parents.

Defence of This Style

> One hand a Mathematique Christall swayes,
> Which, gathering in one line a thousand rayes
> From her[1] bright eyes, Confusion *burnes to death,*
> And all estates of men distinguisheth.
> By it Morallitie and Comelinesse
> Themselves in all their sightly figures dresse.
> Her other hand a lawrell rod applies,
> To beate back Barbarisme and Avarice,
> That follow'd, eating earth and excrement
> And human limbs; and would make proud ascent
> To seates of gods, were Ceremonie slaine.

CHAPMAN: *Hero and Leander,* III, 131.

I believe I am right in saying that the reaction of many readers to the chapter I have just finished might be expressed in the following words. 'You have described exactly what we do *not* call poetry. This manipulation of the audience which you attribute to Milton is just what distinguishes the vile art of the rhetorician and the propagandist from the disinterested activity of the poet. This evocation of stock responses to conventional situations, which you choose to call Archetypal Patterns, is the

---

[1] Those of the goddess Ceremony.

very mark of the cheap writer. This calculated pomp and grandiosity is the sheer antithesis of true poetic sincerity—a miserable attempt to appear high by mounting on stilts. In brief, we always suspected that Milton was bogus, and you have confirmed our suspicion. *Habemus confitentem reum.*' I hardly expect to convert many of those who take such a view; but it would be a mistake not to make clear that the difference between us is essential. If these are my errors they are not errors into which I have fallen inadvertently, but the very lie in the soul. If these are my truths, then they are basic truths the loss of which means imaginative death.

First, as to Manipulation. I do not think (and no great civilization has ever thought) that the art of the rhetorician is necessarily vile. It is in itself noble, though of course, like most arts, it can be wickedly used. I do not think that Rhetoric and Poetry are distinguished by manipulation of an audience in the one and, in the other, a pure self expression, regarded as its own end, and indifferent to any audience. Both these arts, in my opinion, definitely aim at doing something to an audience. And both do it by using language to control what already exists in our minds. The differentia of Rhetoric is that it wishes to produce in our minds some practical resolve (to condemn Warren Hastings or to declare war on Philip) and it does this by calling the passions to the aid of reason. It is honestly practised when the orator honestly believes that the thing which he calls the passions to support *is* reason, and usefully practised when this belief of his is in fact correct. It is mischievously practised when that which he summons the passions to aid is, in fact, unreason, and dishonestly practised when he himself knows that it is unreason. The proper use is lawful and necessary because, as Aristotle points out, intellect of itself 'moves nothing': the transition from thinking to doing, in nearly all men at nearly all moments, needs to be assisted by appropriate states of feeling. Because the end of rhetoric is in the world of action, the objects it deals with appear foreshortened and much of their reality is omitted. Thus the ambitions of Philip are shown only in so far as they are wicked and dangerous, because indignation and moderate fear are emotional channels through which men pass from thinking to doing. Now good poetry, if it dealt with the ambitions of Philip, would give you something much more like their total reality—what it felt like to be Philip and Philip's place in the whole system of things. Its Philip would, in fact, be more *concrete* than the Philip of the orator. That is because poetry aims at producing something more like vision than it is like action. But vision, in this sense, includes passions. Certain things, if not seen as lovely or detestable, are not being correctly seen at all. When we try to rouse some one's hate of toothache in order to persuade him to ring up the dentist, this is rhetoric; but even if there were no practical issue involved, even if we only wanted to convey the reality of toothache for some speculative purpose or for its own sake, we should still have failed if the idea produced in our friend's mind did not include the hatefulness of toothache. Toothache, with that

left out, is an abstraction. Hence the awakening and moulding of the
reader's or hearer's emotions is a necessary element in that vision of concrete reality which poetry hopes to produce. Very roughly, we might almost say that in Rhetoric imagination is present for the sake of passion
(and, therefore, in the long run, for the sake of action), while in poetry
passion is present for the sake of imagination, and therefore, in the long
run, for the sake of wisdom or spiritual health—the rightness and richness of a man's total response to the world. Such rightness, of course, has
a tendency to contribute indirectly to right action, besides being in itself
exhilarating and tranquillizing; that is why the old critics were right
enough when they said that Poetry taught by delighting, or delighted by
teaching. The rival theories of Dr. Richards and Professor D. G. James
are therefore perhaps not so different that we cannot recognize a point
of contact. Poetry, for Dr. Richards, produces a wholesome equilibrium
of our psychological attitudes. For Professor James, it presents an object
of 'secondary imagination', gives us a view of the world. But a concrete
(as opposed to a purely conceptual) view of reality would in fact involve
right attitudes; and the totality of right attitudes, if man is a creature at
all adapted to the world he inhabits, would presumably be in wholesome
equilibrium. But however this may be, Poetry certainly aims at making
the reader's mind what it was not before. The idea of a poetry which exists only for the poet—a poetry which the public rather overhears than
hears—is a foolish novelty in criticism. There is nothing specially admirable in talking to oneself. Indeed, it is arguable that Himself is the very
audience before whom a man postures most and on whom he practises the
most elaborate deceptions.

Next comes the question of Stock Responses. By a Stock Response Dr.
I. A. Richards means a deliberately organized attitude which is substi-
tuted for 'the direct free play of experience'. In my opinion such deliberate organization is one of the first necessities of human life, and one
of the main functions of art is to assist it. All that we describe as con-
stancy in love or friendship, as loyalty in political life, or, in general, as
perseverance—all solid virtue and stable pleasure—depends on organiz-
ing chosen attitudes and maintaining them against the eternal flux (or
'direct free play') of mere immediate experience. This Dr. Richards would
not perhaps deny. But his school puts the emphasis the other way. They
talk as if improvement of our responses were always required in the direction of finer discrimination and greater particularity; never as if men
needed responses more normal and more traditional than they now have.
To me, on the other hand, it seems that most people's responses are not
'stock' enough, and that the play of experience is too free and too direct
in most of us for safety or happiness or human dignity. A number of
causes may be assigned for the opposite belief. (1) The decay of Logic, resulting in an untroubled assumption that the particular is real and the
universal is not. (2) A Romantic Primitivism (not shared by Dr. Richards

himself) which prefers the merely natural to the elaborated, the un-willed to the willed. Hence a loss of the old conviction (once shared by Hindoo, Platonist, Stoic, Christian, and 'humanist' alike) that simple 'experience', so far from being something venerable, is in itself mere raw material, to be mastered, shaped, and worked up by the will. (3) A confusion (arising from the fact that both are voluntary) between the organization of a response and the pretence of a response. Von Hügel says somewhere, 'I kiss my son not only because I love him, but in order that I may love him.' That is organization, and good. But you may also kiss children in order to make it *appear* that you love them. That is pretence, and bad. The distinction must not be overlooked. Sensitive critics are so tired of seeing good Stock responses aped by bad writers that when at last they meet the reality they mistake it for one more instance of posturing. They are rather like a man I knew who had seen so many bad pictures of moonlight on water that he criticized a real weir under a real moon as 'conventional'. (4) A belief (not unconnected with the doctrine of the Unchanging Human Heart which I shall discuss later) that a certain elementary rectitude of human response is 'given' by nature herself, and may be taken for granted, so that poets, secure of this basis are free to devote themselves to the more advanced work of teaching us ever finer and finer discrimination. I believe this to be a dangerous delusion. Children like dabbling in dirt; they have to be *taught* the stock response to it. Normal sexuality, far from being a *datum,* is achieved by a long and delicate process of suggestion and adjustment which proves too difficult for some individuals and, at times, for whole societies. The Stock response to Pride, which Milton reckoned on when he delineated his Satan, has been decaying ever since the Romantic Movement began—that is one of the reasons why I am composing these lectures. The Stock response to treachery has become uncertain; only the other day I heard a respectable working man defend Lord Haw-Haw by remarking coolly (and with no hint of anger or of irony), 'You've got to remember that's how he earns his pay.' The Stock response to death has become uncertain. I have heard a man say that the only 'amusing' thing that happened while he was in hospital was the death of a patient in the same ward. The Stock response to pain has become uncertain; I have heard Mr. Eliot's comparison of evening to a patient on an operating table praised, nay gloated over, not as a striking picture of sensibility in decay, but because it was so 'pleasantly unpleasant'. Even the Stock response to pleasure cannot be depended on; I have heard a man (and a young man, too) condemn Donne's more erotic poetry because 'sex', as he called it, always 'made him think of lysol and rubber goods'. That elementary rectitude of human response, at which we are so ready to fling the unkind epithets of 'stock', 'crude', 'bourgeois', and 'conventional', so far from being 'given' is a delicate balance of trained habits, laboriously acquired and easily lost, on the maintenance of which depend both our virtues and our pleas-

ures and even, perhaps, the survival of our species. For though the human heart is not unchanging (nay, changes almost out of recognition in
the twinkling of an eye) the laws of causation are. When poisons become
fashionable they do not cease to kill.

The examples I have cited warn us that those Stock responses which
we need in order to be even human are already in danger. In the light of
that alarming discovery there is no need to apologize for Milton or for
any other pre-Romantic poet. The older poetry, by continually insisting
on certain Stock themes—as that love is sweet, death bitter, virtue lovely,
and children or gardens delightful—was performing a service not only of
moral and civil, but even of biological, importance. Once again, the old
critics were quite right when they said that poetry 'instructed by delighting', for poetry was formerly one of the chief means whereby each new
generation learned, not to copy, but by copying to make,[2] the good Stock
responses. Since poetry has abandoned that office the world has not bet-
tered. While the moderns have been pressing forward to conquer new
territories of consciousness, the old territory, in which alone man can
live, has been left unguarded, and we are in danger of finding the enemy
in our rear. We need most urgently to recover the lost poetic art of en-
riching a response without making it eccentric, and of being normal without being vulgar. Meanwhile—until that recovery is made—such poetry
as Milton's is more than ever necessary to us.

There is, furthermore, a special reason why mythical poetry ought not
to attempt novelty in respect of its ingredients. What it does with the
ingredients may be as novel as you please. But giants, dragons, paradises,
gods, and the like are themselves the expression of certain basic elements
in man's spiritual experience. In that sense they are more like words—
the words of a language which speaks the else unspeakable—than they
are like the people and places in a novel. To give them radically new
characters is not so much original as ungrammatical. That strange blend
of genius and vulgarity, the film of *Snow-White,* will illustrate the point.
There was good unoriginality in the drawing of the queen. She was the
very archetype of all beautiful, cruel queens: the thing one expected to
see, save that it was truer to type than one had dared to hope for. There
was bad originality in the bloated, drunken, low comedy faces of the
dwarfs. Neither the wisdom, the avarice, nor the earthiness of true dwarfs
were there, but an imbecility of arbitrary invention. But in the scene
where Snow-White wakes in the woods both the right originality and the
right unoriginality were used together. The good unoriginality lay in
the use of small, delicate animals as comforters, in the true *märchen* style.
The good originality lay in letting us at first mistake their eyes for the
eyes of monsters. The whole art consists not in evoking the unexpected,
but in evoking with a perfection and accuracy beyond expectation the

---

[2] 'We learn how to do things by doing the things we are learning how to do,' as
Aristotle observes (*Ethics,* ii, i).

very image that has haunted us all our lives. The marvel about Milton's Paradise or Milton's Hell is simply that they are there—that the thing has at last been done—that our dream stands before us and does not melt. Not many poets can thus draw out leviathan with a hook. Compared with this the short-lived pleasure of any novelty the poet might have inserted would be a mere kickshaw.

The charge of calculated grandiosity, of 'stilts' remains. The difficulty here is that the modern critic tends to think Milton is somehow trying to deceive. We feel the pressure of the poet on every word—the *builded* quality of the verse—and since this is the last effect most poets wish to produce today, we are in danger of supposing that Milton also would have concealed it if he could, that it is a tell-tale indication of his failure to achieve spontaneity. But does Milton want to sound spontaneous? He tells us that his verse was unpremeditated in fact and attributes this to the Muse. Perhaps it was. Perhaps by that time his own epic style had become 'a language which thinks and poetizes of itself.' But that is hardly the point. The real question is whether an *air* of spontaneity—an impression that this is the direct outcome of immediate personal emotion—would be in the least proper to this kind of work. I believe it would not. We should miss the all-important sense that *something out of the ordinary is being done*. Bad poets in the tradition of Donne write artfully and try to make it sound colloquial. If Milton were to practise deception, it would be the other way round. A man performing a rite is not trying to make you think that this is his natural way of walking, these the unpremeditated gestures of his own domestic life. If long usage has in fact made the ritual unconscious, he must labour to make it look deliberate, in order that we, the assistants, may feel the weight of the solemnity pressing on his shoulders as well as on our own. Anything casual or familiar in his manner is not 'sincerity' or 'spontaneity', but impertinence. Even if his robes were not heavy in fact, they ought to *look* heavy. But there is no need to suppose any deception. Habit and devout concentration of mind, or something else for which the Muse is as good a name as any other, may well have brought it to pass that the verse of *Paradise Lost* flowed into his mind without labour; but what flowed was something stylized, remote from conversation, hierophantic. The style is not pretending to be 'natural' any more than a singer is pretending to talk.

Even the poet, when he appears in the first person within his own poem, is not to be taken as the private individual John Milton. If he were that, he would be an irrelevance. He also becomes an image—the image of the Blind Bard—and we are told about him nothing that does not help that archetypal pattern. It is his office, not his person, that is sung. It would be a gross error to regard the opening of *Samson* and the opening of Book III as giving us respectively what Milton really felt, and what he would be thought to feel, about his blindness. The real man, of course, being a man, felt many more things, and less interesting things, about it than are expressed in either. From that total experience the poet selects, for his epic and for his tragedy, what is proper to each. The impatience, the humiliation, the questionings of Providence go into *Samson* because the business of tragedy is 'by raising pity and fear, or terror, to purge the mind of those and such-like passions . . . with a kind of delight stirred up by reading or seeing those passions well imitated'. If he had not been blind himself, he would still (though with less knowledge to guide him) have put just those elements of a blind man's experience into the mouth of Samson: for the 'disposition of his fable' so as to 'stand best with verisimilitude and decorum' requires them. On the other hand, whatever is calm and great, whatever associations make blindness venerable—all this he selects for the opening of Book III. Sincerity and insincerity are words that have no application to either case. We want a great blind poet in the one, we want a suffering and questioning prisoner in the other. 'Decorum is the grand masterpiece.'

The grandeur which the poet assumes in his poetic capacity should not arouse hostile reactions. It is for our benefit. He makes his epic a rite so that we may share it; the more ritual it becomes, the more we are elevated to the rank of participants. Precisely because the poet appears not as a private person, but as a Hierophant or Choregus, we are summoned not to hear what one particular man thought and felt about the Fall, but to take part, under his leadership, in a great mimetic dance of all Christendom, ourselves soaring and ruining from Heaven, ourselves enacting Hell and Paradise, the Fall and the repentance.

Thus far of Milton's style on the assumption that it is in fact as remote and artificial as is thought. No part of my defence depends on questioning that assumption, for I think it ought to be remote and artificial. But it would not be honest to suppress my conviction that the degree to which it possesses these qualities has been exaggerated. Much that we think typically 'Poetic Diction' in *Paradise Lost* was nothing of the sort, and has since become Poetic Diction only because Milton used it. When he writes of an *optic glass* (I, 288) we think this is a poetical periphrasis because we are remembering Thomson or Akenside; but it seems to have been an ordinary expression in Milton's time. When we read *ruin and combustion* (I, 46) we naturally exclaim *aut Miltonus aut diabolus!* Yet the identical words are said to occur in a document of the Long Parliament. *Alchymy* (II, 517) sounds like the Miltonic vague: it is really almost a trade name. *Numerous* as applied to verse (V, 150) sounds 'poetic', but was not. If we could read *Paradise Lost* as it really was we should see more play of muscles than we see now. But only a little more. I am defending Milton's style as a ritual style.

I think the older critics may have misled us by saying that 'admiration' or 'astonishment' is the proper response to such poetry. Certainly if 'admiration' is taken in its modern sense, the misunderstanding becomes disastrous. I should say rather that joy or exhilaration was what it produced—an overplus of robust and tranquil well-being in a total experience which contains both rapturous and painful elements. In the *Dry Salvages* Mr. Eliot speaks of 'music heard so deeply that it is not heard at all'. Only as we emerge from the mode of consciousness induced by the symphony do we begin once more to attend explicitly to the sounds which induced it. In the same way, when we are caught up into the experience which a 'grand' style communicates, we are, in a sense, no longer conscious of the style. Incense is consumed by being used. The poem kindles admirations which leave us no leisure to admire the poem. When our participation in a rite becomes perfect we think no more of ritual, but are engrossed by that *about which* the rite is performed; but afterwards we recognize that ritual was the sole method by which this concentration could be achieved. Those who in reading *Paradise Lost* find themselves forced to attend throughout to the sound and the manner have simply not discovered what this sound and this manner were intended to do. A schoolboy who reads a page of Milton by chance, for the first time, and then looks up and says, 'By gum!' not in the least knowing how the thing has worked, but only that new strength and width and brightness and zest have transformed his world, is nearer to the truth than they.

The Language of *Paradise Lost*

by B. Rajan

Paradise Lost has not one style but several, as Pope was among the first to recognise. There is, at the simplest level of discrimination, an infernal style, a celestial style, and styles for Paradise before and after the fall. But the infernal style itself differs both mechanically and actually, in the heroic preparations of the first book, in the "great consult" in Pandemonium and in Satan's encounter with Sin and Death. The other styles reveal similar and substantial differences of application. In these circumstances it may seem irrelevant to talk of the poem's style at all, but the word, though deceptive, is not wholly beside the point. With all its variations, the language of the poem has a basic homogeneity and in fact one of the pleasures of reading *Paradise Lost* is to discover the wide differences the language can accommodate, without imperilling its unitive power. In this sense also the poem makes alive a basic quality of the reality which it celebrates.

Sublimity is a quality usually conceded to *Paradise Lost,* though it is argued that the sublimity is monolithic, that its price is petrification and that the style marches on irrespective of what is inside it. But perspicuity is not ordinarily associated with the poem, the general impression being that its syntax, its erudition and its latinised usages combine to invest it with a pervasive obscurity. Mr. Eliot is typical in observing that "the complication of a Miltonic sentence is an active complication, a complication deliberately introduced into what was a previously simplified and abstract thought." Although this is from the 1936 essay, we also find Mr. Eliot, in his 1947 recantation, still proclaiming that Milton's style is personal rather than classic, that its elevation is not the elevation of a common style, that in Milton "there is always the maximal, never the minimal, alteration of ordinary language" and that as a poet, Milton is "probably the greatest of all eccentrics." Similarly, Mr. Leavis observes: "So complete, and so mechanically habitual, is Milton's departure from the English order, structure and accentuation that he often produces passages that have to be read through several times before one can see

"The Language of *Paradise Lost*." From *John Milton, Paradise Lost, Books I & II*, edited with an Introduction and Commentary by B. Rajan, Bombay, 1964. Reprinted by permission of the author and Asia Publishing House Private Ltd.

how they go, though the Miltonic mind has nothing to offer that could justify obscurity—no obscurity was intended: it is merely that Milton has forgotten the English language." . . .

Fortunately all generalisations about *Paradise Lost* (including those that offer themselves as truisms) have to encounter and survive the text. The following lines from the ninth book are quoted not only because the syntax is uniformly unorthodox, but also because the unorthodoxy is maintained at a crisis in the action, in other words, under conditions of potentially maximum irrelevance:

> From his slack hand the Garland wreath'd for *Eve*
> Down dropd, and all the faded Roses shed:
> Speechless he stood and pale, till thus at length
> First to himself he inward silence broke.

It should not be necessary to point out how the first inversion sets in motion the succession of linked *a*'s that makes "slack" a reality in the sound and pace of the verse, or how the wreathing of the *e* sound in "wreath'd for *Eve*" is made more vivid by the placing of *"Eve"* at the climax of the line. The plummeting force of "Down dropd" is created both by the inversion and by its dramatic positioning (which the previous inversion has made possible). These departures from the normal word-order indicate how the syntax is being manoeuvred to create a pattern of impact rather than a logical or grammatical sequence. In this context "all the faded Roses shed" is surprising only in analysis. Within the poetry itself, it spreads out of the numbness of "Down dropd," so that Adam's paralysis seems to be measured by the manner in which it passes out into nature, withering the roses with the same shock that withers him. The image succeeds precisely by not calling attention to itself, by being shaped into the situation, into the inert downward movement. The next inversion places "Speechless" at the beginning of the line; both the stressed position and its anchoring by "stood" (the alliteration is, of course, purposive) charge the word with the surrounding sense of deadness. We are made aware that Adam's speechlessness is not ordinary consternation but the mental surface of his "inward silence." The separation of "speechless" and "pale" by "stood" (a favourite Miltonic device) is similarly functional; both in the syntax and in the reality being enacted, the inner condition is precedent and decisive. "Pale," we must also remember, was a stronger word to Milton's contemporaries than it is to us. The suggestion here is of the pallor of death. One recalls the "shuddring horror pale" of the fallen angels and the "pale and dreadful" light of their damnation. In this context, "till thus at length" is creatively ambiguous; the grammatical coupling with "he inward silence broke" is deliberately weakened by the inversion of the fourth line and this enables the emotional link with "Speechless he stood" to become active in the total movement. "First to himself" delays and defines the climax. Adam

is not soliloquising. Rather, he is seeking to achieve a response out of the
momentary paralysis of his being, to create out of inward silence a ground
for interior debate. The movement and tension of the poetry, charged
with meaning beneath the lucid surface, shape and intensify this reality.
Diction, syntax, sound and imagery contribute purposefully to the poetic
result.

This analysis has been pursued in some detail to indicate that the
poetry of *Paradise Lost* can bear and will respond to a far greater pressure of interpretation than it normally receives. It also suggests that
"the complication of a Miltonic sentence" is a creative rather than an
"active complication" if indeed it is a complication at all; the true aim
seems to be the playing of metrical against grammatical forces to form
and embolden the emotional line. This conclusion is not limited to the
"simpler" kind of writing that has been analysed; the following lines
present a characteristically different surface but are modelled by essentially similar forces. The quotation is from one of those passages in the
third book where God the Father turns a school divine, though according
to some of our better scholars, he speaks more like a seventeenth century
rhetorician, an ideal student of Puttenham and Peacham.

> Man disobeying
> Disloyal breaks his fealtie, and Sinns
> Against the high Supremacie of Heav'n
> Affecting God-head and so loosing all,
> To expiate his Treason hath naught left,
> But to destruction sacred and devote,
> He with his whole posteritie must die:
> Die hee or Justice must; unless for him
> Som other able, and as willing, pay
> The rigid satisfaction, death for death.
> Say Heav'nly Powers, where shall we find such love,
> Which of ye will be mortal to redeem
> Mans mortal crime, and just th' unjust to save?
> Dwels in all Heaven charitie so deare?

One is expected to note such touches as the manner in which "high
supremacie" recalls I, 132, tying the human sin to the angelic. Less
obvious, but equally part of the underlying network, is the exact pre-
monition in "But to destruction sacred and devote" of the truth which
breaks into Adam's inward silence (IX, 901) as he faces the finality of
Eve's sin. The irony of "Affecting God-head and so loosing all" has a
sardonic validity in itself but the punishment is also measured by the
presumption and the legal matching of the two is part of the poem's concept of justice. Some may find the use of the images of kingship curious,
but Milton's view that the only true monarchy is that of Heaven (XII,
67-71) is not only consistent but republican. In any case the imagery,
with its legalistic undertone, makes possible the intensification of dis-

obedience into disloyalty and finally into treason, thus dictating the
measured and monolithic verdict: "He with his whole posteritie must
die". One notes how the quasi-rhymes bind the judgment together and
how the crucial words "He" and "die" stand dramatically at the beginning and end of the line. Then comes the concentration, the sudden
swoop of emphasis, as these terminal words are driven and fused together, with both the inversion, the emphatic "hee" and the brief almost
ferocious power of the movement, joining to assert the law in its angry
finality. Everything is to the purpose now. The semicolon after "Die hee
or Justice must" reinforces the compulsive strength of "must" and once
again the inversion strengthens the impact. At the same time the strong
medial pause coming after an auxiliary verb creates a sense of expectation, of basic incompleteness; the movement in its clenched decisiveness
dictates the relaxation into the lines that follow. The body of the verse
begins to react to the awareness of a law transformed by charity. Though
the language of "Som other able, and as willing" remains legalistic, the
fluent movement of the verse, the suggestion of infinite love in "willing"
escapes from and redefines the merely legal. In the next line, the two
tendencies are forced into creative collision. "Death for death" states
the law in its sterile absoluteness, an absoluteness reflected fully in the
conclusive, hammer-like movement. But in "rigid satisfaction" the organic
word plays against and undermines the mechanical. The legal content
of "satisfaction" engages with "rigid" and with "death for death", locking
itself into the circle of crime and punishment. But the overtones of life
and growth in the word point securely to a higher satisfaction, a reality
beyond the exactions of the law. The line is a fortress which only love
can enter but the language in erecting it has also breached it. The relaxation of the movement is now both logical and organic. One need only
note the way in which the two uses of "mortal" preserve the legal
equivalence while opening the way into the wider paradox of "just th' unjust to save". In terms of the "rigid satisfaction" the balance is inequit-
able but the poetry has established a higher reality. It has created a
world in which charity becomes an imaginative fact as well as a theological principle. This is an achievement of peculiar difficulty since sensuous imagery is forbidden by the circumstances, and the animating forces
must therefore be those of syntax, and of word-play precisely and imaginatively controlled. Given these limited resources the result is a triumph
of considerably more than craftsmanship.

These two widely different passages suggest both the variety of Milton's
style and the criteria to which the style is answerable. That the verse will
bear considerable scrutiny is evident and in fact the most difficult temptation to reject in modern criticism is that which seeks to establish complexity, irony, ambiguity and paradox as controlling qualities of Milton's
writing. It is not merely convenient but reassuring to suggest that there
is one right way of using poetic language and that Milton's poetry like

all poetry, can be found true to that way. To deny the complexity of
Paradise Lost would of course, be perverse; but that does not mean that
complexity should be regarded as a principle shaping the local life of the
language. The complexity of Milton's epic is less one of surface than of
reverberation. It arises not so much from the immediate context, as from
the connection of that context to other contexts and eventually to the
context of the whole poem and of the cosmic order drawn into and recreated within it. Svendsen is right in arguing that "the basic mode of
Paradise Lost is ambivalence" and paradox and irony are equally vital in
its total effect. But these qualities operate through the poem's structure
rather than its texture. The surface is not characteristically complex, and
the resources of diction, syntax and imagery cooperate to clarify and intensify, rather than to qualify the main thrust of the poetry. Coleridge
understood this when he observed that "the connection of the sentences
and the position of the words are exquisitely artificial; but the position
is rather according to the logic of passion or universal logic than to the
logic of grammar." A more recent critic, Professor Wright, describes
Milton's style as "unusually clear and forceful" while MacCaffrey begins
a perceptive discussion by stating: "elevation, not breadth is the principal
dimension of epic. Unity and elevation demand that there should be a
single—even, in a sense, a simple—effect produced in the reader, and this
end is not to be accomplished by a style with a verbally complex surface."

All this is clearly as it should be. If the style is to develop its primary
(and symbolic) qualities of sublimity, of propulsive power, of designed
and inexorable movement, it can only do so through a deliberate simplicity of surface. The other qualities which matter are not sacrificed and
indeed are realized to a far greater extent than in any other poem of this
magnitude. They live, however, not so much on the surface, as in the
weight of qualification, connection and commentary which the whole
poem places behind every point on its surface. Milton's observation that
poetry is more simple, sensuous, and passionate than rhetoric is surely
not meant as an attempt to confuse us about the predominant qualities
of his verse. The style is capable of "metaphysical" effects or more correctly, it can frequently draw the metaphysical into the heroic; but it
remains heroic and not metaphysical. The distinction is important not
only in terms of decorum, but as an indication of how to read the poem,
of how to respond to its impact and its tactics. The present writer is
frankly not appalled by the discovery that there is more than one way of
using poetic language or that Milton is Milton because he is not Donne.
The open society of poetry ought to have room for the excellences of both.

Milton's Blank Verse:
The Diction

by F. T. Prince

I

There is a decisive change of tone in Milton's verse after 1638, a sudden access of confidence, which one may well attribute to his Italian travels; and this suggests that those travels themselves may have been undertaken with a precise literary purpose which had found what it sought. It seems possible that Milton's studies had led him to a point, in 1638, at which he found he must seek information in Italy itself concerning the methods and theories of heroic poetry. He went first to Florence for the tradition of critical analysis and discussion; he sought out Manso in Rome and Naples because he wished to find out all he could about Tasso, the only epic poet of modern times of whom he thoroughly approved.

However, even if we can never be sure that the tradition of epic 'magnificence' in Italian was a prime object of Milton's journey, we can assert that, as a result of his experience in Italy, he found it. The evidence of the texts is clear. At some time in these three or four years Milton had seized the idea of the 'magnificent' style in Italian, and decided to adopt its methods in English. His abnormal literary faculty made this seem a comparatively simple matter. There are no signs of faltering in the sonnets; and there is no reason to suppose that, if *Paradise Lost* had been written in the 1640s, it would have been stylistically less perfect than it is.

It becomes less difficult to account for the technical skill of *Paradise Lost* if we place it against the background of Italian Renaissance verse. Just as Milton had several perfectly accomplished Italian models for his type of sonnet, he had an Italian tradition of epic blank verse with which to reinforce the style and diction of *Paradise Lost*. It is true that in Italy no undeniably great work had yet been written in this form; the metre

"Milton's Blank Verse: The Diction." From *The Italian Element in Milton's Verse* by F. T. Prince, Oxford, 1954. Reprinted by permission of the author and The Clarendon Press, Oxford.

was not to attain its full glory there until the eighteenth century, when Parini surpassed all other didactic poets in infusing Virgilian grandeur into the descriptive satire of *Il Giorno*. But this eighteenth century achievement, and the admirable blank verse of the Romantic period which followed it, had itself been prepared for by the experiments of the *Cinquecento*: Milton in England did but develop the Italian epic tradition as it might well have been developed in Italy itself in the seventeenth century, had it not been for the failure of creative power which then came to Italian literature.

Blank verse in Italian was the invention of the *Cinquecento*.[1] Yet the attempts to perfect it as an instrument for epic poetry were for one reason or another unsuccessful. Trissino's *Italia Liberata* failed from sheer poverty of poetic energy and imagination. Caro's translation of the *Aeneid* was a most remarkable performance, but, far from raising his *versi sciolti* to the grave beauty of Virgil's hexameters, Caro rather brought the Roman epic down to the familiarity, ease, and delightful vividness of Tuscan speech.[2] Tasso's *Mondo Creato* was the most ambitious and sustained effort to raise blank verse to the heroic pitch; but it suffered, not only from Tasso's intellectual weaknesses and the weariness of his last years, but from the fact that its matter was not that of the epic proper.

Enough had been done, however, in sixteenth-century Italy, to show the possibilities for epic poetry held out by the new metre. And, moreover, enough had been written by Italian critics to show that they perceived both the dangers and the demands of this form of verse. It was realized that both diction and content must become of special importance when the metre itself imposes so little restraint on the poet. Even before Caro translated the *Aeneid,* the acuteness of a Florentine scholar, Carlo Lenzoni, had defined the problems of blank verse and pointed to its suitability for epic grandeur.

> Since one cannot cover up this verse [he wrote] with the sweetness of rhymes, or excuse oneself by the necessity of closing one's sentences, as in *terzetti* and *stanze;* and because, having been released from these demands, it can no longer make use of licences which are in themselves permissible: it does not allow of incorrectness, either in the language or the composition, it does not submit to harshness in the expression nor to weakness in the rhythm, it does not buoy up weak or empty ideas; and in fine it is not enough for it only to do what is necessary, it must also reject anything

[1] Carducci refers to a thirteenth-century blank-verse poem by Brunetto Latini and to a fourteenth-century Venetian author's use of blank verse for a series of love-epistles in the manner of Ovid; but he makes it clear that the metre only developed fully with the spread of classical studies in the sixteenth century ('Il Parini Maggiore', Storia del 'Giorno', *Opere* [Bologna, 1933], xiv. 279-82).

[2] See Carducci, op. cit., p. 265.

which is not great in itself or which art cannot make great by virtue of or-
namentation and beauty.[3]

Lenzoni thus anticipated by two centuries Johnson's dictum that
'blank verse, if it be not tumid and gorgeous, is but crippled prose'. The
Florentine critic proceeded to argue that these inherent necessities of
blank verse must impel it to the expression of heroic grandeur, both in
the conception and the language:

> Therefore, as being most capable of all gravity and grandeur, and, if one
> may put it so, most desirous of appearing marvellous to the hearer; and dif-
> fering from other forms of verse as the eloquent man is said to differ from
> the pedant: it seeks that point and perfection of excellence contained in the
> idea of perfect heroic poetry. The marvellous beauty of which kind of po-
> etry (though it can be better apprehended by the mind than by the ear) we
> have truly no kind of verse which can show us better or more fully than
> this, coloured not, so to speak, with artificial enamel, but with its own nat-
> ural blood.[4]

From such criticisms as these, and from the various Italian endeavours
to devise an epic form of blank verse, Milton could clearly perceive the
vital connexion here between verse and style, measure and manner. If
blank verse were to succeed, it must be largely by virtue of some special
power or beauty of diction. This was the lesson to be learnt from the
versi sciolti of the sixteenth century, and it included the recommendation
of Virgil as the all-sufficient model for the supreme diction required.

It is in the light of these decisions and discriminations that we must
interpret Milton's own statement of the structural principle of his verse:
'the sense variously drawn out from one verse into another'. The structural power of this principle could be developed fully only in blank verse,
for only in blank verse could its elaborate application be justified. The
basis of both English and Italian prosody was rhyme. Blank verse, having
discarded this, needed to find some other means of enforcing a continuity of pattern, inducing a continuity of expectation in the reader:
hence the play of diction and prosody in forms which produce slowness
and suspense. The Italians worked out this style with the guidance of
such general conceptions as *asprezza*, 'difficulty', and 'magnificence'.
Milton accepted their premises and conclusions, and adopted what he
could of their working methods.

II

It is scarcely possible to give more than a token of the relationship
between the rich Virgilian texture of *Paradise Lost* and Italian experiments in epic diction. This may be done, however, by taking as an ex-

[3] *In difesa della lingua fiorentina e di Dante* (Florence, 1556): quoted by Carducci, op.
cit., p. 281.
[4] Ibid.: Carducci, op. cit., p. 282.

ample a verbal pattern which comes down to the sixteenth century from earlier Italian poetry, and is then turned, with elaborations and variations, to the new purposes; and which Milton also makes a part of his epic diction.

A common usage in Italian poetry from Dante and Petrarch onwards is the addition of a second adjective, as an interjection or afterthought, to an already qualified substantive. This little device was found very useful by Bembo and his followers, and Della Casa employs it frequently as a part of his equipment for suspending the sense and slowing down the movement of his verse:

> *Or viver orbo i gravi giorni e rei*
> Now live bereaved my heavy days and cruel
>
> (Sonetto XIII)
>
> *Dolce rigor; cortese orgoglio e pio*
> Sweet severity, courteous disdain and kind
>
> (Sonetto XI)
>
> Bella *fera* e gentil *mi punse il seno*
> A fair wild beast, and sweet, had pierced my breast
>
> (Sonetto XII)
>
> *Fo mesti i boschi, e pii del mio cordoglio*
> Make sad the woods, and pitiful of my plight
>
> (Sonetto XLI)
>
> *In chiaro foco e memorabil arse*
> In a clear flame and memorable burned
>
> (Sonetto XXXV)

This trick of phrasing is very common in the sonnet form, where there is a constant tendency to arrange words in pairs. Milton introduces it into his English sonnets, and it appears early in *Paradise Lost*:

> Before all Temples th'upright heart and pure
>
> (*P.L.*, Book I, l. 18)

In this, its simplest form, it is indeed one of the marks of Milton's diction, and its appearance in any later writer is enough to stamp the verse as 'Miltonic':

> High matter thou injoinst me, O prime of men,
> Sad task and hard   (*P.L.*, Book V, ll. 563-4)
>
> He comes, and settl'd in his face I see
> Sad resolution and secure   (*P.L.*, Book VI, ll. 540-1)

An easy variation is to separate the second adjective, or adjectival phrase, more widely from the first:

> *Feroce spirto un tempo ebbi e guerrero*
> A fierce soul once I had, and warlike too
>
> (Della Casa, Sonetto XLVIII)

> *Aspro costume in bella Donna e rio*
> Harsh custom in fair lady, and unkind
>
> (Ibid., Sonetto III)
>
> *E di sì mansueta e gentil pria,*
> *Barbara fatta sovr' ogn' altra, e fera*
> And from so mild and well-conditioned once,
> Barbarous made above all others, and wild
>
> (Ibid., Sonetto LXI)
>
> *Così deluso il cor più volte, e punto*
> *Dall' aspro orgoglio, piagne*
> Thus undeceived the heart again, and pierced
> By sharp disdain, will weep   (Ibid., Sonetto V)
>
>   pleasing was his shape,
> And lovely   (*P.L.*, Book IX, ll. 503-4)
>
>   for wide was spred
> That Warr and various   (*P.L.*, Book VI, ll. 241-2)
>
> For many are the Trees of God that grow
> In Paradise, and various, yet unknown
> To us   (*P.L.*, Book IX, ll. 618-20)
>
> Faithful hath been your Warfare, and of God
> Accepted, fearless in his righteous Cause
>   (*P.L.*, Book VI, ll. 803-4)

It will be seen that these patterns grow in complexity, since the adjectives or participles placed in this way may have attached to them qualifying words or phrases, and these in their turn may be disposed in a similar pattern:

> *Ben mi scorgea quel dì crudele stella*
> *E di dolor ministra e di martiri*
> Troth I discerned that day a cruel star,
> And of sorrow ministrant and of pains
>
> (Della Casa, Sonetto XL)
>
> *Ed or di lui si scosse in tutto, e scinse*
> *Tua candida Alma, e leve fatta appieno,*
> *Salìo, son certo, ov' è più il Ciel sereno*
> And now from (earth) shook wholly free, and purged
> Itself, thy white soul, and made light in all,
> Climbed up, I know, where most the heavens are pure
>
> (Ibid., Sonetto XLV)
>
>   the Tree of Life,
> The middle Tree and highest there that grew
>   (*P.L.*, Book IV, ll. 194-5)
>
>   others on the grass
> Coucht, and, now fild with pasture gazing sat,
> Or Bedward ruminating   (*P.L.*, Book IV, ll. 350-2)

> then whom a Spirit more lewd
> Fell not from Heaven, or more gross to love
> Vice for it self   (*P.L.*, Book I, ll. 490-2)

But the full possibilities of such patterns as these only appear when
one looks for them without regard for the precise grammatical nature of
their components. Substantives or verbs can be placed in this way as
easily as adjectives; and the style of *Paradise Lost* is in reality less 'adjectival' than its fullness of statement would suggest. Milton more frequently
uses substantives than adjectives in the pattern in question:

> Amaze,
> Be sure, and terrour seis'd the rebel Host
>   (*P.L.*, Book VI, ll. 646-7)

> when the Scourge
> Inexorably, and the torturing houre
>   (*P.L.*, Book II, ll. 90-91)

> he seemd
> For dignity compos'd and high exploit
>   (*P.L.*, Book II, ll. 110-11)

Italian examples are not far to seek:

> *Ov' è 'l silenzio, che 'l dì fugge, e 'l lume?*
> Where is silence, that the day flees, and the light?
>   (Della Casa, Sonetto L)

> *Già fu valore, e chiaro sangue accolto*
> *Inseme, e cortesia*
> One time were valour and noble blood received
> Together, and courtesy   (Ibid., Sonetto LIV)

> *e ghiaccio*
> *Gli spiriti anch' io sento, e le membra farsi*
>   and ice
> My spirits too I feel, and limbs, become
>   (Ibid., Sonetto LVIII)

Even more constant and varied use is made of substantives combined with
adjectives in this way, because the placing of the adjectives before or
after their nouns can be made to contribute to the deliberate complex
balance:

> *Mansueto odio spero, e pregion pia*
> Mild hatred I may hope, and prison kind
>   (Ibid., Sonetto XXVII)

> *Mai io palustre augel, che poco s'erga*
> *Sull 'ale, sembro, o luce inferma, e lume*
> *Ch'a leve aura vacille, e si consume*
> But I some marshland bird, that scarce can rise

On pinions, seem, or some faint light or lamp
That to a slight breath wavers, and is spent

(Ibid., Sonetto XLIX)

Che più crudo Euro a me mio verno adduce,
Più lunga notte, e dì più freddi e scarsi
For harsher winds to me my winter brings,
A longer night, and days more chilled and drear

(Ibid., Sonetto LVIII)

So pray'd they innocent, and to thir thoughts
Firm peace recoverd soon and wonted calm

(*P.L.*, Book V, ll. 209-10)

his gestures fierce
He markd and mad demeanour, then alone

(*P.L.*, Book IV, ll. 128-9)

for his sleep
Was Aerie light, from pure digestion bred,
And temperat vapors bland, which th' only sound
Of leaves and fuming rills, Aurora's fan,
Lightly dispers'd, and the shrill Matin Song
Of Birds on every bough   (*P.L.*, Book V, ll. 3-8)

The last example illustrates beautifully how such patterns enrich themselves as they unfold, by a sort of natural impetus which they gather; that is to say, once the pattern imposes itself and its movement, numerous floating phrases may be attached to the central statement. Adjectives may be balanced against adverbial phrases or participles:

From Diamond Quarries hew'n & Rocks of Gold

(*P.L.*, Book V, l. 756)

but torture without end
Still urges, and a fiery Deluge, fed
With ever-burning Sulphur unconsum'd

(*P.L.*, Book I, ll. 67-69)

From thence a Rib, with cordial spirits warme,
And Life-blood streaming fresh

(*P.L.*, Book VIII, ll. 467-8)

The following passages show the same movement in various degrees of complexity and force:

Nè quale ingegno è 'n voi colto, e ferace,
Cosmo, nè scorto in nobil arte il vero
Nè retto con virtù tranquillo impero,
Nè loda, nè valor sommo e verace
Neither what mind is in you skilled and keen,
Cosmo, nor spied by noble science truth,
Nor steered with rectitude a peaceful realm,
Nor fame, nor worth exalted and most pure

(Della Casa, Sonetto XXII)

Perocch' a noi, com' alla fertil vite,
Conviensi, o come alla feconda oliva,
Producer largamente i dolci frutti
Because to us, as to the fertile vine,
Becoming 'tis, or to the fecund olive,
To bring forth in abundance our sweet fruits
(Tasso, *Mondo Creato*, Giornata Terza)

but nigh at Hand
Celestial Armourie, Shields, Helmes, and Speares,
Hung high, with Diamond flaming and with Gold
(*P.L.*, Book IV, ll. 552-4)

as with Starrs thir bodies all
And Wings were set with Eyes, with Eyes the Wheels
Of Beril, and careering Fires between
(*P.L.*, Book VI, ll. 754-6)

A comparison between Tasso's and Milton's skill in such writing might be drawn from the following passages, two of them on the whole pedestrian, and two eloquent:

E nell' istesso modo
Fa ritrosa la Luna, e 'l suo bel cerchio
Finge ineguale, e non ritondo appieno,
E la figura le distorce, e 'l corso
And in the self-same manner
Makes err the Moon, and her fair circle feigns
Uneven, and not rounded to the full,
And both her face distorts, and wayward course
(Tasso, *Mondo Creato*, Giornata Quarta)

the floating Vessel swum
Uplifted; and secure with beaked prow
Rode tilting o're the Waves, all dwellings else
Flood overwhelmd, and with them all thir pomp
Deep under water rould; Sea cover'd Sea,
Sea without shoar; and in thir Palaces,
Where luxurie late reign'd, Sea-monsters whelp'd
And stabl'd; of Mankind, so numerous late,
All left, in one small bottom swum imbark't.
(*P.L.*, Book XI, ll. 741-9)

Oh! piaccia a lui, che ne distringe, e lega,
Com' a lui piace, e talor solve, e snoda
I lacci del peccato, e i duri nodi,
Onde 'l fato quaggiù tien l'alme avvinte
Oh! may it please Him who distrains and binds,
As pleases Him, and sometimes melts and solves
The thongs of sin, and those hard knots wherein
Fate here below detains our captive souls
(Tasso, *Mondo Creato*, Giornata Seconda)

> Standing on Earth, not rapt above the Pole,
> More safe I Sing with mortal voice, unchang'd
> To hoarse or mute, though fall'n on evil dayes,
> On evil dayes though fall'n, and evil tongues;
> In darkness, and with dangers compast round,
> And solitude;   (*P.L.*, Book VII, ll. 23-28)

Even within the narrow limits of these quotations it may be seen that the conception of style and the methods of the two poets are identical; and also that there is a greater force and vividness of expression, and freshness of feeling, in Milton than in Tasso.

III

A close comparison between Milton's diction and that of these sixteenth-century Italians suggests that, while English is less capable than Italian of imitating certain details of Latin syntax, our language is, on the other hand, a more flexible instrument and can therefore sustain this rich Virgilian manner with greater ease and variety. Thus we find that the texture of Milton's epic diction is more uniformly fine than that of Tasso's *Mondo Creato,* in which a certain monotony and flatness makes itself felt, and appears clearly in the repetition of phrases such as *i stellanti chiostri* for the sky. The richness and delicacy of Milton's language can bear comparison even with the concentrated beauty of Della Casa's sonnets, in spite of the difference in scale and perspective between epic narrative and a lyric of fourteen lines.

The explanation is probably to be found in part in the relative freedom of English from syntactical bonds. This may be shown even within the limits of the little verbal pattern whose varied possibilities have just been illustrated. While Milton can, for example, use his adjectives very frequently with an adverbial effect, the Italian poets are more restricted to the primary grammatical function of their words. *Paradise Lost* is full of such adverbial adjectives as in this passage:

> for wide was spred
> That Warr and various   (*P.L.*, Book VI, ll. 241-2)

And this use of adjectives is, of course, prevalent as a vulgar solecism in spoken English. In Milton's Italian models such constructions are indeed to be found:

> *chi vede Marte*
> *Gli altrui campi inondar torbido insanò*
> he who sees Mars
> Another's fields inundate turbid and foul
>   (Della Casa, Sonetto XLVI)

> *Nel sacro monte, ov' oggi uom rado viene*
> On the holy hill where now men rarely come
>   (Ibid., Sonetto XXV)

Ov' orma di virtù raro s'imprime
Where print of virtue's foot is rarely pressed
(Ibid., Sonetto XXVI)

And participles in Italian can quite easily be used with this effect:

Ahi venen nova, che piacendo ancide!
Ah novel poison, that by pleasing kills!
(Ibid., Sonetto LIII)

Mira, Padre celeste, omai con quante
Lacrime a Te devoto mi converto
See, Heavenly Father, henceforth with how many
Tears unto Thee devout I do me turn
(Ibid., Sonetto LXVI)

But in Italian the demands of syntax make success in this type of diction more strenuous than in English. Parini's *Il Giorno* is the longest poem in which complexity and richness are sustained from beginning to end; and it is on the scale of the *Georgics* rather than, like *Paradise Lost*, on that of the *Aeneid*.

IV

In the pattern of which various forms have been chosen as examples there is only one constant element, and this would be found in any similar pattern that could be chosen and traced: that is, that the sense of the statement is suspended or interrupted. A quite direct, simple, or 'logical' order of words is avoided in order to provide one in which the completion of the statement is either postponed or anticipated.

In some cases it may even be impossible to say what a 'logical' word-order would be. In the lines,

his gestures fierce
He mark'd and mad demeanour, then alone,

one might choose to say that 'He marked his gestures fierce and mad demeanour, then alone' would be more logical. But rhetoric, which seeks to reproduce the vividness of impressions, or to give the emphasis of passion, is entirely justified in placing the 'gestures' first. And while it might then seem more logical to say 'His gestures fierce and mad demeanour, then alone, he marked', this would also bring about a loss of vividness and emphasis: the expression would decline into flatness and heaviness.

It is clear, then, that the systematic deformation of 'logical' word-order, as it is applied in Milton, is made to serve the poetic effect both in a narrowly technical and in a more general aesthetic manner. By means of the phrasing the sense is suspended and diffused throughout a larger block of words than could otherwise be built into a unity; verses and sentences are thus bound together and brought into animated movement.

Moreover, this intricate word-order is also a conventional method of gaining the effect of emphatic, excited, or passionate modes of speech. This is the language of sublimated emotion and intellectual excitement.[5]

V

Miltonic diction is thus but one aspect of a form of poetry in which everything is unified: matter, meaning, emotion, method. What might appear superficially a mere complexity of ornament, in fact contributes essentially to the structure of the verse, and corresponds to the strength of the 'inspiration', the poetic emotion. The dangers of the style and the diction are obvious enough: the elaboration of language, the complexity of surface, are only justified if the poem requires a fullness of statement which often amounts to pleonasm. The element of pleonasm is one of the foundations of *Paradise Lost*. And, if the dangers of this pleonastic style are obvious, it is equally obvious that throughout the whole immense length of his poem Milton has succeeded in avoiding the worst of these dangers: inflation, the presenting too little matter and meaning in too many words.

His success can be understood in general terms only as a result of extreme intellectual energy, joined with force of character. But there are minor manifestations of this mental energy which deserve recognition, if only because they have received too little attention in the past. These include his addiction to verbal wit, various forms of conceits, and puns. This is not only more characteristic than has always been admitted, but provides also a parallel to certain features of Tasso's style. Milton has his own particular form of *seicentismo,* and this form is anticipated here and there in Tasso, most obviously in the *Mondo Creato*.

In Milton's epic poetry there is an incessant, sometimes obtrusive, activity of mind at the level of verbal wit: there is play upon words, sometimes in puns, sometimes in emphasizing the jingling qualities of words of different or kindred meaning, sometimes in twisting grotesquely ingenious complexities of syntax. These freaks of fancy are combined with a remorseless chopping of logic, above all in the speeches, which has a similar effect. That effect is above all to compensate for the somewhat stupefying power of the 'magnificent' diction, to add possibilities of surprise to a technique of which one of the chief dangers is monotony. The play upon words and the metaphysical or logical conceits are not indeed alien to this epic style, for ingenuity is here omnipresent in one form or another: it is present in the artificial word-order and in the music of the verse no less than in the assiduous search for what is astounding in thought and image and emotion. The whole elaborate machine could only be constructed and kept moving by a constant exercise of the mind, and it is only by way of variety, and not by any abandonment of prin-

[5] See Coleridge, *Biographia Literaria,* chapters xvi-xviii.

ciple, that this mental activity sometimes displays itself in such sports as the following:

> Serpent, we might have spar'd our coming hither,
> Fruitless to me, though Fruit be here to excess
> (P.L., Book IX, ll. 647-8)

> At one slight bound high overleap'd all bound
> Of Hill or highest Wall   (P.L., Book IV, ll. 181-2)

There are straightforward puns like that of the ravens in *Paradise Regained*: but these are rare in comparison with half-puns or jingles:

> Which tempted our attempt, and wrought our fall
> (P.L., Book I, l. 642)

> and to begirt th' Almighty Throne
> Beseeching or besieging   (P.L., Book V, ll. 865-6)

> Sole partner and sole part of all these joyes
> (P.L., Book IV, l. 411)

> On the part of Heav'n
> Now alienated, distance, and distaste
> (P.L., Book IX, ll. 8-9)

> hee to be aveng'd,
> And to repaire his numbers thus impair'd
> (P.L., Book IX, ll. 143-4)

There are instances in which a verbal flourish, sometimes empty enough in itself, is made to give interest or significance:

> Blest pair; and O yet happiest if ye seek
> No happier state, and know to know no more.
> (P.L., Book IV, ll. 775-6)

> A chance but chance may lead where I may meet
> Some wandring Spirit of Heav'n   (P.L., Book IV, ll. 530-1)

> wilt taste
> No pleasure, though in pleasure, solitarie.
> (P.L., Book VIII, ll. 401-2)

> Wonder not, sovran Mistress, if perhaps
> Thou canst, who art sole Wonder,   (P.L., Book IX, ll. 532-3)

Certain Latinisms provide also a touch of surprise, of stimulating difficulty:

> him who disobeyes
> Mee disobeyes,   (P.L., Book V, ll. 611-12)

> Man is not whom to warne: (P.L., Book XI, l. 773)

The grotesque ingenuity of some climaxes plays its part:

> Thoughts, which how found they harbour in thy brest
> *Adam*, missthought of her to thee so dear?
>
> (*P.L.*, Book IX, ll. 288-9)

The following passage is a good example of several of these devices within a small compass: it reminds us that Milton's conversation was 'very satirical', and suggests that his armoury of puns and jingles was drawn upon most frequently when his poetry assumed that tone:

> To these that sober Race of Men, whose lives
> Religious titl'd them the Sons of God,
> Shall yeild up all thir virtue, all thir fame
> Ignobly, to the traines and to the smiles
> Of these fair Atheists, and now swim in joy,
> (Erelong to swim at larg) and laugh; for which
> The world erelong a world of tears must weepe.
>
> (*P.L.*, Book XI, ll. 617-23)

The humour of 'No fear lest dinner cool' and the irony frequently used by Satan are other manifestations of this vein in Milton's poetry. It is a mistake to regard them as occasional and regrettable lapses from epic dignity. Like the almost fantastic ingenuity which Adam displays in speaking to his Creator, and which Eve uses in the face of temptation, they spring from the depths of Milton's mind. When Pope observed that:

> In quibbles angel and archangel join,
> And God the Father turns a school-divine,

he said no more than anyone can see; but his view of the relation of these oddities to Milton's total achievement was that of a superficial critic.

Milton has in fact made this form of interest so much his own that it may seem supererogatory to search for the origins of something so personal in his Italian exemplars. Yet there are in Tasso's *Mondo Creato* some passages which are exactly parallel to Milton's verbal conceits; and Milton may well have regarded these as giving him licence and authority to indulge in what came to him so easily. Tasso has some curious instances of playing upon words:

> *Ma delle piante ancor chi tace il pianto?*
> But of the plants once more who speaks not the plaint?
>
> (*Mondo Creato,* Giornata Terza)

> *Non cupidigia, o fame infame d'oro*
> Not avarice, nor infamous famishment for gold
>
> (Ibid., Giornata Quinta)

> *Altri son della mano a' vezzi avezzi*
> Others are skilled in the charms of the hand   (Ibid.)

> *Basta la vite solo a farci accorto*
> *Di nostra vita*
> Even the vine alone shows us a sign
> Of our own life   (Ibid., Giornata Terza)

The appearance of this kind of verbal conceit in both Tasso's and Milton's blank verse confirms the affiliation between these works of the two poets.[6]

We do not, however, form a complete impression of the kinship and the distinction between the styles of the two poets in this respect, unless we compare *Paradise Lost* also with the *Gerusalemme Liberata*; for it is in Tasso's masterpiece that the conceited qualities of his manner are revealed in all their flamboyancy. An analysis of this aspect of Tasso's poetry provides one of the most memorable passages of De Sanctis's *History of Italian Literature*:

> Learned as he is, his poetic material is full of reminiscences, and he received his notions of the world not directly, but by way of books. He sets to work on his work, refines and sharpens images and conceits: a manner which he calls in its external mechanism '*parlare disgiunto*'; and which is a '*lavoro di tarsie*', as Galilei said.[7]

The whole of this analysis is worth reading in connexion with the origins of Milton's style, although in Tasso the form of the *ottava rima* encourages the tendency to epigram and antithesis of an exaggerated kind and veils the affiliations with *Paradise Lost*. But De Sanctis makes clear that this ingenuity in straining after effect is of the essence of Tasso's conception of the 'magnificent' style:

> The imagination in its visions has always at its side a pedagogue, who analyses and distinguishes with logical precision, as in:
>
> > *Sparsa è d'armi la terra, e l'armi sparse*
> > *Di sangue, e il sangue col sudor si mesce.*
> > Covered with arms the earth is, and th' arms
> > With blood, and blood with sweat is all enmixed.

The poet seeks too great a stress and distinctness, tries to give a significance even to the insignificant; and he seeks this significance in intellectual relationships even when he disposes already of the more powerful resources of imagery and of the most violent emotional excitement, as in:

> > *O sasso amato ed onorato tanto,*
> > *Che dentro hai le mie fiamme e fuori il pianto!*
> > O stony tomb beloved and honoured so,
> > Bearing within my flames, without my woe!

With such play upon words and fancies Tancred laments and Armida raves, and even in the desperation of her suicide makes a very ingenious little speech to her weapons, and concludes:

[6] Playing upon words, and more especially on proper names, was an established device in sonnets in Italian ever since Petrarch had alluded to Laura as a laurel-tree. This trick was given new life by the fashion for heroic and complimentary sonnets in the sixteenth century. Poets who exchanged sonnets with one another would pun upon the name of the recipient as often as they could.

[7] *Storia della Letteratura Italiana* (Bari, 1925), ii. 168.

      Sani piaga di stral piaga d'amore,
      E sia la morte medicina al core! [8]
      May arrow wounds heal wounds of love that smart,
      And death be the physician to my heart!

It may seem a far cry from Tasso's knights and enchantresses to the solemnities of *Paradise Lost,* but there is a real connexion between the poetic tissue of the two epics. The difference is that Milton's subject supported much better the continual seeking after effect which accompanied the idea of 'magnificence'; 'he chose a subject', as Dr. Johnson said, 'on which too much could not be said'. Milton's use of verbal conceits is also controlled by a more severe ideal of art and by a powerful intellectual tension than is to be found in Tasso.[9]

VI

Considered simply as a machine, Milton's epic manner, and in particular his diction, can be seen to fulfil Tasso's ideal more completely than any of Tasso's own essays in 'magnificence'. The differing imaginative powers of the two poets, the differing intellectual climates of the sixteenth century in Italy and the seventeenth century in England, no doubt contributed much to this result. But it is due also to the differing qualities of the two languages, at least at that stage in their development. English in the seventeenth century had fresher and richer resources and was in closer relation to contemporary life and thought than was literary Italian in the sixteenth century. Milton indeed desired 'to use English words in a foreign idiom' and his ideal of style was to remove his poetic diction from common usage; but, despite these dangerous ambitions, he had behind him, and he freely drew upon, the vigorous freedom of Elizabethan English. In contrast, poets in Italy in the sixteenth century, whether or not they were Tuscans (and Tasso was Neapolitan by birth and Ferrarese by adoption), had to write their serious poetry in the dialect of Dante and Petrarch. This literary language, which had been fresh two centuries before, had in their time been carefully refined and codified, so that Della Casa's *Galateo,* for example, is a masterpiece of prose style, but of the prose style of the fourteenth century. Tasso was attempting to impose an artificial diction on a literary language already burdened by exacting demands of grammar and idiom.

---

  [8] *Storia della Letteratura Italiana* (Bari, 1925), ii. 168.

  [9] Verbal cleverness, grotesqueness, and obscurity are perhaps more essential features of epic poetry, or all high poetry, than our critical tradition has always admitted. The 'kennings' of Anglo-Saxon and Scandinavian verse are no more incompatible with 'high seriousness' than Shakespeare's conceits or Dante's constant and sometimes playful circumlocutions. Perhaps Milton's verbal wit and logic-chopping give his epic some qualities akin to these and safeguard it from the perils of neo-classical decorum by breathing into it a primitive or personal zest.

The variety of linguistic resources which might have helped to support epic 'magnificence' was therefore lacking in Italian at this time, and Tasso's blank verse in particular is made of a more monotonous substance, and has a smaller range of verbal harmonies and contrasts, than Milton's. No doubt this also has something to do with permanent differences in the structure and texture of the two languages. The vocabulary of English is less polysyllabic than that of Italian, yet it can offer its Latin element for polysyllabic effects if they are desired; and the greater proportion of monosyllables and the relative lack of inflexions enable the English poet to achieve effects of bareness and simplicity which add greatly to this total range. This is in part a matter of taste. Effects of bareness and simplicity seem to have appealed little to Tasso, while Milton consciously reserves them for some of the finest moments of his poem. But this contrast between the manners of the two poets corresponds also to a contrast between the substances of their native tongues.

Satan and the Technique
of Degradation

by A. J. A. Waldock

. . . [Some] of the major difficulties that we now find in *Paradise Lost* are due, quite simply, to Milton's inexperience in the assessment of narrative problems. It is not, I think, mere folly or presumption to suggest that this is so. Narrative is a special art, and the greatest of poets may not be capable of apprehending instinctively the traps and danger-spots of an especially intricate and difficult theme. There were besides, as we have noted, reasons inherent in the very nature of this theme why Milton was not in a position to appreciate its full complexity. But, in-experienced or not, and unable, as he may have been, to estimate the true explosive qualities of his material, he knew one thing: he had to be interesting. That was the paramount necessity; and it was a necessity that immediately set certain conditions for the delineation of Satan and his fellows.

It was essential, in the first place, that the rebellion should seem credible; and this meant, in turn, that there had to be some uncertainty, or at least some *illusion* of uncertainty, about the facts. It will be remembered that Milton makes his initial statement in carefully generalized terms: the really awkward details come much later, where they will do less harm. At the opening of the poem we hear merely that Satan made a great bid for supremacy and that his motive was pride; the exact occasion of the revolt is left, for the time being, obscure. Again, it is not until we are two-thirds of the way through Book II that we learn what the odds against the rebels were: two to one. We hear this from Death:

> Art thou that Traitor Angel, art thou he,
> Who first broke peace in Heav'n and Faith, till then
> Unbrok'n, and in proud rebellious Arms
> Drew after him the third part of Heav'ns Sons . . . ? (II, 689)

By this time Satan has become in our imaginations so formidable a figure that we take the news in our stride; in any case it is slipped in so

"Satan and the Technique of Degradation." From *Paradise Lost and its Critics* by A. J. A. Waldock, Cambridge, 1947. Reprinted by permission of the Cambridge University Press.

unemphatically that we receive it almost without thinking about it. To have given it earlier and at all pointedly would have been to cast doubt on the quality of Satan's brain. The impression, carefully built up in Book I and confirmed in Book II, is that the rebellion (in the eyes, of course, of the rebels) was a thoroughly rational undertaking, with a fair fighting chance of success. The qualification 'in the eyes of the rebels' is not fatuous: the rebels have to be allowed their estimate. God, the event has now shown, was the stronger; but, as Satan says:

> till then who knew
> The force of those dire Arms?   (I, 93)

The conclusion must now be accepted, says Beëlzebub, that God *is* almighty,

> since no less
> Then such could hav orepow'rd such force as ours.   (I, 144)

We should not gather from this line, and are not meant to, that their party was outnumbered two to one; nor should we have gathered it from Satan's words a little earlier about 'innumerable force of Spirits arm'd'. Indeed, the tone of all the discussion is to keep that fact well out of sight. The rebels shook the throne of God, says Satan, and made him doubt his empire. They endangered Heaven's perpetual King, says Beëlzebub,

> And put to proof his high Supremacy,
> Whether upheld by strength, or Chance, or Fate.   (I, 132)

Up till then, says Satan, God had occupied his throne 'secure',

> but still his strength conceal'd,
> Which tempted our attempt, and wrought our fall.   (I, 641)

As we read through Books I and II we do not check at such lines and remind ourselves that Satan is a liar, nor does Milton expect us to do so. We feel the element of bravado in the language; we know that in such circumstances we cannot look for strict accuracy; we do not take the words of these defeated ones for a perfectly literal report of fact. But the drift of their talk cannot but affect us, and it is meant to affect us. Mr Williams (interested throughout in his key principles of 'derivation' and 'self-love') seems to me to miss completely the narrative impressions that Milton is striving after in these books. 'Milton', he says, 'knew as well as we do that Omnipotence cannot be shaken.' [1] Certainly he did; and for that very reason he must do his best as a narrative poet (it was elementary technique) to make us forget the fact, must try by every craft of narrative at his command to instil into us the temporary illusion that Omnipotence *can* be shaken—until such time, at least, as he has his poem properly moving and Satan securely established in our imaginations as a worthy

[1] [*The English Poems of John Milton*, with Introduction by Charles Williams. World's Classics (Oxford Univ. Press, 1940), p. xv.]

Antagonist of Heaven. The rebellion, we know well, was 'a foolish effort': we know it if we stop to think. But if the net effect of Milton's writing in Book I had been to make us *feel* that it was mere foolishness he might just as well have laid aside his work there and then. 'Much of *Paradise Lost* can be felt to revolve, laughingly and harmoniously, round the solemn and helpless image of pride.' [2] Much of it may; it is quite certain that the great opening books of the poem do not; Milton's chief care has been precisely to see to it that they do not.

Actually, if the text is watched closely it will be seen, I think, that there is a certain equivocation in the use of the word 'omnipotent'. When it is convenient to do so Milton uses it with full literal force; but on occasion it can seem not much more than a grandiloquent synonym for 'supreme'. There is a certain latitude or 'play' in the use of the word; and this for the benefit of the narrative. Similarly, we do not quite know, in reading the first and second books, whether we are to accept as absolutely fixed and definite facts the immortality of the fallen angels and the eternity of their doom. We are pretty sure, of course, where the truth lies. All the same, the questions are kept slightly controversial; and this, again, is for the good of the narrative. The grain of doubt left by such lines as

> Or if our substance be indeed Divine
> And cannot cease to be,   (II, 99)

or

> Suppose he should relent
> And publish Grace to all, on promise made
> Of new Subjection,   (II, 237)

small though it is, helps to make the situation of the rebels interesting and enhances their dignity in debate.

It is much the same with Satan's own inconsistencies. 'Hell is inaccurate', says Mr Williams. So, it may be remarked, is Heaven, if we may take the Son's account of the Fall of Man (already noted) as a fair sample of heavenly accuracy. But it seems obvious that the inaccuracies of Satan are sometimes rhetorical rather than real (inaccuracies of expression rather than of thought), and that when they are real they are often being used as deliberate debating points. A clear example of the first kind is his speech from the throne at the beginning of Book II. Mr Lewis cites it as one of two passages that prove that Satan is already wilting under the doom of Nonsense—that his brain is already in process of decay.

> Powers and Dominions, Deities of Heav'n,
> For since no deep within her gulf can hold
> Immortal vigor, though opprest and fall'n
> I give not Heav'n for lost. From this descent
> Celestial vertues rising, will appear

[2] Ibid p. xi.

> More glorious and more dread then from no fall
> And trust themselves to fear no second fate:
> Mee though just right, and the fixt Laws of Heav'n
> Did first create your Leader, next, free choice,
> With what besides, in Counsel or in Fight,
> Hath bin achievd of merit, yet this loss
> Thus farr at least recover'd, hath much more
> Establisht in a safe unenvied Throne
> Yielded with full consent. The happier state
> In Heav'n, which follows dignity, might draw
> Envy from each inferior; but who here
> Will envy whom the highest place exposes
> Formost to stand against the Thunderers aime
> Your bulwark, and condemns to greatest share
> Of endless pain? where there is then no good
> For which to strive, no strife can grow up there
> From Faction; for none sure will claim in hell
> Precedence, none, whose portion is so small
> Of present pain, that with ambitious mind
> Will covet more. With this advantage then
> To union, and firm Faith, and firm accord,
> More then can be in Heav'n, we now return
> To claim our just inheritance of old,
> Surer to prosper then prosperity
> Could have assur'd us; and by what best way,
> Whether of open Warr or covert guile,
> We now debate; who can advise, may speak.   (II, 11)

Of course there are contradictions in the speech, as there are in a good
epigram or a string of humorous and effective paradoxes. The argument,
indeed, is deliberately tinged with paradox: it has, in such ways, a nicely
calculated appeal. 'Safe unenvied Throne', 'none sure will claim in hell
Precedence': these sallies deserved, and perhaps (we may imagine) got,
the faintest stir of amused response. The wry ironic note is exactly suited
to the occasion; and the more direct implications of 'condemns to greatest
share Of endless pain' would have gone home. When a mother picks up
a hurt child and brings a bleak smile by some quickly improvised comfort we do not examine what she says for 'logic': we judge it by its effect.
So here. The logic of the speech, naturally, is insecure. His throne is safe
and unenvied, argues Satan, because the misery of the rebels is complete;
it follows that every improvement in their state must tend to weaken his
authority (since misery is its basis) and to sap the firmness of their union;
yet the firmness of their union is the very ground he gives for his hope
of victory. This (as Mr Lewis points out) is what the argument means if it
is looked into. But it is not meant to be looked into—it is not that kind of
argument; nor, because of these latent absurdities, is it justifiably branded
as nonsense. On the contrary, it is exceedingly good sense, of the sort that
Satan requires for the moment's ends. The whole aim of the speech, ob-

viously, is to instil a mood, to cheer spirits, to confirm a confederacy that after the shocks it has just been receiving might easily be on the verge of total collapse. If his spurious impromptu reasoning accomplishes those immediate results it will have served the sole use it was meant for. In short it is the kind of speech that able commanders, one supposes, have been making at such critical junctures since the dawn of history. The specious logic betrays, of course, the desperateness of the situation. Nevertheless, to appraise such a speech by logic alone is to bring under the same ban of Nonsense, by implication, half the great oratory of the world.

Satan's other 'nonsensical' speech occurs in Book v. It is his reply to Abdiel, who alone opposed the 'current of his fury'.

> That we were formd then saist thou? & the work
> Of secondarie hands, by task transferd
> From Father to his Son? strange point and new!
> Doctrin which we would know whence learnt: who saw
> When this creation was? rememberst thou
> Thy making, while the Maker gave thee being?
> We know no time when we were not as now;
> Know none before us, self-begot, self-rais'd
> By our own quick'ning power, when fatal course
> Had circl'd his full Orbe, the birth mature
> Of this our native Heav'n, Ethereal Sons.
> Our puissance is our own, our own right hand
> Shall teach us highest deeds, by proof to try
> Who is our equal: then thou shalt behold
> Whether by supplication we intend
> Address, and to begirt th' Almighty Throne
> Beseeching or besieging. This report,
> These tidings carrie to th' anointed King;
> And fly, ere evil intercept thy flight.
>
> (v, 850)

It must be admitted that in the wordy warfare Satan is hard pressed. In Books v and vi Milton allows the truth of things to come more into the open, and Abdiel more than once gets well inside Satan's guard. Abdiel (as Milton's mouthpiece) has just delivered the 'official' view on the creation of angels. The angels, he informs the assembly, were created by the Son himself, acting as the Word. This is a heavy thrust, and even though none 'seconds' Abdiel Satan must say something. He makes two not ineffective rejoinders: first, that the point is new; and second, that Abdiel's account of the creation of himself and other angels must necessarily be based on hearsay. Neither rejoinder is silly. The point *must* be new, or he could not in full assembly say it was. We are not told why it is that Abdiel is so exceptionally well informed; for some reason he is, just as for some reason the rebel angels appear to have been kept in the dark about a number of other facts that good angels know. However that may be, Satan is at a disadvantage and must improvise. I do not think it can be said that he improvises nonsensically. Even the notion of the 'self-begetting' is good enough to serve as an argumentative stop-gap, and that is all that Satan wants it for. Whether this particular thought had ever occurred to him before or ever occurred to him again we naturally do not know; it has all the air of a 'bright idea' caught on the wing. But surely nothing of this tells—or is meant by Milton to tell—very seriously against Satan's intellect. He is making the best show he can and is not undeserving, on debating points, of the 'hoarce murmur' that presently 'echo'd to his words applause'.

Nor, finally, does Milton allow the motive for the revolt which (generalized previously) he now takes occasion to explain in more detail, to impress us as merely fantastic. That, again, would be to spoil Satan too soon, spoil therefore the story, spoil the poem. The motive, actually, would seem to have been made rather more plausible than Milton intended, for God's announcement of the exaltation of the Son has, in plain fact, a distinctly curt and challenging air. Abdiel, again as Milton's spokesman, avers that it was never in God's mind to offer a slight, for

> by experience taught we know how good,
> And of our good, and of our dignitie
> How provident he is, how farr from thought
> To make us less, bent rather to exalt
> Our happie state under one Head more neer
> United.   (v, 823)

The real effect of the appointment, he adds, will be to elevate rather than to depress the status of the angelic host:

> since he the Head
> One of our number thus reduc't becomes.   (v, 839)

It is ingenious, and we understand well that we are to accept this as the official view; but it is not exactly what God said, and it is most decidedly not how God sounded, when he made the declaration of appointment. We cannot with any reasonableness talk of Satan's 'wrongs'. In theory, at least, there are no wrongs, and we know so little about the facts of the matter that we are not in a position to dispute the theory. The background of Satan's revolt is, so to say, nonexistent: we cannot argue from it, because it is not there. If we begin to think about it at all deeply we should be obliged, no doubt, to agree with Sir Herbert Grierson that 'if the third part of a school or college or nation broke into rebellion we should be driven, or strongly disposed, to suspect some mismanagement by the supreme powers'.[3] The alternative, he suggests, would be to 'attribute to the rebels a double dose of original sin'; which in the case of the angelic rebels, at least, would again raise awkward questions, seeing that original sin had not yet been invented. There is no use at all, of course, in probing behind what we are given: we can only take the nar-

---

[3] *Milton and Wordsworth* (1937), p. 116.

rative as we find it; and when we respond naturally, Satan's sense of having been passed over, of having suffered impairment through the appointment of the Son, certainly does not affect us (as Mr Lewis and Mr Williams think it should) as laughable. 'In the midst of a world of light and love, of song and feast and dance, he could find nothing to think of more interesting than his own prestige.' [4] If this had been exactly the impression of the poem, Satan's offended pride perhaps *would* have been nothing less than ridiculous. (Think, for example, of the effect of a jealous Satan planted in the middle of the *Paradiso*.) But it is not exactly the impression of the poem. There is no sign of love in God's speech of appointment. On the contrary, the speech is dictatorial and full of threats:

> him who disobeyes
> Mee disobeyes, breaks union, and that day
> Cast out from God and blessed vision, falls
> Into utter darkness, deep ingulft, his place
> Ordaind without redemption, without end.   (v, 611)

And to repeat, God pays nobody the compliment (unless it be Abdiel) of explaining just why he is taking this momentous step.

Milton's problem, in truth, was very difficult. He must give Satan a reason for revolting, a reason that does not put him outside the pale of our interest—make him merely absurd. But it must still be a bad reason: the revolt must still be strange, unpardonable, abhorrent. The truth surely is that Milton succeeded in suggesting a rather greater degree of provocation for it, and therefore of reasonableness in it, than he ever intended.

Let us return for a little to the Satan of the first two books. There are really no problems for *us* in the Satan of these books: the problems were all for Milton; and the chief risk he had to face seems obvious. Given a writer of even rudimentary narrative instincts there was not much doubt that Satan would be impressive: the danger, of course, was that his impressiveness could so easily get out of control. But there is no puzzle in this, surely; nothing that needs intricate accounting for. Mr Lewis goes deep to explain the primacy of Satan as a character. His theory, briefly, is that a 'bad' character is always easier to draw than a 'good' one, for 'to make a character worse than oneself it is only necessary to release imaginatively from control some of the bad passions which, in real life, are always straining at the leash; the Satan, the Iago, the Becky Sharp, within each of us, is always there and only too ready, the moment the leash is slipped, to come out and have in our books that holiday we try to deny them in our lives'.[5] To draw a 'bad' character, in short, it is only necessary to relax, be oneself; to draw a 'good' one it is necessary to rise above oneself; hence the scarcity of well drawn 'good' characters, the

---

[4] [C. S. Lewis, *A Preface to Paradise Lost* (London, Oxford Univ. Press, 1942), p. 94.]
[5] Op. cit. p. 98.

abundance of well drawn 'bad'. If we needed a theory to account for the pre-eminence of Satan among the characters of *Paradise Lost* this theory would certainly suffice. But the more one ponders the theory (which takes its rise in some basic principles of Mr Lewis's moral thinking) the more one doubts its validity. Numerous examples would appear to tell against it. And what exactly is meant by 'good'? When we talk of drawing a good character we do not usually mean drawing a saint. The character of a saint is perhaps difficult to draw, for at least it takes us into a limiting (in a sense into a freakish) region of human experience. And does not that rather suggest what the real fact may be? Is there not a central range of character and is it not perhaps true that the farther we move out towards *either* extreme, the 'good' or the 'bad', the harder becomes the task?

But whatever the validity of Mr Lewis's theory in general, the application of it to Satan seems quite superfluous. We need none of Mr Lewis's reasons to see why it is that Satan *must* stand out from the other characters of *Paradise Lost*. It is because he is the only character in the story whom in any real sense it was possible to draw at all. 'Set a hundred poets to tell the same story,' says Mr Lewis, 'and in ninety of the resulting poems Satan will be the best character.' [6] Exactly; or not quite exactly, for Mr Lewis's figures are inaccurate: in a *hundred* of the resulting poems (supposing the writers to have even an elementary appreciation of the narrative possibilities of their material) Satan will be the best character. For, to repeat, the simple fact is that he has not, and in such circumstances could not have, any competition whatever.

But quite apart from the inherent conditions of the theme—conditions that almost force him into pre-eminence—Satan, we understand well, was a predestined character for Milton. There need, surely, be no confusion here, no perplexity about the 'sympathy', conscious or unconscious, that Milton felt for his creation. Of course it does not mean that Milton, as we ordinarily use the phrase, was on Satan's side. It means merely that he was able, in a marked degree, to conceive Satan in terms of himself: in terms of the temptations to which he felt his own nature especially liable, and of the values, too, to which his own nature especially responded. I say 'to a marked degree', because there is nothing exclusive in Milton's sympathy with Satan. Milton seems to us often, as he writes of him, to be giving of his own substance, but he can give of his own substance anywhere. In those altercations, for example, between Satan and Abdiel in Books v and vi we *feel* Milton now in the lines of the one, now in the lines of the other, but chiefly, without any doubt, in the lines of Abdiel. In the concluding paragraph of Book v the sympathy is so close that there is virtually an identification: in speaking of Abdiel Milton might (as so many have noted) be speaking of himself: the lines come to

[6] Op. cit. p. 98.

us with the weight of some of the intensest memories of his life behind
them.

There is, I think, a further distinction to be made. Mr Bernard Shaw
once remarked that it is the habit of a sentimentalist to assume that human qualities come in neatly assorted sets, that they are 'matched' in
people's natures like colours. In life, as he pointed out, such harmonious
assortments of matched qualities are not so frequently found: a war hero
may be spiteful and may turn out to be an unexpectedly bad loser at
games; a lovable woman may be greedy, untrustworthy in financial affairs,
and not a strict speaker of the truth; and so on. And just as we have to
admit that lying and spitefulness are reprehensible (even though consist-
ing in the same nature with charm and heroism) so we have to admit
that courage in a gangster is still courage and therefore good. Now when
Mr Lewis writes of Satan he writes for the moment, I think, as a sentimentalist. He wishes to see Satan's character as made up of aesthetically
harmonious qualities—of qualities that match. He is reluctant to admit
that we can condemn Satan for some things and at the same time find
him extremely admirable for others. So he compiles for him a little list of
traits that agree—a list, I think, that quite falsifies the impressions yielded
by the first two books. We have in Satan, he says, an expression of Milton's
'own pride, malice, folly, misery, and lust'.[7] But Milton expresses in
Satan much more of himself than this, and such a picture of the Satan of
the first two books is surely a very partial portrait. We hear about Satan's
pride, see something of it, and have no difficulty in believing in it; the
lust is tossed in gratuitously—I doubt if we ever really believe in it: there
is no particular reason why we should;[8] we see something of his malice,
we can perhaps deduce his folly, and we know that theoretically he and
his mates are in misery. But what we are chiefly made to see and feel in
the first two books are quite different things: fortitude in adversity,
enormous endurance, a certain splendid recklessness, remarkable powers
of rising to an occasion, extraordinary qualities of leadership (shown not
least in his salutary taunts), and striking intelligence in meeting difficulties that are novel and could seem overwhelming. What we feel most of
all, I suppose, is his refusal to give in—just that. How can Milton help
sympathizing with qualities such as these? Obviously he sympathizes

---

[7] Op. cit. p. 99.

[8] Why we should believe in it, that is to say, in the sense in which we believe in his
pride or his courage or his arrogance. In this respect the lust of Satan is not unlike the
'luxury' of Macbeth, which is also something *declared,* something extraneous, properly,
to the portrait: take it away and the portrait is just the same. Take away Satan's lust
and the portrait is just the same, for no matter what Milton may have had at the back
of his mind in introducing it, artistically it is an extra. To say with M. Saurat that Satan
represents 'in particular' sensuality seems to me absurd: absurd, indeed, in precisely the
same way as it would be to say that Macbeth stands especially for viciousness and loose
living.

with them. In this sense and to this extent he *is* on Satan's side, as it was quite proper for him to be.

So far the situation seems very clear. But it is evident that portraiture so sympathetic, drawing such strength from Milton's own life and nature, could be very dangerous for Milton's scheme. Of course it was dangerous; and nothing is more interesting, technically, in the opening books than to note the nervousness that creeps on Milton as he becomes aware of what is threatening. It is an instructive and in some ways an amusing study. If one observes what is happening one sees that there is hardly a great speech of Satan's that Milton is not at pains to correct, to damp down and neutralize. He will put some glorious thing in Satan's mouth, then, anxious about the effect of it, will pull us gently by the sleeve, saying (for this is what it amounts to): 'Do not be carried away by this fellow: he *sounds* splendid, but take my word for it. . . .' We have in fact, once again, the two levels: the level of demonstrating or exhibition, and the level of allegation or commentary; and again there is disagreement. What is conveyed on the one level is for a large part of the time not in accord with what is conveyed on the other. Milton's allegations *clash* with his demonstrations.

The process begins, indeed, quite early in the poem. After Satan's very first speech comes the comment:

> So spake th' Apostate Angel, though in pain,
> Vaunting aloud, but rackt with deep despare.   (I, 125)

Has there been much despair in what we have just been listening to? The speech would almost seem to be incompatible with that. To accept Milton's comment here (as most readers appear to do) as if it had a validity equal to that of the speech itself is surely very naïve critical procedure. I emphasize the point again, because here too it becomes of the first importance for our estimate of what is happening in the poem—for our view, in fact, of what the poem actually *is:* in any work of imaginative literature at all it is the demonstration, by the very nature of the case, that has the higher validity: an allegation can possess no comparable authority. Of course they should agree; but if they do not then the demonstration must carry the day. In the present passage, had Milton very much in mind, one wonders, when he penned his comment? Did he really feel, when he wrote the words, that Satan *was* in 'deep despare'? It seems to me that if he had felt the despair he simply could not have written the speech as it is. Surely the truth is obvious that the phrase is half mechanical: it is the first of a long line of automatic snubs, of perfunctory jabs and growls. Each great speech lifts Satan a little beyond what Milton really intended, so he suppresses him again (or tries to) in a comment.

The procedure has been noted by other critics (though not as a rule, I think, from quite this point of view) and could be illustrated at length. There are the guarding phrases a little later:

> but he his wonted pride
> Soon recollecting, with high words, that bore
> *Semblance of worth not substance,* gently rais'd
> Their fainted courage, and dispel'd their fears.   (I, 527)

In a similar way the speech of Belial in Book II receives its prompt corrective. Belial's speech, as I suppose nearly all readers of the poem feel when they are left to themselves, is one of the most notable of those delivered in the infernal conclave; it is not only eloquent and poetically impressive: it is impregnated with strong common sense. And Belial, besides, counsels what Milton theoretically ought to approve—peace. His advice to his fellows is to stay where they are, to be quiet and unprovocative, to lie low and wait and see. In the circumstances, especially as we know from other sources that they have no hope of grace, it is difficult to see what better advice could have been given. But Milton dislikes Belial. To 'low thoughts' of this sort he much prefers (although he will not say so) dashing villainy. So Belial is snubbed.

> Thus *Belial* with words cloath'd in reasons garb
> Counsel'd ignoble ease, and peaceful sloath,
> Not peace.   (II, 226)

Belial's words are not only 'cloath'd in reasons garb': they *are* reasonable. The ease he counsels may be ignoble, but it would have been interesting to hear what kind of activity Milton could have recommended in place of it, seeing that theoretically the bad angels are in hell to stay. And the distinction between 'peaceful sloath' and 'peace' is very much of the nature of a quibble. Milton's perfectly brazen object, in short, is to discredit Belial. What he gives with one hand he takes away with the other. Having permitted his character to speak well and wisely he then says that he has spoken meanly and foolishly. What he has just affirmed (through a demonstration) he now denies (in a comment).

The method, though entertaining, is a little unfair to the characters concerned, and so are the other devices that Milton uses to the same end. After Beëlzebub has spoken we have this:

> Thus *Bëëlzebub*
> Pleaded his devilish Counsel, first devis'd
> By *Satan,* and in part propos'd: for whence,
> But from the Author of all ill could Spring
> So deep a malice, to confound the race
> Of mankind in one root, and Earth with Hell
> To mingle and involve, done all to spite
> The great Creatour?   (II, 378)

Satan, of course, threw out a suggestion in Book I that the rebels might try their luck against the rumoured new world, or tackle Heaven on some other flank. His main point was that they should make an eruption *somewhere* as soon as possible, and resume the attack.

A few lines farther on we have this (Satan has just accepted the perilous scouting mission to the new world):

> Thus saying rose
> The Monarch, and prevented all reply,
> Prudent, least from his resolution rais'd
> Others among the chief might offer now
> (Certain to be refus'd) what erst they feard;
> And so refus'd might in opinion stand
> His rivals, winning cheap the high repute
> Which he through hazard huge must earn.   (II, 466)

The neutralizing intent is again very clear. Satan has just done, when all is said, a noble thing, but it would be inconvenient to leave that impression untarnished. So Milton proceeds to tarnish it by impressing over it the image of Satan as astute politician.

The technique, indeed, is almost comically transparent and in its nature (we may fairly say) is rather primitive. Using the method of allegation Milton can produce a trump card whenever he wishes. We have no defence against such tactics except, of course, to take due note of what is going on and to decline to play when the trump has appeared too obviously from Milton's sleeve. The most flagrant example of this kind of literary cheating occurs, I think, in Book IV. Gabriel, who has not been markedly successful in debate, retorts on the Adversary:

> And thou sly hypocrite, who now wouldst seem
> Patron of liberty, who more then thou
> Once fawn'd, and cring'd, and servilly ador'd
> Heav'ns awful Monarch?   (IV, 957)

Are we, then, on Gabriel's undocumented assertion, to make an effort to accommodate the Satan we know to a Satan who 'once fawn'd, and cring'd, and servilly ador'd'? Why should we accept this high-handed piece of unsupported calumny? This seems beyond reasonable bounds, this is not keeping to the rules of the game at all.

But in the first two books of the poem such measures are really signs of nervousness and do not affect appreciably the single tremendous impression that Satan (rather in excess of Milton's will) has made. Everybody feels that the Satan of the first two books stands alone; after them comes a break, and he is never as impressive again. If we leave aside the unimportant 'accosting' of Uriel towards the end of Book III we hear him next in the famous 'address to the Sun' (IV, 32) in which he 'falls into many doubts with himself, and many passions, fear, envy, and despare'.

I do not think that it is possible to overestimate the effect of this break. Its significance, I think, is much greater than is usually admitted. It is in every respect, I would suggest, an interruption. It is not merely that the Satan of the first two books re-enters altered: the Satan of the first two books to all intents and purposes *disappears:* I do not think that in any true sense we ever see him again.

Milton's task in this, the second part of the delineation, is of course to trace the development of Satan. Now a character in process of change may affect us in either of two ways. If we have been given the requisite clues the development will seem, as it were, to carry its own guarantees with it. It is so with Macbeth. The preliminary glimpses we have of his nature, few and partial though they may seem to be, are enough; because of them we do not question the curiously unexpected turns his development takes. We could hardly have predicted those turns, but when they come we know that they are the right ones. It is as if the progress is self-proving; the keys with which we have been furnished fit; our feelings give us assurance that the man we saw could and would, in the given conditions, change into the man we see. And the progress of Lady Macbeth (so different in its course) is exactly the same in kind.

The progress of Satan is utterly distinct in its nature, and it seems to me that unless we recognize this we are not seeing the poem aright. The extreme simplification of the method in Books I and II leaves us with a memorable, indeed an overpowering, image: but the image is self-complete, finished. To expect it to develop is like expecting a statue of Michelangelo's to develop. We make, surely, a new start. The Satan of the address to the Sun is not a development from the old, he is not a changed Satan, he is a *new* Satan. We can make the transition from the one to the other, I think, in only one way: by spinning a bridge of theory across and above the visible presentment. A doctrine—that Pride, say, has certain consequences—will carry us across: I would suggest that we cannot make the crossing imaginatively. What it comes to is that we are obliged to take this new Satan, and, indeed, all the steps of this new Satan's subsequent history, on trust.

I do not think, in other words, that the term 'degeneration', applied to the downward course of Satan, has any real validity. Macbeth degenerates—in some respects, at least. A character in a piece of imaginative literature degenerates when we are in a position to check his progress by what we know of him: when we are made to feel that this or that change, once we are shown it, does follow, although we ourselves could not, perhaps, have foretold it. But what we have in the alleged 'degeneration' of Satan is really, on a large scale and in a disguised form, what we have had in the running fire of belittling commentary already noted. It is a pretended exhibition of changes occurring; actually it is of the nature of an assertion that certain changes occur. The changes do not generate themselves from within: they are imposed from without. Satan, in short, does not degenerate: *he is degraded.*

It is not surprising, therefore, that this second part of the presentation of Satan should come, increasingly, to be marked by devices that had no place in the first. In particular one might, perhaps, have predicted that the general weakness of the method would betray itself (as in fact it does) in one special way: in the steady drift towards allegory.

Let us, at all events, review rapidly in the light of this reading the main stages in Satan's downward course. We begin with the soliloquy near the opening of Book IV. It is a speech, of course, utterly different in feeling and texture from any speech that has preceded it. As a piece of writing, indeed, it probably strikes every sensitive reader (whether he has heard of Phillips or not) as a little odd in *Paradise Lost*. There is a reason, as we know, for the oddity. Phillips tells us that the soliloquy had been designed by Milton as the opening speech of a tragedy, and that some lines of it were in writing several years before the poem was begun. It is natural, therefore, that it should have the 'feel' of an extended Elizabethan soliloquy, and numerous resemblances have been noted. Perhaps the most interesting is the likeness in some lines to the prayer of Claudius.[9] The Satan of this speech is another 'limed soul':

> O then at last relent: is there no place
> Left for Repentance, none for Pardon left?
> None left but by submission; and that word
> *Disdain* forbids me.   (IV, 79)

The speech, then, was conceived and in part, at least, composed before Milton began his poem. What is the conclusion? Mr Lewis sees in the fact a clear warning that we must not read any *accidental* quality into the progress of Satan. It is not as if Milton, having blundered in the earlier books by making Satan much more glorious than he ever meant to do, had sought then somewhat belatedly to rectify his errors. I think we may easily accept this, and yet feel that it is not quite fair to the total impression to say that Milton in the first two books is occupied merely in putting 'the most specious aspects of Satan' in their proper place, at the beginning of the poem: letting Satan have his head, so to say, at the outset, giving him a run for his money; the implication being that while all this is going on Milton has his mind firmly fixed on the goal towards which everything is moving, the important soliloquy of doubt and self-torture already conceived.

Do creative artists work in quite this way? In a sense, no doubt, the soliloquy was the conception from which Milton started: in the sense that he had already thought of it and in parts written it. But surely nothing is more evident than that when Milton changed over from his tragedy to his epic the whole equilibrium of what he was about to do suffered a shift. It was hardly any longer a question of the old soliloquy controlling the new work: the question was rather whether it could find a quite satisfactory niche in the new context at all, whether, as it stood, it was usa-

---

[9] Hanford pointed out the resemblance (*Studies in Philology*, 1917, p. 190) thinking that it had not been noticed previously. But Newton had observed it.

ble. As it turned out it was usable; but the difference of texture is enough to cause a slight feeling of strangeness, and I do not think any reader can escape a sense of abruptness in the placing.

The abruptness seems to me everything. In the projected tragedy this magnificent soliloquy would have borne on us with its full weight, would have made a direct, unhindered impact. It would have put a stamp on the work that nothing thereafter could have erased. Everything that followed would necessarily have been referred back to it. It would have given us our dominant lead, would have decided, in the first few minutes, what our characteristic attitude to Satan was to be. Milton designed the soliloquy, wrote part of it and put it away. Then, still keeping it by him for use, he began his epic. But now our key, our centre, is quite different; and just as in the other case it would have been impossible to nullify, or even very much to modify, that opening all-powerful impression, so here in the epic the cue is given past alteration: the Satan of the first two books is established once and for all and nothing will avail against him.[10]

For it is too much to ask of us, at the beginning of Book ɪᴠ, that we should come to terms, unwarned, unprepared, with this sudden new Satan who finds, when on the brink of his attempt, that he has brought Hell with him in his breast. Why? What faintest signs were there that anything like this could happen? What filaments, however tenuous, stretch back from this speech of horror and uncertainty and trouble to the Satan of the first books? The soliloquy is a masterpiece, and yet it is to it, properly speaking, that the 'speciousness' belongs. It is specious in

[10] Mr Musgrove ('Is the Devil an Ass?', *The Review of English Studies*, October 1945, p. 302) makes the point that we start the poem with certain presumptions about Satan, and that these presumptions give us the power to override to a considerable extent the impression that Satan makes in the first two books. We know that the 'real' Satan will come on the scene in due course; our business in the meantime is not to take the first Satan too seriously.

I think that Mr Musgrove tends to exaggerate the place and importance of presumptions in literature. It is obvious that we start any book about any well-known character, from Joseph to Joan of Arc and beyond, with presumptions; we start *Paradise Lost* itself with some fairly strong presumptions about God. But a great deal of the interest of reading consists in the process—which starts automatically—of checking the presumptions we have brought with us against the impressions we receive; and if we hang back and fight against the impressions—as it seems to me Mr Musgrove does—we at least run the risk of robbing ourselves of a great deal of the interest of reading new books about well-known people.

Mr Musgrove cites the authority of Horace. But Horace, strictly speaking, had nothing to say to *readers* on this score: in his dictum about 'following report' he was addressing writers; and it is by no means certain that he would have approved of Milton's procedures. So many powerful and unmistakable *departures* from the traditional reports of Satan—so early in the poem—might well have struck him as unwise in the extreme (as in a sense, of course, they were).

I cannot feel that Mr Musgrove's attempt to discount the earlier Satan on the score that we are looking at him in Hell (his natural place) and against a background that flatters him ('evil') touches the realities of the case. Surely that is to allow oneself to be swayed by mere words.

its context because the Satan who now begins to unsay all that the other
Satan said, who all of a sudden recognizes his 'Pride and worse Ambition'
for what they are, who is softened by remorse ('Ah wherefore! he deserv'd
no such return'), who realizes belatedly that the service of God was not
hard at all, who knows now that he himself is Hell, who lectures per-
spicuously on his helpless case and example—this is a Satan that we have
not felt before, not even dimly felt. And now that he is put before us we
still cannot see the connection.

What follows has really, then, nothing to do with 'character'. Perhaps
Satan never was a 'character' in the full sense of the word: a tremendous
emblem, rather, giving the illusion, through two tremendous books, of
life. I do not think he gives that illusion any longer. *Why* does Satan de-
teriorate? Milton could not say, for 'pride' is no sufficient answer. The
whole process is abstract. The point, of course, is that we do not, and in
the peculiar circumstances cannot, know the roots of anything, for it was
never possible to endow Satan in any real sense with a 'nature', and without such a basis of reference we are at a loss. We have in what follows a
series of levels: we meet Satan now on the one level, now on the other:
sometimes he is more like the Satan we knew, sometimes less; but nothing
truly explains the shifts and alternations. The 'character', in short, dis-
integrates into what is really a succession of unrelated moods; and with
this disintegration new and inferior techniques begin to enter.

Consider, for an immediate instance, the passage in Book IV, shortly
after the 'address to the Sun' soliloquy itself, that describes the irruption
of the arch-felon into the garden. Disdaining due entrance he leaps the
wall, then flies up on to the Tree of Life and sits there like a cormorant:

> Yet not true Life
> Thereby regaind, but sat devising Death
> To them who liv'd; nor on the vertue thought
> Of that life-giving Plant, but only us'd
> For prospect, what well us'd had bin the pledge
> Of immortalitie. So little knows
> Any, but God alone, to value right
> The good before him, but perverts best things
> To worst abuse, or to thir meanest use.   (IV, 196)

What a fall is here! Here, surely we may say, the poem reaches one of its
really low spots, here is *manipulation* with a vengeance. Satan perched
on his bough, neglecting his opportunities, put to incidental, momentary
use as a sort of illustration to a trivial homily! This is Sunday-school-
motto technique. It was mean of Milton to use his Satan so.

There is a recovery almost at once. The Satan who stands 'in gaze' at
Adam and Eve (IV, 356) is a Satan restored nearly to his original linea-
ments, for we accept without strain his momentary rapture at the sight
of the pair; and his sadness that such beauty must be destroyed is not too
deep. Presently (and the more Satan he) he slips into the mocking vein.

The speech is an interesting one. Mr Empson wonders whether the accepted view of it is wholly right—the view that, from the word 'league' on, it expresses a brutal irony rather in the manner of Satan's address to his artillerymen during the war in heaven. Satan, he suggests, may genuinely mean his offer. The devils can carry on life in hell: perhaps man can too: Satan at any rate is not in a position to know that he cannot. So when he says:

> League with you I seek,
> And mutual amitie so streight, so close,
> That I with you must dwell, or you with me
> Henceforth; my dwelling haply may not please
> Like this fair Paradise, your sense, yet such
> Accept your Makers work; he gave it to me,
> Which I as freely give; Hell shall unfould,
> To entertain you two, her widest Gates,
> And send forth all her Kings,   (IV, 376)

he may be half or wholly sincere. Mr Empson draws attention, in particular, to the ring of the last three lines: 'their melancholy and their grandeur is that of Milton's direct statements; he does not use *all*, his key word, for any but a wholesale and unquestioned emotion; what we are to feel here is the ruined generosity of Satan and the greatness of the fate of man.' [11]

I do not think the interpretation can possibly hold, though the three lines that Mr Empson speaks of have, without any question, the effect he describes. The tone takes on, for the moment, a more direct eloquence than is really appropriate, the irony for the moment seems to disappear. It is not, surely, intentional. It is simply that Milton, slightly forgetful, injects just a little too much power—power, at least, of the wrong sort—so that we note a difference. If the three lines (or as much of them as Mr Empson quotes) ended the passage, his conjecture would be more plausible: but they do not. The passage continues:

> there will be room,
> Not like these narrow limits, to receive
> Your numerous ofspring; if no better place . . .

where the irony, if it was ever lost, comes back with a rush.

But perhaps it is true (if one looks very closely at it) that the speech does not make a perfect imaginative whole: that between the different elements of it there is a faint but real discord. Satan's feeling, up to the word 'league', has a kind of reality. He is really impressed, really sad, really regretful. And then his visage changes—too suddenly. It is as if he had slipped on another face, a wolfish one. The verse makes him seem to lick his lips as he looks at the pair: he could squeeze them to death ('mutual amitie so streight, so close') and the sardonic tone continues un-

[11] *Some Versions of Pastoral* (1935), p. 168.

til it is broken into by the three lines of unadulterated grandeur. If the
grandeur had been sustained any longer it would have been troublesome:
we should not have been able to harmonize it with the general drift of
the speech. But it ceases now; and the tide of the irony is strong enough
to carry us over the interval. It would be pleasant to think that Satan
spoke the phrase 'public reason just', towards the end of his speech, with
a sarcastic glitter in his eye— a 'leer malign'—but it is unsafe to think so.
Milton catches up and carries on the phrase in his own quite serious comment:

> So spake the Fiend, and with necessitie,
> The Tyrants plea, excus'd his devilish deeds.

The passage is interesting in one further way. Here, superficially at
least, is conflict; here could be drama.

> And should I at your harmless innocence
> Melt, as I doe . . .

The late Professor Elton felt that the moment really was dramatic. 'He
goes back, if only in fancy, upon his purpose.' [12] It is true, of course, that
he does: but it *is* only in fancy. The reality of the speech we feel, surely,
to be in the mockery, and this is partly because we relate it, with such
certainty and immediacy, to the Satan of the earlier books.

Indeed I find it impossible, now or at any other point in the poem, to
feel that the 'real tragedy' (as Professor Elton expressed it) is being
'played out in the breast of Satan'.[13] The simple truth, as it seems to me,
is that we cannot believe sufficiently (for reasons already discussed) in the
reality of the conflicts adumbrated. This speech, and the great soliloquy
at the opening of the book, give us glimpses of a tragedy that might have
been—if the foundations for it had ever really been laid. The elements
of tragic characterization are here; they are forever approaching, forever
drawing together, but no spark can fuse them. The 'tragedy' of Satan is
essentially a shadow-show: he is put through the motions of a tragic conflict, that is all. In the whole of his history, I would suggest, there is no
moment of drama comparable to the moment when Adam hears Eve's
confession and faces his decision: *that* is authentic drama indeed.

From this point on, at any rate, the possibility of genuine tragedy becomes less and less; and, conversely, Milton's *interference* in the presentation becomes more and more marked. Satan is very much himself again
in the interview with Zephon and Ithuriel. 'Not to know mee argues your
selves unknown': this is his old form regained. But Milton will not let
him be—cannot, indeed, afford to—for there is only one way now of
keeping the contract of the poem, and that is by energetically pressing
Satan down and down. So he is made to be 'abasht' by the youthful

[12] *The English Muse* (1933), p. 239.
[13] Op. cit. p. 239.

Cherub (IV, 846). It was not like the Satan we knew to let himself be abashed by anyone, and Milton himself seems to have but little faith in what he has written, for he follows immediately with a second, and much more plausible, cause for Satan's discomfiture:

> but chiefly to find here observd
> His lustre visibly impar'd. (IV, 849)

The progressive impairment of the lustre, however, is merely another kind of 'interference', taking us a step farther on the road to downright allegory: as is Satan's 'imbruting' of himself in animal forms. He feels his disgrace in this, it is said. He is made to, of course.

> O foul descent! that I who erst contended
> With Gods to sit the highest, am now constraind
> Into a Beast, and mixt with bestial slime,
> This essence to incarnate and imbrute,
> That to the hight of Deitie aspir'd;
> But what will not Ambition and Revenge
> Descend to? who aspires must down as low
> As high he soard, obnoxious first or last
> To basest things. (IX, 163)

But the passage illustrates pointedly enough how far we have travelled from the character and quality of the first books. Satan has become hardly more than a helpless symbol, an exhibit, endowed with the capacity to point his own moral. This second 'passion' soliloquy is surely in a different realm of art from the opening addresses of Satan, and the short 'stupidly good' soliloquy, a little later, is no improvement on it. Both are somewhat clumsily information-giving ('Of these the vigilance I dread', 'for I view far round'), and in the second, as in the first, Satan is in the position very much of a patient who is being forced hypnotically to insult himself. The allegorical vein has developed still farther, and we learn that pain has made inroads in Satan's strength. The true 'degeneration' is not in Satan but in the method.

The final stage is in some respects the most interesting of all, and it tells the whole story of what has been happening. This is the scene of the transformation of the bad angels into serpents and the chewing of the ashes, the true technical nature of which has never, as far as I know, been pointed out. The technique of this famous scene is the technique of the comic cartoon. This is not just a way of being rude to Milton. It is most interesting to observe that the technique of it is *exactly* that of the comic cartoon. The method of the cartoon is to allow the villain of the piece to reach a pitch of high confidence and vainglory, and then to dash him down. The whole point is that he is dashed down, the essence of cartoon-technique being to bring your adversary to grief by unfair means—in short, by some form of practical joke. This, of course, is precisely how Satan is treated here. What happens to him parallels in the exactest manner what used to happen in religious plays to the Devil and Herod, what happens in war-posters to our enemies, and what happens in film comedies to the Big Bad Wolf. Milton of course does it superbly, and it is hardly necessary to add that in sheer verbal power and expressiveness the passage has scarcely its match in *Paradise Lost*. And the construction of it, the timing, are as masterly: each ludicrous, uproarious calamity being succeeded by another still more ludicrous and uproarious, until the climax is reached with the final 'aggravation' (in both senses of the word the very essence of the art of cartoon) and the miserable tricked victims begin to eat.

It is a scene we would not give up for worlds, but to treat such a scene (as would seem to be usually done) as if it were in sober verity the conclusion and climax of a valid development is surely to lapse into a critical absurdity. To attempt to link such a scene as this with what happens in the first two books of *Paradise Lost* is to try to bring incommensurables together, for the kind of art exemplified in this passage and the kind of art with which the presentment of Satan began have simply no meeting-point. They are in different realms of discourse. The scene is amusing, and the writing of it is superb: but about Satan it proves literally nothing whatever.

I finish the chapter with a note on Milton's Hell, which has some peculiar features.

Theology supplies us with a diversity of hells, but they all, I think, have one quality in common. Whether the punishments are conceived literally or not, whether the true suffering is in the mind or the body, whether the pain itself is continuous or intermittent, whatever the internal economy of hell may be: in a true hell the damned have come to the end of their road; hell is their terminus. What activity remains for them is of the nature of a meaningless round, an endless marking-time:

> saxum ingens volvunt alii, radiisve rotarum
> districti pendent: sedet aeternumque sedebit
> infelix Theseus.

That is the true type of hell. In the *Inferno* it is the same. The sinners symbolize their sin through all eternity, perpetually relive the past, or else stay fixed—grotesque mounted specimens—in horrible parody of their guilt. Without such fixity, literal or in effect, hell loses most of its meaning.

This is precisely what Milton's Hell does. While Milton desired to make his Hell impressive as a place of punishment (drawing local colour for it, legitimately enough, from his classical precedents) he also desired, somewhat inconsistently, to cram it as full as he possibly could with human interest. This was for the good of the poem, and the result is superb. But what in the meantime happens to Hell as such? It is obvious that as the conclave proceeds Hell, for all the effective pressure it exerts on our consciousness, has as good as vanished. The livid flames become mere torches to light the assembly of the powers. A little later, when there is leisure, Milton recollects his duty, resumes his account of the infernal landscape and adds further items to his (somewhat meagre) list of tortures. But as he has just proved to us in the clearest way how little the rebels are inconvenienced by their situation it is impossible for us to take these further lurid descriptions very seriously. The plain fact of it, of course, is that Milton's Hell is very much a nominal one: it is less a hell than a vast concentration camp: less even that than a vast, remote, somewhat gloomy and uncomfortable shelter where the defeated rebels can rest, recover their strength and 'regroup'.

It is really very curious to note how little the bad angels *are* inconvenienced.

> Part curb thir fierie Steeds, or shun the Goal
> With rapid wheels, or fronted Brigads form.   (II, 531)

We might be in the Elysian fields, where we most decidedly should not be. It is as if for the moment Milton were thinking (improperly) in terms of Hades. The details, in fact, if we care to dwell on them, become very confusing. What are the conditions in Hell supposed to be? There is of course a kind of lull during Books I and II—there has to be one. Conditions, we understand from various remarks, were much worse before we arrived on the scene and may become much worse later on; that is partly why Belial advises extreme caution: better not stir God up. Yet conditions, even while the action is in progress, are (theoretically) bad enough: 'torture without end Still urges' (I, 67); 'these raging fires Will slack'n, if his breath stir not thir flames' (II, 213); in spite of which, organized field sports are possible. The reason for these and other vaguenesses in the picture is fairly evident: Milton was trying his best to accomplish two incompatible things at the same time. He wanted to convey, as far as he could, the effect of a genuine hell; but he also wanted, still more, to make the drama in Hell intense. Hell therefore as a locality has to serve a double duty: it is a place of perpetual and unceasing punishment, in theory; and it is also, in the practice of the poem, an assembly ground, a military area, a base for future operations. The two conceptions do not very well agree.

But the chief un-hell-like characteristic of Milton's Hell is simply the atmosphere of busy planning, of life nearly as lively as ever, of energies unquenched. The legitimate Hell in *Paradise Lost* is the Hell that is conveyed in such lines as

> A Dungeon horrible, on all sides round
> As one great Furnace flam'd, yet from those flames
> No light, but rather darkness visible
> Serv'd only to discover sights of woe,

> Regions of sorrow, doleful shades, where peace
> And rest can never dwell, hope never comes
> That comes to all;   (I, 61)

or

>   and feel by turns the bitter change
> Of fierce extreams, extreams by change more fierce,
> From Beds of raging Fire to starve in Ice
> Thir soft Ethereal warmth, and there to pine
> Immovable, infixt, and frozen round,
> Periods of time, thence hurried back to fire.   (II, 598)

But amid the teeming interests of Books I and II such passages make on us only a minor and insignificant impression. They are merely the setting, of which for most of the time we are naturally oblivious, for the great consult: not much more than a decorative fringe or border, attended to by Milton when his more pressing preoccupations allow. And the plain truth about the giant personalities who absorb all our interest here— who take up their lives pretty well at the point where they left them, who persist in their natures, who preserve their energies and wills, who plan for the future, who mean at the very least to make themselves comfortable, who feel no remorse—is that they have never in any true sense been in 'hell' at all.

For this reason, and for others, I do not see how Mr Lewis's ingenious modern analogies for the states of the fallen angels can possibly hold. 'Each of them is like a man who has just sold his country or his friend and now knows himself to be a pariah.' [14] But do the rebels, in fact, feel that they have 'sold' anything? Not one of them feels guilt. They are in a painful position, defeated, that is all: the only true modern analogy, surely, is with *that*. There is not the slightest moral resemblance between Moloch and a traitor who sees the true nature of his deed and whose impulse is to 'rush blind-headed' at the thing he has wronged; or between Belial and a false lover who in 'one last unforgettable conversation' with the woman he has cheated sees himself as he is and perceives all he is losing. Moloch is angry because he has been ejected from a good place where he thinks he still has a right to be—that is all. Belial is not sorry, except for the fact that the war has landed him and his fellows in this plight; he does not shrink from the thought of what he did, he is not bothered in the slightest about the true quality of his offence: he is miserable, that is all. Mr Lewis's chapter on 'Satan's Followers' is, I would suggest, of the nature, not so much of criticism, as of a sermon—an extremely suggestive and stimulating sermon, to be sure. A sermon is entitled to use its text less as a subject for rigorous interpretation than as a convenient springboard for disquisition on moral truth. Mr Lewis, I think, uses the followers of Satan in very much the same way. And

---

[14] Op. cit. p. 101.

though he anticipates and meets the charge that he is treating the poem for the moment as allegory, that, I think, is what he is really doing all the same: only in that way could the analogues he brings forward become valid.

Milton's Counterplot

by Geoffrey Hartman

Milton's description of the building of Pandemonium ends with a reference to the architect, Mammon, also known to the ancient world as Mulciber:

> and how he fell
> From Heav'n, they fabl'd, thrown by angry *Jove*
> Sheer o'er the Crystal Battlements: from Morn
> To Noon he fell, from Noon to dewy Eve,
> A Summer's day; and with the setting Sun
> Dropt from the Zenith like a falling Star,
> On *Lemnos* th'Ægæan Isle (*Paradise Lost* I, 740-6).

These verses stand out from a brilliant text as still more brilliant; or emerge from this text, which repeats on several levels the theme of quick or erring or mock activity, marked by a strange mood of calm, as if the narrative's burning wheel had suddenly disclosed a jewelled bearing. Their subject is a Fall, and it has been suggested that Milton's imagination was caught by the anticipation in the Mulciber story of a myth which stands at the center of his epic. Why the "caught" imagination should respond with a pastoral image, evoking a fall gradual and cool like the dying of a summer's day, and the sudden, no less aesthetically distant, dropping down of the star, is not explained. One recalls, without difficulty, similar moments of relief or distancing, especially in the cosmic fret of the first books: the comparison of angel forms lying entranced on the inflamed sea with autumnal leaves on Vallombrosa's shady brooks, or the simile of springtime bees and of the dreaming peasant at the end of Book I, or the applause following Mammon's speech in Book II, likened to lulling if hoarse cadence of winds after a storm, or even the appearance to Satan of the world, when he has crossed Chaos and arrives with torn tackle in full view of this golden-chained star of smallest magnitude.

The evident purpose of the Mulciber story is to help prick inflated Pandemonium, and together with the lines that follow, to emphasize

"Milton's Counterplot." From *ELH*, XXV (1958), 1-12. Reprinted by permission of the author and The Johns Hopkins Press. The present reprint contains a few minor alterations requested by the author.

that Mammon's building is as shaky as its architect. This fits in well with the plot of the first two books, a description of the satanic host's effort to build on hell. But the verses on Mulciber also disclose, through their almost decorative character, a second plot, simultaneously expressed with the first, and which may be called the counterplot. Its hidden presence is responsible for the contrapuntal effects of the inserted fable.

The reader will not fail to recognize in Milton's account of the progress of Mulciber's fall the parody of a biblical rhythm: "And the evening and the morning were the (first) day." The thought of creation is present to Milton, somehow associated with this fall. Moreover, the picture of *angry* Jove blends with and gives way to that of *crystal* battlements, and the imperturbability of the summer's day through which the angel drops:

> from Morn
> To Noon he fell, from Noon to dewy Eve,
> A Summer's day;

while in the last part of his descent an image of splendor and effortlessness outshines that of anger or ignominy:

> and with the setting Sun
> Dropt from the Zenith like a falling Star.

In context, of course, this depiction is condemned as mere fabling, and there is nothing splendid or aloof in the way Milton retells the story:

> thus they relate,
> Erring; for he with his rebellious rout
> Fell long before; nor aught avail'd him now
> To have built in Heav'n high Tow'rs; nor did he scape
> By all his Engines, but was headlong sent
> With his industrious crew to build in hell. (746-51)

Yet for a moment, while moving in the charmed land of pagan fable, away from the more literal truth in which he seeks supremacy over all fable, Milton reveals the overwhelming, if not autonomous drive of his imagination. Mulciber draws to himself a rhythm reminiscent of the account of the world's creation, and his story suggests both God and the creation undisturbed (Crystal Battlements . . . dewy Eve) by a fall which is said to occur later than the creation, yet actually preceded it. Here, surely, is a primary instance of Milton's automatically involving the idea of creation with that of the Fall. But further, and more fundamental, is the feeling of the text that God's anger is not anger at all, rather calm prescience, which sees that no fall will ultimately disturb the creation, whether Mulciber's fabled or Satan's real or Adam's universal Fall.

Milton's feeling for this divine imperturbability, for God's omnipotent knowledge that the creation will outlive death and sin, when expressed in such an indirect manner, may be characterized as the counterplot. For it does not often work on the reader as independent theme or subplot, but lodges in the vital parts of the overt action, emerging from it like good from evil. The root-feeling (if feeling is the proper word) for imperturbable providence radiates from many levels of the text. It has been given numerous interpretations in the history of criticism, the best perhaps, though impressionistic, by Coleridge: "Milton is the deity of prescience: he stands *ab extra* and drives a fiery chariot and four, making the horses feel the iron curb which holds them in." Satan's fixed mind and high disdain are perverted reflectors of this same cold passion, but doomed to perish in the restlessness of hell, and its compulsive gospel of the community of damnation. So deep-working is this spirit of the "glassy, cool, translucent wave," already invoked in *Comus*, that other poets find hard to resist it, and, like Wordsworth, seek to attain similar virtuosity in expressing "central peace, subsisting at the heart Of endless agitation." Milton's control is such, that even in the first dramatic account of Satan's expulsion, he makes the steady flame of God's act predominate over the theme of effort, anger, and vengefulness: in the following verses "Ethereal Sky" corresponds to the "Crystal Battlements" of Mulciber's fall, and the image of a projectile powerfully but steadily thrust forth (evoked in part by the immediate duplication of stress, letter and rhythmic patterns) recreates the imperturbability of that other, summer space:

> Him the Almighty Power
> Hurl'd headlong flaming from th'Ethereal Sky
> With hideous ruin and combustion down
> To bottomless perdition, there to dwell
> In Adamantine Chains and penal Fire . . . (44-8)

One of the major means of realizing the counterplot is the simile. Throughout *Paradise Lost*, and eminently in the first two books, Milton has to bring the terrible sublime home to the reader's imagination. It would appear that he can only do this by way of analogy. Yet Milton rarely uses straight analogy, in which the observer and observed remain, relative to each other, on the same plane. Indeed, his finest effects are to employ magnifying and diminishing similes. Satan's shield, for example, is described as hanging on his shoulder like the moon, viewed through Galileo's telescope from Fiesole or in Valdarno (I, 284-91). The rich, elaborate pattern of such similes has often been noted and variously explained. Certain details, however, may be reconsidered.

The similes, first of all, not only magnify or diminish the doings in hell, but invariably put them at a distance. Just as the "Tuscan Artist" sees the moon through his telescope, so the artist of *Paradise Lost* shows hell at considerable remove, through a medium which, while it clarifies, also intervenes between reader and object. Milton varies points-of-view shifting in space and time so skilfully, that our sense of the reality of hell, of its power vis-a-vis man or God, never remains secure. Spirits, we know, can assume any shape they please; and Milton, like Spenser, uses this imaginative axiom to destroy the idea of the simple location of good and evil in the spiritual combat. But despite the insecurity, the abyss momentarily glimpsed under simple event, Milton's main effort in the first books is to make us believe in Satan as a real and terrible agent, yet never as an irresistible power. No doubt at all of Satan's influence: his success is writ large in religious history: which may also be one reason for the epic enumeration of demonic names and place-names in Book I. Nevertheless, even as we are closest to Satan, presented with the hottest view of hell's present and future appeal, all suggestion of irresistible influence must be expunged, if Milton's two means of divine justification, man's free will and God's foreknowledge of the creation's triumph, are to win consent.

These two dominant concepts, expressed through the counterplot, shed a calm and often cold radiance over all of *Paradise Lost,* issuing equally from the heart of faith and the center of self-determination. The similes must persuade us that man was and is "sufficient to have stood, though free to fall" (III, 99), that his reason and will, however fiercely tempted and besieged, stand on a pinnacle as firm and precarious as that on which the Christ of *Paradise Regained* (IV, 541 ff) suffers his last, greatest, archetypal temptation. They must show the persistence, in the depth of danger, passion or evil, of imperturbable reason, of a power working *ab extra.*

This they accomplish in several ways. They are, for example, marked by an emphasis on place names. It is the *Tuscan* artist who views the moon (Satan's shield) from the top of *Fesole* or in *Valdarno* through his optic glass, while he searches for new Lands, Rivers, Mountains on the spotty globe. Do not the place names serve to anchor this observer, and set him off from the vastness and vagueness of hell, its unnamed and restless geography, as well as from his attempt to leave the earth and rise by science above the lunar world? A recital of names is, of course, not reassuring of itself: no comfort accrues in hearing Moloch associated with *Rabba, Argob, Basan, Arnon,* or sinful Solomon with *Hinnom, Tophet, Gehenna* (I, 397-405). The point is that these places were once neutral, innocent of bloody or holy associations; it is man who has made them what they are, made the proper name a fearful or a hopeful sign (cf. XI, 836-39). Will Valdarno and Fiesole become such by-words as Tophet and Gehenna? At the moment they are still hieroglyphs, words whose ultimate meaning is in the balance. They suggest the inviolate shelter of the created world rather than the incursions of a demonic world. Yet we sense that, if Galileo uses the shelter and Ark of this world to dream of other worlds, paying optical rites to the moon, Fiesole, Valdarno, even Vallombrosa may yield to the tug of a demonic interpretation and soon become a part of hell's unprotected marl.

Though the figure of the observer *ab extra* is striking in Milton's evo-

cation of Galileo, it becomes more subtly patent in a simile a few lines
further on, which tells how the angel forms lay entranced on hell's inflamed sea

> Thick as Autumnal Leaves that strow the Brooks
> In *Vallombrosa*, where th'Etrurian shades
> High overarch't imbow'r; or scatter'd sedge
> Afloat, when with fierce winds *Orion* arm'd
> Hath vext the Red-Sea Coast, whose waves o'erthrew
> *Busiris* and his *Memphian* Chivalry,
> While with perfidious hatred they pursu'd
> The sojourners of *Goshen,* who beheld
> From the safe shore thir floating Carcasses
> And broken Chariot Wheels (302-11)

A finer modulation of aesthetic distance can hardly be found: we start at
the point of maximum contrast, with the angels prostrate on the lake, in
a region "vaulted with fire" (298), viewed as leaves fallen seasonally on a
sheltered brook vaulted by shade; go next to the image of sea-weed scattered by storm, and finally, without break of focus, to the Israelites watching "from the safe shore" the floating bodies and parts of their pursuers.
And, as in music, where one theme fading, another emerges to its place,
while the image of calm and natural death changes to that of violent and
supernatural destruction, the figure of the observer *ab extra* becomes explicit, substituting for the original glimpse of inviolable peace.

Could the counterplot be clearer? A simile intended to sharpen our
view of the innumerable stunned host of hell, just before it is roused by
Satan, at the same time sharpens our sense of the imperturbable order of
the creation, and of the coming storm, and of the survival of man through
providence and his safe-shored will. Satan, standing clear of the rout,
prepares to vex his legions to new evil:

> on the Beach
> Of that inflamed Sea, he stood and call'd
> His Legions, Angel Forms, who lay intrans't
> Thick as Autumnal Leaves . . .

but the scenes the poet himself calls up mimic hell's defeat before Satan's
voice is fully heard, and whatever sought to destroy the calm of autumnal
leaves lies lifeless as scattered sedge. The continuity of the similes hinges
on the middle image of Orion, which sketches both Satan's power to
rouse the fallen host and God's power to scatter and destroy it. In this
"plot counterplot" the hand of Satan is not ultimately distinguishable
from the will of God.

A further instance, more complex still, is found at the end of Book I.
Milton compares the host gathered in the gates of Pandemonium to bees
at springtime (768 ff). The wonder of this incongruity has been preserved by many explanations. It is clearly a simile which, like others we

have adduced, diminishes hell while it magnifies creation. The bees are fruitful, and their existence in the teeth of Satan drowns out the sonorous *hiss* of hell. Their "straw-built Citadel" will survive "bossy" Pandemonium. As Dr. Johnson kicking the stone kicks all excessive idealism, so Milton's bees rub their balm against all excessive demonism. But the irony may not end there. Are the devils not those bees who bring food out of the eater, sweetness out of the strong (Judges 15: 5-19)?

It may also be more than a coincidence that the most famous in this genre of similes describes the bustle of the Carthaginians as seen by storm-exiled Aeneas (*Aeneid* I, 430-40). Enveloped in a cloud by his divine mother, Aeneas looks down from the top of a hill onto a people busily building their city like a swarm of bees at summer's return, and is forced to cry: "O fortunati, quorum iam moenia surgunt!"—o fortunate people, whose walls are already rising! Then Vergil, as if to dispel any impression of despair, adds: *mirabile dictu*, a wonder! Aeneas walks among the Carthaginians made invisible by divine gift.

Here the counterplot thickens, and we behold one of Milton's amazing transpositions of classical texts. Aeneas strives to found Rome, which will outlast Carthage. The bees building in Vergil's text intimate a spirit of creativity seasonally renewed and independent of the particular civilization. The bees in Milton's text represent the same privilege and promise. Aeneas wrapped in the cloud is the observer *ab extra*, the person on the shore, and his impatient cry is of one who desires to build a civilization beyond decay, perhaps even beyond the wrath of the gods. An emergent, as yet invisible figure in Milton's text shares the hero's cry: he has seen Mammon and his troop build Pandemonium, Satan's band swarm triumphant about their citadel: despite this, can the walls of creation outlive Satan as Rome the ancient world?

All this would be putative or extrinsic if based solely on the simile of the bees. For this simile, like the middle image of Orion vexing the Red Sea, is indeterminate in its implications, a kind of visual pivot in a series of images which act in sequence and once more reveal the counterplot. Its indeterminacy is comparable to Milton's previously mentioned use of proper nouns, and his overall stylistic use of the *pivot*, by means of which images and words are made to refer both backwards and forwards, giving the verse period unusual balance and flexibility. The series in question begins with the trooping to Pandemonium, and we now give the entire modulation which moves through several similes:

> all access was throng'd, the Gates
> And Porches wide, but chief the spacious Hall
> (Though like a cover'd field, where Champions bold
> Wont ride in arm'd, and at the Soldan's chair
> Defi'd the best of *Paynim* chivalry
> To mortal combat or career with Lance)
> Thick swarm'd, both on the ground and in the air,

> Brusht with the hiss of rustling wings. As Bees
> In spring time, when the Sun with *Taurus* rides,
> Pour forth thir populous youth about the Hive
> In clusters; they among fresh dews and flowers
> Fly to and fro, or on the smoothed Plank,
> The suburb of thir Straw-built Citadel,
> New rubb'd with Balm, expatiate and confer
> Thir State affairs. So thick the aery crowd
> Swarm'd and were strait'n'd; till the Signal giv'n,
> Behold a wonder! they but now who seem'd
> In bigness to surpass Earth's Giant Sons
> Now less than smallest Dwarfs, in narrow room
> Throng numberless, like that Pigmean Race
> Beyond the *Indian* Mount, or Faery Elves,
> Whose midnight Revels, by a Forest side
> Or Fountain some belated Peasant sees,
> Or dreams he sees, while over-head the Moon
> Sits Arbitress, and nearer to the Earth
> Wheels her pale course, they on thir mirth and dance
> Intent, with jocund Music charm his ear;
> At once with joy and fear his heart rebounds. (761-88)

The very images which marshall the legions of hell to our view reveal simultaneously that the issue of Satan's triumph or defeat, his real or mock power, is in the hand of a *secret arbiter,* whether God and divine prescience or man and free will. In the first simile the observer *ab extra* is the Soldan, who as a type of Satan overshadows the outcome of the combat between pagan and christian warriors in the "cover'd field." The second simile is indeterminate in tenor, except that it diminishes the satanic thousands, blending them and their war-like intents with a picture of natural, peaceful creativity, Sun and Taurus presiding in place of the Soldan. "Behold a wonder!" echoes the *mirabile dictu* of Vergil's story, and prepares the coming of a divine observer. The mighty host is seen to shrink to the size of Pigmies (the third simile), and we know that these, the "small infantry," as Milton had called them with a pun reflecting the double perspective of the first books, can be overshadowed by Cranes (575-6). The verse period then carries us still further from the main action as the diminished devils are also compared to Faery Elves glimpsed at their midnight revels by some belated Peasant. From the presence and pomp of hell we have slowly slipped into a pastoral.

Yet does not this static moment hide an inner combat more real than that for which hell is preparing? It is midnight, the pivot between day and day, and in the Peasant's mind a similar point of balance seems to obtain. He is not fully certain of the significance or even reality of the Fairy ring. Like Aeneas in Hades, who glimpses the shade of Dido (*Aeneid* VI, 450-5), he "sees, Or dreams he sees" something barely distinguishable from the pallid dark, obscure as the new moon through clouds. What an intensity of calm is here, reflecting a mind balanced on the critical pivot, as a point of stillness is reached at greatest remove from the threats and reverberations of hell! But even as the man stands uncertain, the image of the moon overhead becomes intense, it has sat there all the time as arbiter, now wheels closer to the earth, and the Peasant's heart rebounds with a secret intuition bringing at once joy and fear.

The moon, clearly, is a last transformation of the image of the observer *ab extra*, Soldan, Sun and Taurus, Peasant. What was a type of Satan overshadowing the outcome of the real or spiritual combat is converted into a presentment of the individual's naive and autonomous power of discrimination, his free reason, secretly linked with a superior influence, as the moon overhead. The figure of the firmly placed observer culminates in that of the secret arbiter. Yet this moon is not an unambiguous symbol of the secret arbiter. A feeling of the moon's uncertain, changeable nature—incorruptible yet spotty, waxing and waning (I, 284-291; II, 659-666; see also "mooned horns," IV, 978, quoted below)—is subtly present. It reflects this series of images in which the poet constantly suggests, destroys and recreates the idea of an imperturbably transcendent discrimination. The moon that "Sits Arbitress" seems to complete the counterplot, but is only the imperfect sign of a figure not revealed till Book IV. Thus the whole cycle of to and fro, big and small, Pigmies or Elves, seeing or dreaming, far and near, joy and fear, this uneasy flux of couplets, alternatives and reversals, is continued when we learn, in the final lines of Book I, that far within Pandemonium, perhaps as far from consciousness as hell is from the thoughts of the Peasant or demonic power from the jocund, if intent music of the fairy revelers, Satan and the greatest of his Lords sit in their own, unreduced dimensions.

We meet the Peasant once more in *Paradise Lost,* and in a simile which seems to want to outdo the apparent incongruity of all others. At the end of Book IV, Gabriel and his files confront Satan apprehended squatting in Paradise, a toad at the ear of Eve. A heroically contemptuous exchange follows, and Satan's taunts finally so incense the Angel Squaddron that they

> Turn'd fiery red, sharp'ning in mooned horns
> Thir Phalanx, and began to hem him round
> With ported Spears, as thick as when a field
> Of *Ceres* ripe for harvest waving bends
> Her bearded Grove of ears, which way the wind
> Sways them; the careful Plowman doubting stands
> Lest on the threshing floor his hopeful sheaves
> Prove chaff. On th'other side *Satan* alarm'd
> Collecting all his might dilated stood,
> Like *Teneriff* or *Atlas* unremov'd:
> His stature reacht the Sky, and on his Crest
> Sat horror Plum'd; nor wanted in his grasp

> What seem'd both Spear and Shield: now dreadful deeds
> Might have ensu'd, nor only Paradise
> In this commotion, but the Starry Cope
> Of Heav'n perhaps, or all the Elements
> At least had gone to rack, disturb'd and torn
> With violence of this conflict, had not soon
> Th'Eternal to prevent such horrid fray
> Hung forth in Heav'n his golden Scales, yet seen
> Betwixt *Astrea* and the *Scorpion* sign,
> Wherein all things created first he weigh'd,
> The pendulous round Earth with balanc'd Air
> In counterpoise, now ponders all events,
> Battles and Realms . . . (978-1002)

The question of Satan's power does not appear to be academic, at least not at first. The simile which, on previous occasions, pretended to illustrate hell's greatness but actually diminished hell and magnified the creation, is used here just as effectively against heaven. Milton, by dilating Satan, and distancing the spears of the angel phalanx as ears ready for reaping, creates the impression of a balance of power between heaven and hell. Yet the image which remains in control is neither of Satan nor of the Angels but of the wheatfield, first as its bearded ears bend with the wind, then as contemplated by the Plowman. Here the counterplot achieves its most consummate form. *Paradise Lost* was written not for the sake of heaven or hell but for the sake of the creation. What is all the fuss about if not to preserve the "self-balanc't" earth? The center around which and to which all actions turn is whether man can stand though free to fall, whether man and the world can survive their autonomy. The issue may not therefore be determined on the supernatural level by the direct clash of heaven and hell, only by these two arbiters: man's free will, and God's foreknowledge. The ripe grain sways in the wind, so does the mind which has tended it. Between ripeness and ripeness gathered falls the wind, the threshing floor, the labour of ancient *ears*, the question of the relation of God's will to man's will. The ears appear to be at the mercy of the wind, what about the thoughts, the "hopeful sheaves" of the Plowman? The fate of the world lies between Gabriel and Satan, but also between the wind and the ripe ears, but also between man and his thoughts. Finally God, supreme arbiter, overbalances the balance with the same pair of golden scales (suspended yet between Virgin and Scorpion) in which the balanced earth weighed at its first creation.

Characters and Drama

by Douglas Bush

. . . *Paradise Lost* is by far the most important survivor of the many heroic poems which were being written all over Europe in the seventeenth century, so that it is often regarded as a solitary and peculiarly Puritan work. But Milton's choice of a biblical subject was in full accord with the European movement, since the effect of both the Reformation and the Counter Reformation had been to turn epic ambitions away from secular to Christian material. Milton himself had early contemplated a British subject, which would of course have been Christian, but he settled on one of much broader and deeper significance, one which had already attracted other European poets.

When we compare Milton's poem with the ancient epics, we see that his subject involved special difficulties, difficulties of a kind apparent to some degree in Virgil. These are mostly comprised in one large fact, the widening gulf between material and theme. In Homer material and theme were indivisible; all the spiritual values of life were concentrated in the active courage of the warrior and the traveler in a dark world of flux and futility. The *Aeneid,* however, moves on more than one level, and we feel a partial disharmony between the prescribed pattern of war and voyaging, the traditional stuff of the epic, and the abstract theme. And Virgil's abstract theme is not single. It obviously presents the glory of the Italian past and the Italian destiny. But in a larger way it presents what C. S. Lewis has called "a transition in the world-order, the shift of civilization from the East to the West, the transformation of the little remnant, the *reliquias,* of the old, into the germ of the new." [1] And, thirdly, there is the more positively religious and ethical idea of a pilgrim's progress; Aeneas is led, through trial and suffering, by divine providence and a sense of duty. The second and third of these themes may be said to have their parallels in Milton's poem. But a concrete pattern and material already inadequate for the philosophic Virgil were not

"Characters and Drama." From *Paradise Lost in Our Time* by Douglas Bush, Ithaca, N.Y., 1945. Copyright © 1945 by Cornell University. Reprinted by permission of the author and Cornell University Press. The present selection includes pages 58-79 of the above book, with minor omissions in two places indicated by ellipsis marks.

[1] *A Preface to* Paradise Lost (London: Oxford University Press, 1942), pp. 34-35.

less so for a poet of the seventeenth century, and the gulf between Milton's material and his theme was increased by the special nature of his fable. That fable was, for most men of his century, a record of one of the two greatest events in the history of the world and, as I said, it had attracted other poets, but as characters it had of course only supernatural beings and two scarcely normal human beings. The wonder is not that Milton did not overcome all his problems but that he triumphantly overcame so many of them. One of Mr. Eliot's most quoted asides is this: "Milton's celestial and infernal regions are large but insufficiently furnished apartments filled by heavy conversation; and one remarks about the Puritan mythology its thinness." [2] Well, a critic with as little sympathy for Dante as Mr. Eliot has for Milton might say that *The Divine Comedy* presents a small but crowded prison and a somewhat gloomy visitor's painful interviews with the convicts, which are happily concluded by a chat with the Warden's daughter. Milton's insufficiently furnished apartments contain the marvelous pictures of hell and of vast space, and the heavy conversation includes the defiant speeches of Satan and the greatly dramatic debate in Pandemonium. And the "thin" story of Satan and Adam and Eve was not a Puritan invention. Indeed there is very little of the specifically Puritan in *Paradise Lost* or in the whole body of Milton's poetry.

The poet's consciousness of at least some of his problems is made clear by the repeated apologies put into the mouth of Raphael when he tells Adam of the war in heaven and the Creation:

> and what surmounts the reach
> Of human sense, I shall delineate so,
> By lik'ning spiritual to corporal forms,
> As may express them best, though what if Earth
> Be but the shadow of Heav'n, and things therein
> Each to other like, more than on earth is thought?

Often we cannot be sure at what point in his own mind Milton distinguished the imaginative and symbolic from what he and his age regarded as historical. That he allowed himself a large license is amply evident when we put *Paradise Lost* beside the *Christian Doctrine* and find, for example, that in the treatise only a few lines are given to Satan and little more to the revolt of the angels and the war in heaven. This last episode is a good illustration of the difficulty of handling abstract ideas in the concrete terms of the traditional epic. The long account of the war is a picture of ambitious pride attempting to overthrow righteousness and order and bringing about utter chaos and destruction. As a whole it is done with imaginative power and energy such as only Milton can command, yet in parts it is too unreal for an epic, in parts too real-

---

[2] *Selected Essays* (London: Faber and Faber, 1932), p. 307; (New York: Harcourt, Brace, 1932), p. 279.

istic for a symbol. Another example might be God's proclamation of Christ as Messiah, the event which inflames Satan to revolt. The situation is the same as that in *Macbeth* when Macbeth is aroused by Duncan's nomination of Malcolm as heir-apparent. But Milton is not making God into a human and dynastically minded king, still less is he giving a philosophic explanation of the origin of evil; he is establishing Christ in His place as the Son of God, the Mediator between God and man, the active agent of good in the world. The nature and necessities of epic narrative, however, convert a spiritual symbol into a concrete dramatic incident.

But we must turn from generalities to the characters. Bestriding our path is the colossal figure of Satan, who has misled not only a host of angels and Adam and Eve but a host of critics as well. Since the romantic age, which misinterpreted a number of great works, it has been conventional to regard Satan as the real hero of *Paradise Lost*. We can readily understand how revolutionary poets like Blake and Shelley could make over Milton in their own image; what is less understandable is the persistence of that attitude. . . .

The argument is in brief that, since God is so unpleasant and Satan is a being of such magnificent vitality, Milton, in spite of his consciously different purpose, must have put his heart and soul into the projection of Satan. We might find a partial parallel in the *Aeneid,* in which, we are often told, the stuffy nominal hero is greatly overshadowed by a character with whom we were not intended to sympathize. For many readers, especially for those who, like many readers of *Paradise Lost,* know only the first few books, Virgil's most vital and central figure is Dido. She alone is humanly and tragically real, while Aeneas, the embodiment of Roman virtue, and Jupiter, Divine Providence, are, like Milton's Adam and God, pallid, self-righteous, and irritating. To persons of this way of thinking, or feeling, there seems to be a central discord in both poems, a conflict between the poet's intention and the result. Both Dido and Satan, it appears, are much too great and attractive for their functional role as villains. But Dido would certainly have been an ineffectual villain if she had not had magnetism enough to charm Aeneas (and us), and Satan would certainly have been an ineffectual villain if he had not had magnetism enough to sway a host of followers (and us). To put the case in that manner, though, might suggest that Virgil and Milton sat down to calculate in cold blood how much vitality they could allow such characters and made a mistake in their arithmetic. The notion sounds much better in this form—that Virgil and Milton had it in their heads to set forth certain orthodox principles but were carried away unwittingly by their hearts and imaginations. No doubt artists have sometimes produced effects different from what they intended, have produced works with internal antinomies, but if any artists in the world have given the impression of knowing what they are about, it is Virgil and Milton.

That these poets should in their major works reveal a fundamental religious and moral contradiction one may find it quite impossible to conceive.

But let us glance at a clearer case, at a poet much closer in time and outlook to Milton. When we come upon the speeches in which Iago, Edmund, Macbeth, and the rest concoct their diabolical plans against the good, do we exclaim, "Here is the real Shakespeare, the poet who was of the devil's party without knowing it?" No one disputes the vitality of these great villains, but one doubts if even the most crackbrained of Shakespearian critics, and there are many, have ever suggested that Shakespeare was at heart an Iago or Edmund or Macbeth who forgot his principles in creating such congenial characters. And Shakespeare is only one of the multitude of serious authors who have treated serious themes and created great bad characters in the process. Were all these authors on the side of evil, or is Milton to be the solitary victim of an astonishing naïveté?

Of course it is said, with a romantic transmutation of values, that Satan is really "right," and that brings us to deeper and more disastrous reasons for the misunderstanding of Milton. We can indeed see the same reasons at work in the interpretation of Shakespeare, even if it stops short of the palpable absurdities just imagined. Mr. Eliot, who may be cited as an influential representative of many, appears to sum up Shakespeare's philosophy as "the mixed and muddled scepticism of the Renaissance." [3] Students of Renaissance thought, however, would say that, no matter how far and wide Shakespeare's imagination traveled, his plays were solidly built on the traditional Renaissance orthodoxy of order and degree in the soul, in society, and in the cosmos. And that same orthodoxy, developed with more philosophic learning and more positive religious zeal, is central in Milton. The fact is simply that the modern world has moved quite away from the old assumptions and doctrines of religious, ethical, social, and cosmic order and right reason. It is perhaps a fair guess that among the general reading public three out of four persons instinctively sympathize with any character who suffers and rebels, and pay little heed to the moral values and responsibilities involved, because in such cases the sinner is always right and authority and rectitude are always wrong. We have much more sympathy with *virtù*, which is always exciting, than with virtue, which is always smug. This instinctive response has of course grown the stronger as religion and morality have been increasingly sapped by romantic naturalism and sentimentalism. So thoroughly are we debauched by these flabby "liberal" doctrines that when we encounter an artist who passionately affirms the laws of justice, reason, and righteousness, the laws that grow not old, we cannot understand his high convictions and purposes and either turn from them in

[3] *Selected Essays* (London: Faber and Faber, 1932), p. 137; (New York: Harcourt, Brace, 1932), p. 117.

disgust or explain them away. The moment such principles are associated with a poet, he becomes automatically a timid and conventional reactionary or, in the case of Milton, too simple-minded to understand human experience. To celebrate Milton therefore as the great champion of a religious and ethical orthodoxy is to bring ignominy upon him. As Hooker said in opening his defense of divine and human reason against dogmatic and irrational Calvinism, a rebel always finds a ready and admiring audience, whereas one who maintains things established has to meet a number of heavy prejudices. And Milton, the great Puritan enemy of the Anglican church, was in the same tradition of Christian humanism as Hooker.

But, it may be asked, what then becomes of the bold rebel and pamphleteer against ecclesiastical and civil authority? Certainly Milton was a great rebel, on one plane, but on another he was not, and it is fatal to ignore the difference. Milton was a rebel like his own Abdiel, the faithful angel whom Satan could not seduce and who received from God the noble praise:

> Servant of God, well done, well hast thou fought
> The better fight, who single hast maintain'd
> Against revolted multitudes the Cause
> Of Truth, in word mightier than they in Arms;
> And for the testimony of Truth hast borne
> Universal reproach, far worse to bear
> Than violence: for this was all thy care
> To stand approv'd in sight of God, though Worlds
> Judg'd thee perverse.

Or one might think of such a "rebellious" servant of God as Socrates, who has also suffered sometimes from the charge of personal arrogance. For the modern "liberal," knowing no absolute imperatives and having no beliefs, in the old meaning of the word, can think of no explanation except arrogant self-righteousness for the inward strength, "Unshak'n, unseduc'd, unterrifi'd," of one to whom life means obedience to God.

The many readers who glorify Satan of course regard Milton's God as an almighty King Charles, a tyrant against whom it was glorious to rebel. I trust that that wild notion has been exploded by what was said before about Milton's conception of God as the supreme source and symbol of love, mercy, justice, reason, and order. For an eloquent summary of that conception I may quote the last words of Hooker's first book:

> Wherefore that here we may briefly end: of Law there can be no less acknowledged, than that her seat is the bosom of God, her voice the harmony of the world: all things in heaven and earth do her homage, the very least as feeling her care, and the greatest as not exempted from her power, both Angels and men and creatures of what condition soever, though each in different sort and manner, yet all with uniform consent, admiring her as the mother of their peace and joy.

This is the sacred and sublime law, the divine harmony, that Satan seeks to overthrow.

The common fallacy begins with a basic misapprehension of the beginning of *Paradise Lost,* namely, Satan's first speech delivered as he surveys his followers rolling in the fiery gulf, confounded though immortal. Before we look at the speech we may remind ourselves that Milton's dramatic methods are much the same as those of the Elizabethan playwrights. In a soliloquy uttered later on his way to Eden—a soliloquy originally written, we are told, as the first speech for the drama Milton had planned—Satan condemns himself with a thoroughness which even God could hardly amplify. Such an open avowal of wickedness by a villain we may assign to the naïve plane of dramaturgy, though we have it everywhere in Shakespeare and his fellows. But the dramatists, and Milton, also use a more dramatic and sophisticated method. They contrive a speech in such terms that, without being a direct confession of evil, it will be so opposed to accepted ideas and values as to invite condemnation by the audience; and that desired response may also be guided through the reaction of a character of recognized goodness. Milton's narrative and descriptive medium encouraged still more direct guidance of our response, though he too could use purely dramatic irony without comment.

In the case of this first speech, our response is prepared for through the picture of the archangel torn by wholly evil passions. But even if there were no such preparation, the speech itself in every line should arouse horror and repulsion. It is a dramatic revelation of nothing but egoistic pride and passion, of complete spiritual blindness. The "Potent Victor in his rage" is a blind and blasphemous description of God. Nothing that that Victor can inflict will make Satan "repent or change." This phrase, which Shelley remembered as glorious at the end of *Prometheus Unbound,* is a repudiation of all Christian teaching; and one might quote Lord Vansittart on the Germans' national fallacy that only the weak repent. Satan's "injur'd merit" is a figment of his own egoism, quite the opposite of the real and selfless merit of Christ.

> What though the field be lost?
> All is not lost. . . .

These famous lines embody, not the spirit of the Puritan armies, but the spirit of Hitler. Satan sees only a conflict between himself, the world conqueror, and a temporarily superior force; he cannot see that it is a conflict between evil and good. "The unconquerable Will" is not the religious and ethical will, it is the irreligious and naturalistic will to power. "Study of revenge" and "immortal hate" brand themselves.

> Courage never to submit or yield

is not true courage, it is the courage of a wolf at bay, of Hitler again, desperate perseverance in evil. In short, if we think defiance is splendid, regardless of what is defied, if we read this speech with a thrill of sympathy, we ought to feel the same thrill in reading the speeches of Iago and Edmund and Macbeth. Certainly Milton did no less than Shakespeare to guide our reaction. But anything is possible to romantic sentimentalism combined with indifference to the principles on which Milton, like Shakespeare, stood. Even Walter Savage Landor, a romantic revolutionary and neopagan who loathed Milton's theology, could see that "There is neither truth nor wit . . . in saying that Satan is hero of the piece, unless, as is usually the case in human life, he is the greatest hero who gives the widest sway to the worst passions."

I have dwelt on this first speech of Satan's because, as I said, it is for so many readers and critics the beginning of error. There is no antinomy here between Milton's intention and the result, and there is none later, even when he leaves dramatic speech to create its own effect. Those who admire the rebel of the first speech also admire him when he declares:

> Here at least
> We shall be free. . . .
> To reign is worth ambition though in Hell:
> Better to reign in Hell, than serve in Heav'n.

But to those who comprehend and feel Milton's principles, which are everywhere made clear, such words tell how far Satan is from understanding true liberty, how far slavery to pride and passion is from Him in whose service is perfect freedom. Or take the great moment when Satan, his face entrenched with deep scars of thunder, surveys the host he has led to ruin and can hardly speak:

> Thrice he assay'd, and thrice in spite of scorn,
> Tears such as Angels weep, burst forth: at last
> Words interwove with sighs found out thir way.

If, again, one has an impulse to admire a powerful leader momentarily remorseful in defeat, one may think of Hitler explaining his later campaigns. Satan is of course a far grander figure than Hitler, but their motives are closely parallel. In fact Milton uses what was for the sixteenth and seventeenth centuries the equivalent of Hitler in repeatedly likening Satan to a Sultan; Richard Knolles in 1603 had summed up western feeling when he began his history with the phrase "The glorious empire of the Turks, the present terror of the world." The tyrant of Milton's poem, as some readers have seen, is not God but Satan.

Of course Satan has heroic qualities. A character of Mr. Aldous Huxley's remarks: "Indeed, you can't be really bad unless you *do* have most of the virtues. Look at Milton's Satan for example. Brave, strong, generous, loyal, prudent, temperate, self-sacrificing. And let's give the dictators the credit that's due to them; some of them are nearly as virtuous as Satan. Not quite, I admit, but nearly. That's why they can achieve so much evil." [4] And if Satan has heroic virtues, so has Macbeth. Both characters possess the emotional advantage—if we do not feel the values involved—of fighting against odds, while the representatives of goodness and right have irresistible power. The situation is in fact essentially the same. Satan is overthrown when Christ is armed with the might of God; Macbeth, who has leagued himself with the powers of Satan, is overthrown by the English army, which is, says Malcolm, the instrument of the powers above. Both poets, though imaginatively capable of creating a great villain, are constrained by their traditional faith in Providence and the ultimate triumph of good to bring divine power to the defeat of evil—which is not to say that Shakespeare and Milton always saw good triumphant here and now—and, compared with the dauntless archangel and the bloody tyrant at bay, Christ and Malcolm may not win much of our sympathy.[5] But to revert again to a more immediately conclusive example, whatever sentimental aberrations may cloud the minds of readers of poetry, few countries or persons seem to be filled with sympathetic admiration for Germany because it has been fighting bravely against the three strongest powers of the world.

Satan's first speech has proclaimed him a great outlaw, a Titan of the Hebrew and Christian cosmogony, and his spiritual state receives concrete illustration in the loss of his archangelic grandeur when he arrives in Eden to pursue his campaign against man. He is compared with a wolf and he takes the actual shape of various creatures, finally a toad and a serpent. But these bestial transformations are less interesting than his metamorphosis into a very human villain. At his first sight of Adam and Eve in their blissful innocence he can indulge in the sardonic humor of Richard III:

> League with you I seek,
> And mutual amity so strait, so close,
> That I with you must dwell, or you with me
> Henceforth.

Witnessing the two

> Imparadis't in one another's arms,

he feels the sensual sting of Iago or Leontes. Later he approaches Eve with the flattering guile of Iachimo.

But we must leave Satan and observe the far more elaborate humaniz-

---

[4] *After Many a Summer Dies the Swan* (London: Chatto and Windus, 1939), p. 115; (New York: Harper, 1939), p. 130.

[5] In speaking of *Macbeth* and *Paradise Lost,* one might add that the discussion between Malcolm and Macduff, concerning the wicked and the ideal king, is commonly regarded by modern readers as a curious layer of unpoetic dullness, and as such it may be linked with Milton's council in heaven; for the modern reader does not share the traditional convictions about divine, public, and individual order on which both passages are based.

ing process in Milton's treatment of Adam and Eve. As we first see them, they are ideal man and ideal woman, ideal husband and ideal wife, wholly happy in their relations with each other and with God, living in a natural world of eternal spring and incomparable beauty. One line, by the way, in Milton's first picture of them,

> Hee for God only, shee for God in him,

has evoked both mirth and annoyance; but it simply embodies the hierarchical view of order and degree which, as we have seen, was a universal heritage, and which Shakespeare appealed to at the end of *The Taming of the Shrew.*

The place of right reason in Milton's conception of man and life and God is nowhere more strikingly illustrated than in his account of love between man and woman. This has been regarded, with favor or otherwise, as the Puritan ideal of marriage set forth in a versified Puritan conduct book. The Puritan ideal was certainly not low, nor ascetic, but Milton's ideal has some distinctive characteristics. For one thing, he is decidedly more emphatic and outspoken than most Puritans in exalting the physical expression and enrichment of love. The importance he gives to "Love's due Rites" has a metaphysical basis, namely, his belief in the essential oneness of matter and spirit, yet this emphasis is part of, and not at odds with, his larger emphasis on the rational nature of human love. True love, as opposed to sensual passion, is

> Founded in Reason, Loyal, Just, and Pure.

It

> is the scale
> By which to heav'nly Love thou may'st ascend.

Even

> smiles from Reason flow,
> To brute deni'd, and are of Love the food,
> Love not the lowest end of human life.

If to us such phrases sound starched and chilling, it is because we do not understand and do not feel the positive and emotional values contained in the idea of reason.

When Milton turns from the cosmic to the human stage, epic technique largely gives place to intimate drama. An elaborate chain of incident and motive leads up to the fall. Readers who find Adam and Eve somewhat stodgy in their idyllic pastoral happiness must have missed the tragic irony through which the pair are viewed. Milton's description of primeval beauty, harmony, love, and joy is not mere exuberance, it comes after Satan has entered the garden; the contrast between present and future indeed draws expressions of pity not only from the poet but from the malignant tempter. Many passages which may seem to be merely idyllic have their dramatic value. Eve's account of her first moments of existence and her first meeting with Adam gives, through veiled adapta-

tions of the myths of Narcissus and of Apollo and Daphne, the first hint
of her vanity and of his passion. Later Satan, planning his campaign,
decides that, since Adam and Eve are happy in humble ignorance and
obedience, he will kindle an ambitious desire for superhuman knowledge.
In the fancy of the sleeping Eve he forges a dream which, in great distress, she tells Adam when she is awakened. An angel, she dreamed, had
persuaded her to eat of the forbidden fruit which would make her among
the gods a goddess. Eve rejoices that it was only a dream; yet, if her
waking conscience is sound, her uncensored dream had revealed the
seeds of vanity and ambitious pride. Adam's psychological explanation
of dreams, though in this case inadequate, brings comfort,

> So all was clear'd, and to the Field they haste.

Since Satan's activity has only begun, there is irony too in the magnificent
canticle in praise of God's creation which Adam and Eve utter before
going to their daily work.

At this point the angel Raphael is sent down from heaven to instruct
Adam and reinforce the admonitions he has already received. Raphael's
long narrative, which runs from book five through book eight, is of
course the recapitulation of the past that we have in the *Odyssey* and
the *Aeneid,* though Milton's purpose and materials are very different.
Raphael commences, as we saw, with a picture of divine order, the traditional chain of being, and he emphasizes Milton's own metaphysical
doctrine of the unity of matter and spirit and the perpetual transformation of matter into spirit. Then, both as a necessary part of the cosmic
and epic story and as a lesson to Adam, Raphael tells of the revolt and
overthrow of Satan and of the creation of the world. In the eighth book
we come closer to Adam's business and bosom in the discourse on astronomy and the danger of intemperance in knowledge, of vain speculation on things remote. Adam fully agrees that the prime wisdom is the
religious and moral insight needed for the problems of daily life. But
as he goes on to tell the angel the story of his own experience he betrays
what is to be his tragic flaw. Recalling his first union with Eve, he says:

> here passion first I felt,
> Commotion strange, in all enjoyments else
> Superior and unmov'd, here only weak
> Against the charm of Beauty's powerful glance.

He knows he should not be so carried away by an inferior being,

> yet when I approach
> Her loveliness, so absolute she seems
> And in herself complete, so well to know
> Her own, that what she wills to do or say,
> Seems wisest, virtuousest, discreetest, best;
> All higher knowledge in her presence falls

> Degraded, Wisdom in discourse with her
> Loses discount'nanc't, and like folly shows;
> Authority and Reason on her wait,
> As one intended first, not after made
> Occasionally; and to consummate all,
> Greatness of mind and nobleness thir seat
> Build in her loveliest, and create an awe
> About her, as a guard Angelic plac't.

Those who sympathize with Satan will here sympathize with Adam and resent the frowning angel's rebuke, since for romantic naturalism the road of excess, in Blake's words, leads to the palace of wisdom—or, for another expression of the same idea:

> Who liketh loving over-well
> Shall look on Helen's face in Hell.
> But he whose love is thin and wise
> Shall see John Knox in Paradise.

Milton was not a romantic naturalist or sentimentalist, but we have seen how he glorifies love and might assume that he is here condemning it only in the way and degree in which he condemned science, or condemned Greek thought and literature in *Paradise Regained*. In all three cases he is upholding the hierarchic scale of religious and moral values against threatened violation. Adam's expression of his love for Eve is not by any means wholly bad, it is a quite human compound of right and wrong. His error is twofold. He, God's prime creature, is subordinating his reason (and we remember what Milton means by reason) both to his own senses and, partly because of his senses, to a being of inferior wisdom; and the implication of this double error is that he may allow his love for Eve to cloud his love for God. If we are disposed to call the author's attitude harshly Miltonic, or harshly Puritan, or anything but genuinely Christian, we may, for instance, remember some words of St. Teresa: "Cursed be that loyalty which reaches so far as to go against the law of God. It is a madness common in the world, and it makes me mad to see it. We are indebted to God for all the good that men do to us, and yet we hold it to be an act of virtue not to break a friendship of this kind, though it lead us to go against Him. Oh, blindness of the world!" [6]

Adam's answer to the angel emphasizes the chief joy of companionship and indicates that his heart is more right than his words had been, yet we are left aware of a possible weakness which temptation may bring out. Adam changes the awkward subject by asking how angels love, and his celestial visitor, after assuring him with a blush that the angelic equivalent is quite satisfactory, thinks it is time to depart. He does so with a last warning against letting passion mislead reason and will, a last reminder of Adam's responsible freedom of choice.

[6] *St. Teresa of Jesus*, ed. J. J. Burke (New York: Columbus Press, 1911), p. 23.

Adam and Eve are now left alone. The war between God and Satan had been only a macrocosmic illustration of, and background for, Milton's real theme, the war between good and evil in the soul of man; and while Satan had been defeated in heaven he is to be victorious on earth. . . .

Creation

by W. B. C. Watkins

I

"In the beginning was the Word, and the Word was with God, and the Word was God." Of Milton's great themes Creation is most completely and serenely realized in his work. It is closest to his heart. He too is an artificer of the word and no other theme offers him such rich correspondence with all he most prizes. For how could he use his own supreme gift more supremely than in celebrating God's great gift of life?

Not yet twenty, Milton writes awkwardly in *A Vacation Exercise:*

> I have some naked thoughts that rove about
> And loudly knock to have their passage out;

still vaguely but with more fire one of these naked thoughts emerges:

> Such where the deep transported mind may soar
> Above the wheeling poles, and at heaven's door
> Look in, and see each blissful deity
> How he before the thunderous throne doth lie . . .

Then, with growing mastery in his *Ode on Christ's Nativity,* he first attempts Creation itself:

> Such music (as 'tis said)
> Before was never made,
> But when of old the sons of morning sung,
> While the creator great
> His constellations set,
> And the well-balanced world on hinges hung,
> And cast the dark foundations deep,
> And bid the weltering waves their oozy channel keep.

This same voice attains full timbre and assurance only after years of training and waiting and living, until the Creator, who earlier in artful

indirect discourse "bid the weltering waves their oozy channel keep,"
speaks out with magnificent authority:

> "Silence, ye troubled waves, and thou deep, peace,"
> Said then the omnific word, "your discord end:"
> Nor stayed, but on the wings of cherubim
> Uplifted, in paternal glory rode
> Far into chaos, and the world unborn;
> For chaos heard his voice . . .
>
> *P.L.*, VII, 216-21

Theologians may worry over Milton's shifting conception of the Trinity—why in some passages all Three Persons go forth together, why in these lines God sends Christ forth, why elsewhere the Holy Ghost hatches out the universe. But the Divine creative act is clear, as is its inauguration:

> And thou my word, begotten Son, by thee
> This I perform, speak thou, and be it done:
> My overshadowing spirit and might with thee
> I send along, ride forth, and bid the deep
> Within appointed bounds be heaven and earth.
>
> *P.L.*, VII, 163-67

Christ is the Word. Milton is creating with the word. Of course he explicitly recognizes the difference between any grandeur he can achieve and God's, as well as the limitation of time-bound human speech; yet he unquestionably feels passionate assurance of divine direction when he rides forth, like Christ, to re-create in poetry God's Work.

In this task no other poet has equalled him. Michelangelo alone, when he painted the single section of the Sistine Ceiling which lives up to its superb conception, can compare with Milton's achievement. Dante gives us Hell and Purgatory and Paradise, but only incidentally celebrates the *act* of creation; whereas Milton, though relegating Raphael's story to a single book, never lets us forget from beginning to end the Divine creative process. It is both substance and structure of his epic.

To God, who foresaw and foreknew all at one stroke, Creation is not fulfilled till Adam's final vision of Christ's Coming and Judgment. Without confusing us, Milton makes clear that there are two times in *Paradise Lost*, of far greater significance than the ingenious double-time in *Othello:*

> Immediate are the acts of God, more swift
> Than time or motion, but to human ears
> Cannot without process of speech be told,
> So told as earthly notion can receive.
>
> *P.L.*, VII, 176-79

By deliberately dislocating time sequence, by his mastery of cumulative effects, by his genius for energy and movement in language, he secures the illusion that what is past is still present at the end when all is at last rounded out.

As the poem opens, in our chronology, God looks out and sees Satan and his host lying prostrate in Hell after the Fall; the world has already been created out of Chaos.[1] But just as Milton keeps always fresh in our minds the physical sense of Satan's fall, "hurled headlong flaming from the ethereal sky," by having his followers constantly recalling it with shuddering terror, by describing it over and over from different points of view—as seen from below in Hell by Sin and Death, from the middle region by Chaos, from above by Raphael, God and his Angels; so, by distributing accounts of Creation in the mouths of various characters— Satan (as rumor), Uriel, Raphael, the chorusing angels, Adam, Eve—he keeps always alive throughout the poem God's continuous creativity.

With the announcement of subject at the opening we are reminded:

> In the beginning how the heavens and earth
> Rose out of chaos,

while the heavenly spirit

> with mighty wings outspread
> Dove-like satest brooding on the vast abyss
> And madest it pregnant.

At the end, after his vision, Adam returns to find new activity:

> for now too nigh
> The archangel stood, and from the other hill
> To their fixed station, all in bright array
> The cherubim descended; on the ground
> Gliding meteorous, as evening mist
> Risen from a river o'er the marsh glides.
> . . . High in front advanced,
> The brandished sword of God before them blazed
> Fierce as a comet . . .
>
> P.L., XII, 625 ff.

God's never-resting deputies are still at work, this time closing the gate on Paradise to start that creation of human history leading to Christ and Judgment—history which by characteristic dislocation of man's time in an approximation of God's simultaneity, we have just experienced.

But Creation is far more deeply interfused in *Paradise Lost* than these surface devices indicate. Miss Mahood has brilliantly, if perhaps too ingeniously, demonstrated how it forms the design and movement of the poem:

> Like the Creator, who, as described in Book VII, begins His work by setting a compass upon the face of the deep, Milton in the opening line

[1] *P.L.*, I, 50-58; II, 349; III, 56-76; VII, 131 ff. Action proper begins with Satan's recovery in Hell. The Six Days evidently occur while Satan lies stunned and immobile.

of his epic transfixes the centre of his cosmos—the earth, human life—and
the nodal point of his action—the Fall of Man. The fine Invocation to
the Holy Spirit which follows is dominated by the idea of flight, and
thus prepares us for the outward movement of the poet's imagination
towards the circumference, through which he swings the other foot of his
compasses in the opening words of his second paragraph:

> Say first, for Heav'n hides nothing from thy view
> Nor the deep Tract of Hell . . .

On this circumference, everything is in motion. As a natural philosopher,
Milton's main objection to the Ptolemaic astronomy seems to have been that
it postulated an incredible speed in the revolutions of the outer spheres
around 'this punctual spot,' the earth. . . . But as a poet, Milton accepted
the geocentric universe as the framework to his epic for this very reason
that it comprised a still centre and a violently moving periphery.[2]

Miss Mahood demonstrates how the various great shifts in the poem
back and forth between Heaven and Earth and Hell parallel the action,
the thematic development, the various arcs described by God's compasses
—always proceeding from and returning to the focal point, the still and
fixed world at the center of this vortex, "with its womb-like security." In
her analysis, the main features are outlined by the plunge *in medias res*
during the first four books; the formal perfection is revealed by the slow
outward and receding movement of the next four; and the last three
books serve to restore the symmetry, hitherto flawless, which transgression
in the ninth has marred.

Thus the movement of the various actors in this drama, the shifts in
focus of attention, the contrasts between motion and rest, sound and
silence—all directly enforce the rational meaning to be found in the
actors' speeches and Milton's running comment. And by endowing the
whole poem with his own amazing sensuous capacity, shared alike by
animate and inanimate—even the unformed matter of Chaos, those "em-
bryon atoms"—Milton in his anatomy of the Universe makes all from
clod to God one body.

II

Lessing insists on dividing Time-Space between poetry and painting.
Joyce meditates ingeniously throughout *Finnegans Wake* on the Time-
Space problem confronting man; to him time is masculine change, space
feminine permanence. But it is Milton who confounds theory by creat-

---

[2] M. M. Mahood, *Poetry and Humanism* [New Haven, 1950], 178 ff. Miss Mahood anticipates my own view so effectively in this respect that it is a privilege to endorse her,
with the sole reservation that she tends (in writing of the Fifth, Sixth, Eleventh,
Twelfth Books, for instance) to confuse perfection of conception with perfection of
execution.

ing in time a sense of space that remains unsurpassed even by Dante, who surpasses him in conveying mystic union with God, not through sight, hearing, taste, touch, smell, but through the intense light only of all-pervading love.

To both poets creation is the traditional imposing of order on chaos; that Milton is magnetically drawn to Dante's medieval sense of order is clear from his deliberate adaptation of the Ptolemaic system, though he cannot, like Dante, use it without reservation.[3] For this reason Dante's Hell, Purgatory, Paradise are more precisely calculated in their relation to the earth and each other than Milton's and more intricately detailed. Nonetheless, we cannot grasp Dante's total scheme without resort to diagrams, mainly because his urgent desire is to reach upward to Paradise, in true Platonic-Christian fashion leaving so far as possible the material senses behind; his imagery in *Paradiso* sloughs off earth and water for fire and air. At each stage of his pilgrimage he puts out of mind the terrain he has passed through.

Milton's fundamental conception of matter as indistinct from spirit[4] is different, and of course his whole purpose is different, centered on earth not Paradise, requiring constant journeying back and forth between Empyrean and Hell and to all corners of the Universe in circular progression. Dante, with his detailed traditional map in mind, knows every step of his way. Milton is his own Mercator, pacing out his map as he progresses and marking out, as if for the first time, the distances, the heights, the depths.

Milton's account of actual Creation is postponed till halfway through the poem, so that we are already familiar with the general outline, the space and its division into components, the scale, the materials before we review the process which articulates this order.[5] We have lain in Hell and explored it; we have with Satan struggled through that unarticulated remnant of primordial matter in Chaos; we have circled the earthly universe and entered the Garden; and finally we have climbed with the Heavenly Muse to the Empyrean, and fallen again with the Rebellious Angels back to Hell. During all this time Milton has been impressing on us in manifold ways the *scale* of Creation, its immensity.

Joyce makes the law of falling bodies—an increase in velocity of "thirty-two feet per second per second"—in the figure thirty-two a chief

[3] Milton solves this problem simply. Once he has constructed in our minds his imagined neo-Ptolemaic Universe, he can afford to bring in the Copernican (*PL.*, VIII, 122 ff.) on a quibble of Raphael's overlegitimate and illegitmate knowledge.

[4] Dante himself is not always consistent, sometimes considering the *prima materia* the direct creation of God, sometimes (*Paradiso*, XIII) something external acted upon by God and only imperfectly responding.

[5] To use an analogy from painting, Milton does not move from finished detail to detail until he is done, but with swift strokes blocks in broadly the general design; then roughly marks off values of light and shadow, gradually bringing the whole surface of the canvas simultaneously to completion.

key to his account of man, since falling is man's nature. Not so scientif-
ically exact, Milton also repeatedly relies on elapsed time, though he
occasionally indicates specific distances. "From the center thrice to the
utmost pole" gives a particular distance between Empyrean and the floor
of Hell (a distance that we have already fallen six times before we are
halfway through the poem). Thus Satan falls thrice the distance from
the earth to the *primum mobile* or outer crust of the universe. Voyaging
through Chaos in the Second Book, Satan strikes a vacuum and instantly
drops a fraction over eleven miles (10,000 fathoms): he would still be
falling but for an unlucky updraft of air.

But Milton does not work out his super-Brobdingnagian scheme like
Swift in exact figures. These few concessions to human literalness only
indicate that all creation is as precisely measurable by God as the frag-
ments within our ken by us. The real sense of the awesome depth of
Satan's fall from on high comes from the *time* it took him to fall and to
recover from his ensuing daze. Hephaestus when thrown out of Jove's
heaven fell a whole summer's day before landing. But as for Satan and
his crew, *nine days they fell.* Even if we do not think in terms of thirty-
two-feet-per-second every second, we have all acquired in infancy a realistic enough sense of falling speed to grasp the awful implied distance.
No wonder the shock of such disaster leaves the heretofore-pain-free Angels unconscious and prostrate

> *Nine times* the *space* that measures day and night.
>
> P.L., I, 50

Milton here deliberately identifies space and time, just as he speaks of
blindness in terms of deafness.

I have already mentioned his extraordinary use of sound and reverberation in building his huge structure. Again and again he dwells on
the volume of sound when one-third of these enormous beings who are
God's Angels fall in full battle array for nine days to crash on the floor
of Hell. And he suggests the time needed for that sound to travel over
infinite distance to the ears of Sin, Death, Chaos and old Night, and the
time needed for the echoes to bounce back in seemingly endless reverberation. Nor does he neglect the force of displaced air and of the sound
waves themselves: if earth had been created then "all earth had to her
center shook."

So far we have been considering dimension only. One way Milton
causes the heavens and earth to rise out of Chaos with the solidity and
form of an actual sphere (as well as vast dimension) is simply by animating Mercator's projection of the earth. This depends on sight and motion.
In simplest terms it is movement of the eye as its focus shifts. We come
upon it early in the best-known sequence of Milton's similes, which conveys a sense of the superheroic size and multitudinous number of Satan's
host, while simultaneously dramatizing their rise from quiescence to

vigorous life and movement, from abject defeat to reborn power, and also creates the vault of Hell.

In the First Book Satan floating on the fiery lake "many a rood" is like a vast whale lying off *Norway*. When he moves toward shore his shield is like the moon which Galileo sees at evening from *Fiesole* or in *Valdarno*. His spear dwarfs the tallest pine on *Norwegian* hills. Thus two widely separated geographical points are established for the two feet of the compass, from Norway in the north to Italy in the south. And this is of course only the beginning of a cumulative process. Satan looks back to see the confusion of his host on the lake of fire:

> Thick as autumnal leaves that strew the brooks
> In *Vallombrosa,* where the Etrurian shades
> High over arched embower; or scattered sedge
> Afloat, when with fierce winds Orion armed
> Hath vexed the *Red Sea coast,* whose waves o'er-threw
> Busiris and his Memphian chivalry . . .
>
> *P.L.*, I, 302-307

We are again swept with an ease possible only to imagination and dreams from the second focal point, the Arno river in northern Italy, east and south across the Mediterranean and Near East to the Red Sea opening on the Indian Ocean. Those who are map-conscious (and today for different reasons we are more so than even the exploring seventeenth century) will feel however faintly a sense of here-to-there section of a globe. Fifty lines later in another figure we have shifted back to where the "populous north" pours forth her hordes to cross

> *Rhene or the Danaw,* when her barbarous sons
> Came like a deluge on the south, and spread
> *Beneath Gibraltar to the Libyan sands.*
>
> *P.L.*, I, 353-55

This time the arc sweeps from the vast steppes beyond the Rhine and Danube westward and southward below Gibraltar, then across the Mediterranean to the Libyan desert reaching into the heart of Africa.

After thus drawing and quartering Europe and fringes of neighboring Asia and Africa, we are imaginatively prepared for the vastness of Hell with its four great rivers, its frozen and flaming continents. And, lest we think only in terms of length and breadth, we soon receive (*P.L.*, II, 636 ff.) another arc indicating the height of Hell's roof, together with a swift suggestion of the time and effort needed to cover such distance, and the dwarfing of enormous Satan seen afar:

> As when far off at sea a fleet descried
> Hangs in the clouds, by equinoctial winds
> Close sailing *from Bengala, or the isles*
> *Of Ternate and Tidore,* whence merchants bring
> Their spicy drugs: they on the trading flood

Through the wide Ethiopian to the cape
Ply stemming nightly toward the pole.

This time our arc sweeps from the Malay archipelago off East Asia across the Indian Ocean to the southern tip of Africa.

This last figure shows how Milton, having established map-consciousness and space-through-eye movement, adds actual physical movement (both of flying and of sturdily plowing ships) as Satan starts the first of many journeys. Circling with him over the whole universe familiarizes us with the vast locale of the poem, thoroughly explored muscularly with swift ease or laborious difficulty by flying, walking, crawling, wading, swimming, climbing. We are even privileged through Satan's eyes to see the whole world, not just the earth, in relation to Empyrean from outside, shrunk to relative insignificance in the immense cosmos:

> And fast by hanging in a golden chain
> This pendent world, in bigness as a star
> Of smallest magnitude close by the moon.[6]
>
> > *P.L.*, II, 1051-53

After we have leaped over an unguarded towering wall into Eden with Satan, lurked there with him in secret to spy on Adam and Eve, been thrown out by Gabriel, the poem shifts point of view for four books. On our return to Satan in the Ninth Book, with that imaginative privilege of poetry to go backward in time, we re-spend those seven intervening days traveling with Satan about the globe—three days circling the earth at the equator from east to west, and four circling from pole to pole (*P.L.*, IX, 63 ff.). In between our parting from Satan and rejoining him we have lived through Raphael's account of God's Six Days. For those vast sweeping arcs described by the Golden Compasses we were amply prepared. Satan's seven-fold circling of the earth, coming just afterwards, continues the persistent circular movement and the spherical form of perfection.

III

In Milton's Universe nothing is at rest except Heaven, earth, and Hell, and even these are giving forth and receiving influences. All else is moving at various speeds, either in complex harmony like the spheres or violent turbulence like Chaos. The planets are inhaling and exhaling. On earth, land and sea are in ferment. No wonder the poem pulses with life.

Milton's special genius for motion is more easily experienced than explained. It is so marked that Miss Mahood considers him more tactile

---

[6] Milton resorts to double-scale as well as double-time. Here our world is shrunk to a speck; yet Satan falls only one and one half its diameter (*P.L.*, I, 73-74).

than oral or aural.[7] Motion is in Milton a kind of sixth sense expressed in imagery, in mimetic rhythms, and by an electric charge which he manages to put into ordinary words, making even nouns, adverbs, adjectives, participles behave like active verbs.[8] This is why kinetic sympathy is aroused by the geographical similes we have just been examining and by Satan's busy travels, as

> He *scours* the right hand coast, sometimes the left.
> Now *shaves with level wing* the deep, then *soars* . . .
>
> *P.L.*, II, 633-34

Neither Satan nor any of the other angels tamely fly from here to there. Each flight has its special quality, often its particular angle. Instinctively the flyer seems to test air resistance, seek or avoid air currents. We always know the state of the atmosphere—whether the pure serene of upper regions or the density of lower—as well as the state of mind and purpose, registered by leisurely coasting or meteor speed. An angel can *spring upward like a pyramid of fire, glide* like Uriel on a sunbeam "swift as a shooting star," *throw his steep flight in many an airy wheel, stoop* like a down-swooping hawk. Milton himself, we remember, *soars* over the Olympian hill "above the flight of Pegasean wing," and all these fantasies of flight during his blindness must have been based on earlier close observation of birds as well as knowledge of natural laws. In each instance the rhythm of the verse helps convey the quality of flight, yet it is hardly more responsible than the nice calculation of effort needed to form the words chosen.

As no one tamely flies no one simply falls. Even in a passing allusion to Mulciber-Hephaestus the quality of the human body as a projectile is there. First he is flung sailing in a wide arc:

> From heaven, they fabled, thrown by angry Jove
> *Sheer o'er the crystal battlements:*

then inexorably he turns straight downward with the fascination of slow motion:

> from morn
> To noon he fell, from noon to dewy eve,
> A summer's day;

[7] M. M. Mahood, *Poetry and Humanism*, 201. This is a refreshing change from regarding Milton as predominantly aural; but we have already seen how misleading it is to concentrate on any single sense with Milton.

[8] Milton's great fondness for Latinisms, far from being pedantry, is largely explained by their active literal meanings. *Insult*, for example, is literally *to leap on* or *at; tempt* is *to handle, touch.* D. C. Allen (*The Harmonious Vision* [Baltimore, 1954], 107) remarks: "It is not only Satan who is made visible by motion; whole scenes are made flesh *by this forceful use of verbs.*"

but he gathers speed, just as the sun, so long sinking in the west, draws
close to the horizon and suddenly drops below:

> and with the setting sun
> *Dropped from the zenith like a falling star*
> On Lemnos the Aegaean isle . . .
>
> P.L., I, 741-46

The whole violence of Satan's more terrible fall is in the phrase *hurled
headlong,* requiring for its utterance violent expulsion of breath; then
comes the turn in air: *flaming from the ethereal sky,* the quickening
rhythm; *with hideous ruin and combustion down.* The sense of falling is
conveyed by our *making,* not just hearing, the sounds and rhythms.

Cited often for metrical daring are three lines which are more justly
famous for their varying quality of effort and motion. The fiend, eager
as a thief escaping with the loot,

> O'er bog or steep, through strait, rough, dense, or rare,
> With head, hands, wings or feet pursues his way,
> And swims or sinks, or wades, or creeps, or flies . . .
>
> P.L., II, 948-50

At the other extreme is the magical ease with which Pandemonium, that
fabulously huge edifice, *rose like an exhalation.*

The sun rarely *shines* in Milton. He *impresses his beams* or *smites* or
gently penetrates. And earth may be the stationary center of this wheeling
universe, but it is fermenting with its own life and motion. Streams by a
kind of osmosis

> through veins
> Of porous earth with kindly thirst updrawn
>
> P.L., IV, 227-28

spring into fountains. Satan recoils from Abdiel's stroke,

> as if on earth
> Winds under ground or waters forcing way
> Sidelong, had pushed a mountain from his seat
> Half-sunk with all his pines.
>
> P.L., VI, 195-98

The terrain of Hell is such

> as when the force
> Of subterranean wind transports a hill
> Torn from Pelorus, or the shattered side
> Of thundering Etna, whose combustible
> And fueled entrails thence conceiving fire,
> Sublimed with mineral fury, aid the winds . . .
>
> P.L., I, 230 ff.

To convey terrific energy Milton taps all the natural and cosmic sources he can think of—volcano, earthquake, comet, planetary collision, explosion. Satan when discovered by Ithuriel does not merely change from disguise back to his proper likeness; he *explodes* from toad to angel:

> As when a spark
> Lights on a heap of nitrous powder, laid
> Fit for the tun some magazine to store
> Against a rumored war, the smutty grain
> With sudden blaze diffused, inflames the air:
> So started up in his own shape the fiend.
>
> *P.L.*, IV, 814-19

Menaced by Death, Satan kindles like a comet; the threatened encounter between the two is that of thunderheads. Angels in the Battle of Heaven in their cataclysmic impact are colliding planets.

Motion Milton identifies with life itself. Some of his creatures cannot wait to be fully born before displaying energy. The waters flow together and at once the dolphins play, Leviathan "draws in and at his trunk spouts out the sea." Trees rise *dancing* like the Pleiades.

> The grassy clods now calved, now half appeared
> The tawny lion, *pawing to get free*
> *His hinder parts, then springs as broke from bonds,*
> And rampant shakes his brindled mane; the ounce,
> The libbard, and the tiger, as the mole
> *Rising, the crumbled earth above them threw*
> In hillocks . . . *scarce from his mold*
> Behemoth biggest born of earth *upheaved*
> His vastness . . .
>
> *P.L.*, VII, 463 ff.

Adam has hardly opened his eyes when "raised by quick instinctive motion" he springs erect.

"The grassy clods now *calved*" is significant. Geography, astronomy, meteorology, geometry, dynamics—all these serve merely to describe not explain this vital energy. These purely masculine abstractions—even the superb Golden Compasses drawing the circle of perfection—have done all they can to conceive and project the mystery. Adam remains inert in all his symmetry till God breathes in his nostrils the breath of life. He is ineffectual till God gives him "female for race." Milton has already admitted through the back door at the very beginning the animating principle which Raphael admits only obliquely:

> and other suns perhaps
> With their attendant moons thou wilt descry
> Communicating male and female light,
> *Which two great sexes animate the world.*
>
> *P.L.*, VIII, 148-51

IV

This pregnant admission of Raphael's comes at the end of his account of the Six Days of Creation. Only in connection with the moon, with her mysterious power over tides and women, is light ever female in Milton. Elsewhere it is always male, as his larger symbolism in which God is Light, requires. On the First Day comes the authoritative Word, "Let there be light," and, already in existence, the "co-eternal beam" springs from the deep to be the generating principle of all life.

"Female light" [9] reveals a difficulty Milton has in elaborating the simple thread of the Genesis story which he so punctiliously follows. He has somehow to introduce a female element into a purely masculine cosmic scheme. He discards with a few glancing allusions the cabalistic sephiroth, with which he was familiar, probably for essential simplicity and with the conviction that it is no concern of his to explain more than is explained in Genesis.

Raphael's various speculations with Adam in the Eighth Book admit without resolving these difficulties. However the female element got into the Universe before the creation of Eve, from the start two great sexes animate the world. In the universe within Adam's ken the sun is the source of light and the fertilizing agent. Raphael in his additional revelations stresses an obvious fundamental fact: without the "deep" or the earth the sun is sterile:

> Whose virtue on itself works no effect,
> But in the fruitful earth; there first received
> His beams, unactive else, their vigor find.
>
> *P.L.,* VIII, 95-97

When we come to Satan we shall discover how this sterility can manifest itself in naked aggression. But before Satan's advent in Adam's universe all light shares this fertilizing function—even the faint stars to the extent of fomenting, nourishing, warming, shedding down

> Their stellar virtue on all kinds that grow
> On earth, made hereby *apter to receive*
> *Perfection from the sun's more potent ray.*
>
> *P.L.,* IV, 671-73

We have already seen how the rising sun shoots down his rays to "warm earth's inmost womb" (*P.L.,* V, 300 ff), and to each inward part of the whole universe

[9] Of course, that the female moon's paler light is mere reflection of the sun's fits neatly Milton's belief in subordination of woman to man—"He for God only, she for God in him." But this secondary symbolism conflicts with and confuses the primary. . . .

> With gentle penetration, though unseen,
> Shoots invisible virtue even to the deep.
>
> *P.L.*, III, 585-86

These key passages are as much uterine as phallic.

The boldness and candor of this physiological comment and imagery show the untroubled, unembarrassed acceptance of sex without which Milton could convey neither his imaginatively convincing picture of innocence between man and woman nor vitality in Creation. So full-blooded a poet as Milton, so passionate a vitalist, could not help pouring enormous sexual energy into *Paradise Lost,* both consciously and unconsciously. This does not in the slightest impair his deep reverence. His view of sex is one with his view of God, all facets of whose creation he finds good. While leaving unmistakable the physical relation between Adam and Eve, he relegates this sexual imagery to the surrounding universe to vigorously express God's generative abundance.

If Milton cannot rival Dante's sense of mystic union in God's love, he portrays better than Dante God's joy in abundance. Never before or since was such plenitude as when at the moment of Creation God says to Christ:

> Boundless the deep, because *I am who fill*
> *Infinitude,* nor vacuous the space.
>
> *P.L.*, VII, 168-69

And it is this plenitude boldly expressed which vitalizes what would otherwise be only a geometrically-perfect deistic machine whirling through its mechanical rounds. Toward the end Michael still once more reminds Adam that God's

> omnipresence fills
> Land, sea, and air, and every kind that lives,
> *Fomented by his virtual power and warmed.*
>
> *P.L.*, XI, 336-38

Milton has fused them so skilfully that we do not at first realize he is using two distinct methods in dramatizing Creation, two different sets of images and symbols: abstract and concrete, spirit and matter, mind and body, the spontaneous existence as if by magic with the spoken word and natural biological evolution through time. Both methods are in the opening paragraph of the poem, where, as if by a power inherent in the words as they are voiced

> heavens and earth
> Rose out of chaos;

whereas a moment later we find that the heavenly spirit for an indeterminate period

> Dove-like satest brooding on the vast abyss
> And madest it pregnant.

Thus Milton, long before Raphael stresses them, tacitly accepts the "two great sexes" animating the world. By passing constantly from one method and one set of symbols to the other he manages to infuse this brooding warmth into his abstractions, so that when we come to the Golden Compasses drawing swift arcs over Chaos the image seems more biological than geometric. Without Milton's committing himself metaphysically, matter is to all intents and purposes the feminine aspect of God. In his immensely effective and yet simple account of the Six Days, this earthly universe is born of the brooding spirit from the "womb of unoriginal night and chaos wild":[10]

> Darkness profound
> Covered the abyss: but on the watery calm
> His brooding wings the spirit of God outspread,
> And vital virtue infused, and vital warmth
> Throughout the fluid mass . . .
>
> *P.L.*, VII, 233 ff.

Then with no confusion Milton shifts to the other method. Light is summoned forth, divided into day and night, parceled out to sun, moon, stars by a divine magic which even in the poem (as in Michelangelo's greatest panel—creation of sun and moon) makes it seem to come into being as its name is uttered.

But earth does not rise like an exhalation. However miraculous, the creation of earth combines the two methods, beginning with biological, time-consuming birth:

> The earth was formed, but in the womb as yet
> Of waters, embryon immature involved,
> Appeared not: over all the face of earth
> Main ocean flowed, not idle, but with warm
> Prolific humor softening all her globe,
> Fermented the great mother to conceive,
> Satiate with genial moisture,

then the wizard voice:

> when God said
> "Be gathered now ye waters under heaven
> Into one place, and let dry land appear."
> Immediately the mountains huge appear
> Emergent, and their broad bare backs upheave
> Into the clouds . . .
>
> *P.L.*, VII, 276 ff.

And so in this extraordinary combination of magician's wand and homely birth the Six Days pass, with their evening rests and musical

[10] This phrase I have transposed from a quite different context (*P.L.*, X, 476-77) where it is threatening—a seeming contradiction which I shall consider later.

intervals initiating the music of the spheres, until the great angelic hymn on the Seventh:

> "Open, ye everlasting gates," they sung,
> "Open, ye heavens, your living doors; let in
> The great Creator from his work returned
> Magnificent, his six days' work, a world . . .
>
> *P.L.*, VII, 565 ff.

The Seventh is the day of rest, "but not in silence holy kept." Characteristically Miltonic and unpuritanically Puritan is the celestial Sabbath, with its blazing gold, heavenly music of instruments and voice, clouds of incense fuming from golden censers—all to delight eye, ear, nose. This *Gloria* of the angelic choir echoes at its close the command of plenitude which God has laid in turn on sea, on land, on humankind:

> And multiply a race of worshipers
> Holy and just: thrice happy if they know
> Their happiness.
>
> *P.L.*, VII, 630-32

Against this emergent cosmos of unspeakable grandeur Milton must place without too much disparity the human couple. This disproportion is the most serious problem in the entire epic; but at the opening of the Eighth Book the shift in scale is easy, partly because Milton focuses the attention of the angelic choir on man's entrance and also returns to Raphael, the narrator whom we have completely forgotten during his narrative; mainly because this is the familiar transition in the second chapter of Genesis, which Milton follows almost word for word, with some help from Job and the Psalms (and of course the hexaemeral tradition). After the symphonic grandeur of the Seventh Book, Adam's own story is like a solo on a reed instrument; nonetheless, it is simply another variation on the same theme of creation and plenitude.

Quickening personal interest compensates for abrupt shift in scale, for this is our own ancestral experience. Significantly, Adam's recollection is nothing more than the original awakening of the senses: first *touch,* as he becomes aware of the soft flowery grass on which he lies and the feel of the warm sun evaporating his "balmy sweat"; then *sight,* as his gaze is at once drawn *upward* to the ample heaven; then *motion,* as instinctively he springs erect; then *sound* and *smell* (the senses soon begin their normal coalescence), as he hears birdsong and discovers that "all things smiled with fragrance." *Taste* comes last, in his dream, when prophetically the fruit

> that hung to the eye
> Tempting, stirred in me sudden appetite
> To pluck and eat.
>
> *P.L.*, VIII, 307-309

Yet his first oral manifestation, typically, is not eating but speech. After scrutinizing himself limb by limb, Adam recognizes instinctively the life force, *light* of the sun and *enlightened* earth, almost as if he had heard the last words of the angelic choir singing: "Thrice happy if they know their happiness:"

> Tell me, how may I know him, how adore,
> From whom I have that thus I move and live,
> And feel that I am happier than I know.
>
> *P.L.*, VIII, 280-82

In Genesis, after commanding Adam not to eat of the tree of knowledge, God remarks at once: *It is not good that man should be alone; I will make him an help meet for him.* From this text Milton departs slightly. His Adam, after naming the beasts of the field and seeing their inferiority, before God has time to divulge further plans, recognizes his own loneliness and incompleteness. Further, Adam boldly ventures even to dispute with God on the questions of equality and Unity in Trinity. Having lost the seventeenth century passion for disputation, we find God's pleasure in Adam's sudden suspiciously-Arian argumentative skill faintly humorous, like a father with a precocious child. But Milton departs from Genesis deliberately to stress an essential point of his creed: God creates man with independent God-like reason which awakens as naturally as his senses and at the same time. Rousseau's Instinctive Innocent has blurred for us Milton's (Augustinian) Intellectual Innocent.

Adam takes Eve with thanksgiving but in the spirit of an Old Testament patriarch, almost as a vassal. If this now discredited seventeenth-century view of woman alienates modern readers, it makes all the more poignant Adam's eloquent tribute to Eve, his "mysterious reverence" for the "genial bed." [11] Immediately the verse takes on the lyrical quality of epithalamion and a Tennysonian lilt:

> To the nuptial bower
> I led her blushing like the morn: all heaven,
> And happy constellations on that hour
> Shed their selectest influence; the earth
> Gave signs of gratulation, and each hill;
> *Joyous the birds; fresh gales and gentle airs*
> *Whispered it to the woods, and from their wings*
> *Flung rose, flung odors from the spicy shrub,*
> Disporting, till the amorous bird of night
> Sung spousal, and bid haste the evening star
> On his hilltop to light the bridal lamp.
>
> *P.L.*, VIII, 510-20

"Transported touch" indeed sweeps Adam from Reason's mooring. He reminds himself of woman's inferiority of mind and spirit, her slighter

---

[11] As usual, Milton intends not only the secondary meaning, *festive*, but the primary meaning of *genial—pertaining to generation.*

resemblance to the Divine Image (being a copy of a copy), yet wonders if perhaps God in creating her did not take more than a rib from his side:

> yet when I approach
> Her loveliness, so absolute she *seems*
> And in herself complete, so well to know
> Her own, that what she wills to do or say,
> *Seems* wisest, virtuousest, discreetest, best;
> All higher knowledge in her presence falls
> Degraded, wisdom in discourse with her
> Loses discountenanced, and like folly shows:
> *Authority and reason on her wait,*
> *As one intended first, not after made*
> *Occasionally;* and to consummate all,
> Greatness of mind and nobleness their seat
> Build in her loveliest, and create an awe
> About her, as a guard angelic placed.

P.L., VIII, 546-59

Woman has seldom received higher praise, even when we discount Milton's intent to foreshadow, so soon after Eve's creation, the passion which will shortly cause Adam's downfall, and after him Samson's. She *seems* complete in herself; he *knows* she is complete only in him. Raphael with a frown reproves this excess, this abdication of the male, warning Adam: "Be not diffident." Surprisingly, diffidence lies behind much of Milton's aggressive masculinity.

And they were both naked, the man and his wife, and were not ashamed. This verse in Genesis Milton develops with exultation and contempt for "these troublesome disguises which we wear." Having already surrounded with rich imagery of generation the universe which Adam and Eve inhabit, he has only to gather them silently into the rhythm of plenitude, so that they seem, till eating the forbidden fruit, never self-conscious, each aware only of the other and of sharing in a general process of nature. Except, as we have just noticed, Adam is already beginning to worry over his passionate transport; and Eve we soon find restless for more privacy. It is not long till both are ripe for Satan.

For the most part Milton serenely accepts the beauty of this naked love, but once or twice his tone, not Adam's and Eve's behavior, is aggressive:

> Straight side by side were laid, nor turned I ween
> Adam from his fair spouse, nor Eve the rites
> Mysterious of connubial love refused:
> Whatever hypocrites austerely talk
> Of purity and place and innocence,
> Defaming as impure what God declares
> Pure, and commands to some, leaves free to all.

Our maker bids increase, who bids abstain
But our destroyer, foe to God and man?

P.L., IV, 741-49

The ancient doctrine of plenitude, which Chaucer, Shakespeare, Spenser accept as a matter of course, Milton has to defend against a new conspiracy of silence. With none of the hesitation of St. Paul, Raphael on entering Eden greets Eve:

Hail mother of mankind, whose fruitful womb
Shall fill the world more numerous with thy sons
Than with these various fruits the trees of God
Have heaped this table.

P.L., V, 388-91

The unself-conscious purity of these marital relations in Paradise, difficult to render at best, sometimes a little bruised by Milton's belligerence, is perhaps most apparent in casual moments like Adam's awakening to feast his eyes on Eve in a fashion so different from Satan's voyeurism:

he on his side
Leaning half raised, with looks of cordial love
Hung over her enamored, and beheld
Beauty, which whether waking or asleep,
Shot forth peculiar graces . . .

P.L., V, 11-15

But Eve herself had not slept well, her hair is disarranged, her face is flushed. Satan has already got to her in a dream. Knowing the insuperable problem of portraying purity that is sensuous and full-blooded, Milton wisely cuts short the state of absolute innocence before Satan enters and by his presence in the Garden at once touches it with incipient decay.

All things considered, Milton succeeds remarkably in giving an illusion of innocence, of the unknowable. When we question some of Adam's knowledgeable conversations with Eve before he has been instructed by Raphael, we must remember that Milton not only has to transpose into our vocabulary what presumably they said, but also that not till a later generation was the human mind considered a *tabula rasa* at birth. Original Sin in ourselves explains why our Great Parents do not come fully alive for us until they are tempted and fall.

Adam, our true father, cannot bear to let Raphael go without satisfying one final curiosity. How do the angels express their love:

by looks only, or do they mix
Irradiance, virtual or immediate touch?

Raphael smiles a "celestial rosy red, love's proper hue" and answers Adam as he and Eve might answer us:

> Let it suffice thee that thou knowest
> Us happy, and without love no happiness.
> Whatever pure thou in the body enjoyest
> (And pure thou wert created) we enjoy
> In eminence, and obstacle find none
> Of membrane, joint, or limb, exclusive bars . . .

P.L., VIII, 616 ff.

V

Such bliss was Archangel Satan's till his rebellious mind gave birth full-grown to Sin, whom he first despised, then loved too well:

> and such joy thou tookest
> With me in secret, that my womb conceived
> A growing burden.

P.L., II, 765-67

This time birth, as recounted by Sin, is hideous travesty of plenitude:

> my womb
> Pregnant by thee, and now excessive grown
> Prodigious motion felt and rueful throes.
> At last this odious offspring whom thou seest
> Thine own begotten, breaking violent way
> Tore through my entrails, that with fear and pain
> Distorted, all my nether shape thus grew
> Transformed: but he my inbred enemy
> Forth issued, brandishing his fatal dart
> Made to destroy: I fled and cried out "Death;"
> Hell trembled at the hideous name, and sighed
> From all her caves, and back resounded "Death."
> I fled, but he pursued (though more, it seems,
> Inflamed with lust than rage) and swifter far,
> Me overtook his mother all dismayed,
> And in embraces forcible and foul
> Engendering with me, of that rape begot
> These yelling monsters that with ceaseless cry
> Surround me, as thou sawest, hourly conceived
> And hourly born, with sorrow infinite
> To me, for when they list into the womb
> That bred them they return, and howl and gnaw
> My bowels, their repast . . .

P.L., II, 778 ff.

Nothing in the whole poem stuns us more with the impact of the fall than this monstrous transformation of love into double incest, rape, cannibalism, fearful deformity. And as Satan goes about the universe, tarnished but still magnificent, he carries with him this horrible secret of his own progeny in Hell, nor can we exorcize them from memory. Generation degenerates. . . .

Satan plots against God and at the very instant of plotting begins to corrupt all he touches. Love at once becomes lust. Serene, untroubled generation yields to sexual guilt and fear, as if Satan's own sin were a decomposing body dropped into a pool, spreading ever wider circles of scum over the clear waters of Creation. Foreseeing this, God simultaneously with Satan's defection creates a world in Hell opposite to that of Eden, which eventually it contaminates:

> A universe of death, which God by curse
> Created evil, for evil only good,
> Where all life dies, death lives, and nature breeds,
> Perverse, all monstrous, all prodigious things,
> Abominable, inutterable, and worse
> Than fables yet have feigned, or fear conceived,
> Gorgons and hydras, and chimeras dire.
>
> > *P.L.*, II, 622-28

Here is the sum of mankind's nightmares. In this region of polymorphous perverse, so terrible that Milton only hints it, sex becomes unclean, terrifying, threatening yet compulsive. Here at the nether end of the Universe whose very soul is order and shapeliness we meet "on either side a formidable shape." Male and female—so beautiful in their harmonious interaction in Empyrean Heaven, in sun and earth, in Adam and Eve—are transformed to the ultimate horror:

> The one *seemed* woman to the waist, and fair,
> But ended foul in many a scaly fold
> Voluminous and vast, a serpent armed
> With mortal sting: about her middle round
> A cry of hell hounds never ceasing barked
> With wide Cerberean mouths full loud, and rung
> A hideous peal; yet, when they list, would creep,
> If aught disturbed their noise, into her womb,
> And kennel there . . . Far less abhorred than these
> Vexed Scylla bathing in the sea . . .
> Nor uglier follow the night-hag, when called
> In secret, riding through the air she comes
> Lured with the smell of infant blood . . .

And together with her

> The other shape,
> *If shape it might be called that shape had none*
> Distinguishable in member, joint, or limb.
> . . . black it stood as night,
> Fierce as ten furies, terrible as hell,
> And shook a dreadful dart; what seemed his head
> The likeness of a kingly crown had on.
>
> > *P.L.*, II, 650 ff.

Furthermore, to heap horror on horror's head Milton takes advantage of the patristic notion that the Fallen Angels afterwards become heathen gods; he pours on them all the ancient prophets' distilled hatred of the idolatrous and lewd practices which again and again seduced the Children of Israel from God—the "lustful orgies" enlarged under Solomon even to "that hill of scandal." In particular two among Satan's followers are symbols of spiritual rather than physical disgust, projections of Satan's depravity without relief of any virtue:

> Belial the dissolutest spirit that fell,
> The sensualest, and after Asmodai
> The fleshliest incubus . . .

> *P.R.*, II, 150-52

Asmodeus' unbridled lust for Sarah causes him to murder in turn seven husbands before he is driven off. Unlike Satan, Belial loves vice for itself: "a spirit more lewd fell not from heaven"; one whose altar is in no special place but wherever lust and violence reign in the hearts of men:

> And when night
> Darkens the streets, then wander forth the sons
> Of Belial, flown with insolence and wine.
> Witness the streets of Sodom, and that night
> In Gibeah, when the hospitable door
> Exposed a matron to avoid worse rape.

> *P.L.*, I, 500-505

To rape, incest, abortive deformity are added the special vices of Sodom and Gomorrah. But Sodom and Gomorrah, so prominent in Proust's portrait of social decay, which Joyce in turn transforms into the tragicomedy of infant chatter about those "bad pities of the plain" (*F.W.*, 564), are in Milton's nightmare only incidental to the monstrous distortions of normal sex in the classic human crime—incest, doubled in Satan and Sin, Sin and Death.

All this imagery of fear and horror follows everywhere close on the heels of Satan, who cannot obliterate what he has called into being in the Universe. Like Macbeth, he is "in blood stepped in so far" that to return would be as difficult as to go on. Throttling his fears and doubts, he accomplishes his mission, as he is careful to boast on his return to Hell:

> Long were to tell
> What I have done, what suffered, with what pain
> Voyaged the unreal, vast, unbounded deep
> Of horrible confusion . . . but I
> Toiled out my uncouth passage, forced to ride
> The untractable abyss, plunged in the womb
> Of unoriginal night and chaos wild . . .

> *P.L.*, X, 469 ff.

But in the great Generative Process Satan is more than a link in the chain leading to Death and all this world of formless horrors. He is part of the force coming into being when God changes from static to dynamic. At first glance he seems even to initiate the creation of man, since by depleting the angelic hosts he causes God to create the new race and new world. Yet movement actually starts when God decides to become manifest in the Trinity. In his account Milton *assumes* this initial phase of creation, thus avoiding many theological commitments, and begins with the elevation of pre-existent Christ, which crystallizes Satan's dissatisfaction into open action and precipitates creation, fall, and redemption of mankind.[12]

Once started—partly because it has to be transposed into human terms to be comprehensible—the drama seems to vibrate between a polarity of good and evil, to be a cosmic contest in which God finally through Christ checkmates Satan, the Adversary. Yet whatever else he is, Milton is no Manichean dualist. Everything, including Satan, is one with God. On the First Day, before summoning Light into action, the spirit of God infuses warm virtue into the fluid mass:

> but downward purged
> The black tartareous cold infernal dregs
> Adverse to life . . .
>
> P.L., VII, 237-39

These "infernal dregs adverse to life" are not obliterated but merely pushed down into Hell and dark pockets in the Universe of Light. With them, though born himself of light, Satan has affinity. With his penetration into Eden, they rise again to our world. He wins over Eve, then Adam, because he already has an ally within the gates, for they too have an affinity with the dregs adverse to life. In making Creation a continuous process—not just placing man in static innocence—Milton must recognize and justify these disparate elements.

While dramatizing an essential process in human development and relation to God, Satan also in a deeply reverent poem drains off harmlessly these natural antithetic and anti-social drives: self-love, pride, envy, hatred, frustration, unbridled desire, all lusts of the ego, together with their nightmare fear and guilt. Through him, after doing his best with God's reasoning on unfathomable mysteries, Milton, without fear of being struck by divine wrath, can speak back all the doubts, the violent objections to things as they are. With Milton we go through the ritual-release of damning ourselves in Satan, yet admiring what we damn, since he is essential to the only cycle of being we know—life-death-life—to which even God, become Man in Christ, submits.

We have seen how effectively in concrete imagery Milton brings home to us the consequences of Satan's fall, disrupting but not destroying God's

---

[12] No other epic can equal the beautifully articulated simplicity of Milton's double plot, in which the fall of man not only parallels the fall of Satan but is caused by it, and is redeemed by Christ, the cause of Satan's fall.

plenitude. What of his first revolt, which Milton makes the biological as well as spiritual conception of Sin? Essentially it is of course rebellion against authority brought to a head by God's elevating Christ to the Trinity. Before that, Satan's attitude toward God seems to have been ambivalent yet restrained.

In essence what is this but a law of life, the eternal need of the son to supplant the father, to deny authority? Gabriel strips bare Satan's heroic pretensions:

> And thou sly hypocrite, who now wouldst seem
> Patron of liberty, who more than thou
> Once fawned, and cringed, and servilely adored
> Heaven's awful monarch? wherefore but in hope
> To dispossess him, and thyself to reign?
>
> *P.L.,* IV, 957-61

Later Abdiel warns him, trying to avert inevitable disaster:

> *As by his word the mighty father made*
> *All things, even thee . . .*
> . . . Cease then this impious rage,
> And tempt not these: but hasten to appease
> The incensed father, and the incensed Son
> While pardon may be found in time besought . . .
>
> *P.L.,* V, 836 ff.

But by now Satan's reckless, no-longer-restrained ego insanely denies the Father, as we in solipsism deny, yet at the same time affirm, Creation each time we sin in thought or deed:

> who saw
> When this creation was? rememberest thou
> Thy making, while the maker gave thee being?
> We know no time when we were not as now;
> Know none before us, *self-begot, self-raised*
> *By our own quickening power* . . .
>
> *P.L.,* V, 856-61

With this denial promptly the precarious ambivalence, love-hate, is split. Hate is loosed upon the world. Envious of God's authority, jealous of Christ and later of Adam, the new favorite, henceforth Satan is given over to fraud and malice, determined to destroy man at whatever cost to himself. Worst of all, in suicidal rage and despair Satan curses the sun, the light, symbol supreme of love and life:

> O thou that with surpassing glory crowned,
> Lookest from thy sole dominion like the god
> Of this new world: at whose sight all the stars
> Hide their diminished heads; to thee I call,

> But with no friendly voice, and add thy name
> O sun, to tell thee how *I hate thy beams* . . .
>
> *P.L.,* IV, 32 ff.

That this whole speech is cast in the form of self-searching dramatic soliloquy was early noted by Phillips; these first-composed lines epitomize Satan in what was to become the central symbolism of the poem as light-murderer. Satan's theme is announced a dozen lines earlier: "Now conscience wakes despair." Furthermore, the speech is filled with echoes of that earlier drama of damnation, Marlowe's *Doctor Faustus,* and brings into the open what the imagery has already conveyed:

> for within him hell
> He brings, and round about him, nor from hell
> One step no more than from himself can fly . . .
>
> *P.L.,* IV, 20-22

Satan, who has many functions in the poem—personification, scapegoat, lightning rod, champion—is here completely humanized in the most awesome of tragedies: a man facing damnation of his soul. It is impossible not to feel for him as we feel for Faustus and for Saul, from whom God likewise turns away His face and His mercy.

Heretofore, though Milton has already made clear a planned deterioration, Satan has been a magnificent hero-villain, brilliantly endowed in mind and heart and body, more human in his super-humanity than Milton dares to make God.[13] For when in the poem does God feel the compassion which makes Satan at one point speechless?

> Thrice he essayed, and thrice in spite of scorn,
> Tears such as angels weep, burst forth . . .
>
> *P.L.,* I, 619-20

At creation Satan, like Adam after him, is endowed with the reason which enables him to dispute with God Himself. Just as he is granted sympathy, he is allowed to argue with a freedom which Milton finds impossible to grant his conception of God as Abstract Reason. No wonder Blake is misled into his brilliant but partial intuition of the poem. Into Satan Milton pours all the power of his own passionate way of thinking; for God he reserves a purely theoretical process to arrive at the Absolute, and so the rational justification is foredoomed. Even the philosophical powers of Aquinas would not have enabled Milton to make completely logical what is supralogical, a matter for faith only; nor did

---

[13] To the extent that Satan is a dramatic characterization (which he is not consistently), Milton shows the influence of Marlowe, Shakespeare, and Jacobean drama. On a few occasions, as during the Battle in Heaven, Milton endows Satan with a somewhat debatable sense of humor. But the attempt of Charles Williams and C. S. Lewis to turn him into a figure of farce is the fault more of their own boredom and lack of sympathy with Milton than Milton's lapse. Lewis, too, argues usually from a strongly held personal theology.

the three hundred bishops at Nicaea have much better fortune. Milton himself recognizes this clearly in what amounts to an ironic comment on his own foolhardiness, when he says that the Fallen Angels in Hell

> reasoned high
> Of providence, foreknowledge, will and fate,
> Fixed fate, free will, foreknowledge absolute,
> *And found no end, in wandering mazes lost.*
>
> *P.L.*, II, 558-61

Dante wisely avoids this problem by never letting God personally intrude into his poem. But Milton, unaware of his own mixed feelings toward reason, like Satan tries to usurp God's place, to reason for God. What Blake overlooks, however, is that this failure on the rational level neither completely invalidates nor exhausts Milton's characterization of the Deity, whose creativeness remains unimpaired. Milton is not so wise nor so honest in questioning and answering as that old Hebrew poet who wrote Job, but in the end he too finds sufficient answer in the magnitude and wonder of Creation.

If like Blake we allow ourselves to get caught in the maze of Milton's theological shortcomings and misguided ambition, we fail to appreciate another level on which the poem beautifully succeeds. For if the bold introduction of God is disastrous to Milton's justification by limited logic, it is essential to his marvelous portrayal of Creation, which, if any justification is needed, is enough.

Even the justifications and explanations which, when placed in God's mouth, inevitably put Him on the defensive and make Him open to fallacy, carry more conviction when Satan, as a character in a drama, utters them in his supreme moment of self-recognition:

> Ah wherefore! he deserved no such return
> From me, whom he created what I was
> In that bright eminence, and with his good
> Upbraided none; nor was his service hard.
> What could be less than to afford him praise,
> The easiest recompense, and pay him thanks,
> How due! yet all his good proved ill in me,
> And wrought but malice; lifted up so high
> I 'sdained subjection, and thought one step higher
> Would set me highest, and in a moment quit
> The debt immense of endless gratitude,
> So burdensome still paying, still to owe . . .
>
> *P.L.*, IV, 42 ff.

The why, the wherefore, is purely rhetorical. Here is the heart of human frailty, that restless boredom of the ego which, while recognizing clearly the need to love, lacks the power to lose itself in love.

Believing passionately in the oneness of mind and body, Milton yet at the crucial point divorces too fatally passion and reason, granting all passion and much reason to Satan, while in those barren moments of needless self-justification stripping God of any warmth at all. Except always the warmth of Creation. Nothing shows more strikingly Milton's incapacity for that free and instinctive surrender to love found in Dante and Spenser than his approach to Christ, some aspects of whom he seems unconsciously, like Satan, to resent in his intolerance of any mediation between himself and God. Yet Christ is the key; Him, like Satan, we murder symbolically with our sin in the crucifixion, letting the dregs adverse to life blot out the light till the resurrection purges them downward again.

Milton's faltering reluctance toward Christ, however, is least apparent in *Paradise Lost,* where He appears as the Word, the Creator; for Milton's joy in creation is unalloyed. Though the last two books of the poem flag in inspiration, the triumph of God's plenitude is clear, and Milton's distrust of Romanism in abeyance, when Adam, echoing Raphael's beautiful first greeting to Eve, sings his Ave Maria:

> Virgin mother, hail,
> High in the love of heaven, yet from my loins
> Thou shalt proceed, and from thy womb the Son
> Of God most high . . .
>
> *P.L.,* XII, 379 ff.

The ambivalence of love-hate, life-death at the core of human life and the heart of Creation, personified in Milton's division between Satan and God, is no longer a question to be logically answered, but a mystery resolved. The faith is more mature (*Paradise Regained* seems to show it also less secure) but essentially the same as the Elder Brother's:

> But evil on itself shall back recoil,
> And mix no more with goodness, when at last
> Gathered like scum, and settled to itself
> It shall be in eternal restless change
> Self-fed, and self-consumed . . .
>
> *Comus,* 592 ff.

Unloosed hate is not merely yoked uneasily again with love but completely absorbed. Just as in the beginning by some strange alchemy, evil comes of good, so in the end this supreme manifestation of God's love brings forth good from evil—even, Milton firmly believes, greater good than was at first. Those who overstress the evangelical pessimism of *Paradise Lost* [14] should ponder:

> O goodness infinite, goodness immense!
> That all this good of evil shall produce,

[14] For example, Sir Herbert J. C. Grierson, *Milton and Wordsworth* [Cambridge, 1937], 97. Out of its seventeenth-century context Milton's austerity often seems merely grim to us.

And evil turn to good; more wonderful
Than that which by creation first brought forth
Light out of darkness! full of doubt I stand,
Whether I should repent me now of sin
By me done and occasioned, or rejoice
Much more, that much more good thereof shall spring,
To God more glory, more good will to men
From God, and *over wrath grace shall abound.*

P.L., XII, 469-78

This from a blind old poet, whose long years of service to the Commonwealth of Saints had come to nought, whose political ideals had collapsed into the most dissolute of monarchies!

Not through reason, as he had planned, but through faith in God's grace, Creation comes full circle, ending as it begins, in Light.

The War in Heaven

by Arnold Stein

If the war in heaven is approached as Milton's fulfillment of his epic obligations, if we regard it as a realistic war to be taken quite literally—then we cannot escape Dr. Johnson's verdict that the "confusion of spirit and matter" fills the whole narrative with "incongruity." How can we believe in the fiction of a raging battle in which immortal spirits uncomplainingly confine themselves in hindering armor and, in between verbal debates, use material weapons that lessen their might? But suppose the material action of the war does not exist for its literal and independent meaning, but is instead part of a complex metaphor? That is the view that this study proposes taking.

We are told before the narrative begins that it will be metaphorical:

> what surmounts the reach
> Of human sense, I shall delineate so,
> By lik'ning spiritual to corporal forms,
> As may express them best.   (V, 571 ff.)

But still, this is preceded by what seems to be an echo of Aeneas' polite prologue to Dido (which would anticipate a direct historical tale), and it is followed by Raphael's enigmatic questioning of the metaphor:

> though what if Earth
> Be but the shaddow of Heav'n, and things therein
> Each to other like, more then on earth is thought?   (V, 574 ff.)

Presumably, though, the metaphor has not been discredited but further qualified, for when he concludes his account Raphael emphasizes the metaphorical point of view again: "Thus measuring things in Heav'n by things on Earth/At thy request." In between, besides the constant indirect touches more significant to fallen than to unfallen man, there have been some deliberate gestures toward the understanding of the immediate audience—some of them charming in their thoughtfulness (like grandfather translating remote events into the terms of grandchild's familiar experi-

"The War in Heaven." From *Answerable Style: Essays on Paradise Lost* by Arnold Stein, Minneapolis, 1953. Copyright © 1953 by the University of Minnesota. Reprinted by permission of the author and University of Minnesota Press. The present selection constitutes the first half of Mr. Stein's chapter by this title.

ence). When God's legions march forth upon the air, it is as when all the birds came summoned "to receive/Thir names of thee." When heaven resounds, all the earth, "had Earth bin then," "had to her Center shook." When Michael and Satan meet, it is as if nature's concord should break and two opposing planets clash. But this, the deliberate framework of metaphor, does not take us far, though it invites us to build on the angel's hint.

From the opening of Book I the war in heaven seems more than a simple, finished event. In the invocation we have the authorized formal side presented: the war was ambitious, impious, proud, vain, and resulting in ruin. Satan's first speech implies that there was another side—even after we have partly discounted the personal tones of the defeated leader who speaks of the good old lost cause, "hazard in the Glorious Enterprize." That too is a formal side, presented by the losing actor in the drama. Then Satan goes on, to reveal, before he can pull himself together in defiance, something more:

> into what Pit thou seest
> From what highth fal'n, so much the stronger provd
> He with his Thunder: and till then who knew
> The force of those dire Arms? (I, 91 ff.)

A little later the surprise has been bolstered with a kind of indignation:

> but still his strength conceal'd,
> Which tempted our attempt, and wrought our fall. (I, 641 f.)

We soon learn that we cannot get answers in hell, but we begin to see certain questions, and the possibility that their answers may appear when we see the dramatic presentation of the rebellion. For one thing, Satan's "innumerable force" receives a definite tally later—it is only one third of the angels. And this fact will look different when we learn that God opposes the enemy force with an equal number only, and then puts a fixed limit on the individual strength of the contestants, and then sends only the Son against the rebels, and with His strength limited too. Satan puts so much store on his having shaken the throne of God, against "His utmost power"—"Who from the terrour of this Arm so late/Doubted his Empire"—that we begin to wait for the actual presentation of the conflict. In his long soliloquy at the beginning of Book IV, though Satan tells us much, he answers none of the questions he has raised in our minds about the war. His silence is no doubt a commentary; so complete a fact requires no mention, once the forensic necessity has been removed, but we cannot know this at the time.

The clash with Gabriel at the end of Book IV provides us with a sudden new viewpoint; it will prove to be a true anticipation of what happens in the battles, even though we cannot know this yet. For the first time, with Satan present, an actor on the scene, we see him entirely from the outside; and the external view is one of complete ridicule. It is Gabriel's

> O loss of one in Heav'n to judge of wise,
> Since *Satan* fell, whom follie overthrew.   (IV, 904 f.)

The dominating spirit of the encounter, on both sides, is that of scornful ridicule. Gabriel's most telling point is directed at Satan's *discipline*. The fight itself never takes place because Satan, in spite of his blind defiance, has been forced by experience to recognize that ultimate *strength* is external. He obeys God's sign, even though he has just been defying, with words, God's chariot once more. Gabriel's final comment brings the three themes together again—strength, ridicule, discipline:

> *Satan,* I know thy strength, and thou knowst mine,
> Neither our own but giv'n; what follie then
> To boast what Arms can doe, since thine no more
> Then Heav'n permits, nor mine.   (IV, 1006 ff.)

Perhaps this sounds like a piece of ceremonial tournament chivalry—at least to our merely human understanding. If so, it may be because the ceremony is made of symbolic gestures that are founded upon truth. It is not ceremony to Gabriel, but direct truth, the truth of innocent inexperience that has not (according to Satan's taunt) tried evil. And Satan has experienced that truth.

Within the larger frame of the angel's narration to Adam there is another major frame that governs our perspective of the rebellion. The dominant mood of the war is like nothing so much as a scherzo, a kind of great scherzo, like some of Beethoven's—with more than human laughter, too elevated, and comprehensive, and reverberating not to be terribly funny. God sets the mood when he comments to the Son on the budding rebellion:

> Neerly it now concernes us to be sure
> Of our Omnipotence, and with what Arms
> We mean to hold what anciently we claim
> Of Deitie or Empire . . .
> Let us advise, and to this hazard draw
> With speed what force is left, and all imploy
> In our defence, lest unawares we lose
> This our high place, our Sanctuarie, our Hill.   (V, 721 ff.)

The Son, as usual, reflects the Father's meaning:

> Mightie Father, thou thy foes
> Justly hast in derision, and secure
> Laugh'st at thir vain designes and tumults vain.   (V, 734 ff.)

Throughout the serious events of the foreground, in the spacious North, the great laugh, omniscient and uncircumscribed, cannot fail to be heard.

Before proceeding to the more central ridicule, and to some of the sig-

nificant reverberations, it is worth noting how much of the war is conducted in terms of external ridicule. In one sense, at least, the conflict is
between God's mockery and Satan's. Anticipations of this begin early.
We have already noted the "till then who knew/The force of those dire
Arms" and the "tempted our attempt." There is the suggestive mockery
(that is meant to do more than perform its immediate practical function)
when Satan rouses his followers from the burning lake:

> or have ye chos'n this place
> After the toyl of Battel to repose
> Your wearied vertue, for the ease you find
> To slumber here, as in the Vales of Heav'n?
> Or in this abject posture have ye sworn
> To adore the Conquerour?   (I, 318 ff.)

We have testimony from the other fallen angels that ridicule was an
important attitude in the conflict. Moloch remembers

> When the fierce Foe hung on our brok'n Rear
> Insulting, and pursu'd.   (II, 78 f.)

(This is not literally accurate, but it has its truth; the "insulting" I take
to have both its familiar and its Latinate meaning. If Moloch is mostly
remembering what happened to him in a small skirmish, when he fled
bellowing (VI, 362), that makes an interesting, and true, synecdoche.) To
the extent that the conflict still exists, ridicule continues to be an active
attitude. Belial's precise verb, in a context where any sort of resounding
phrase might have been expected, touches the situation metaphorically.
God's legions scout far and wide, he says, "Scorning surprize" (II, 134).
And God himself "All these our motions vain, sees and derides" (II, 191).
And Belial, for good measure, introduces his own God-like imitated perspective of irony:

> I laugh, when those who at the Spear are bold
> And vent'rous, if that fail them, shrink and fear
> What yet they know must follow, to endure
> Exile, or ignominy, or bonds, or pain,
> The sentence of thir Conquerour.   (II, 204 ff.)

Still concerning ourselves with external ridicule, let us look at the
scenes in heaven for the beginnings of this attitude we have been exploring. From the start it is not only God who mocks, though God omnis-
ciently sets the mood first. There are, of course, the formal flytings traditional in literary battles, but these do more than provide the usual
variety and relief. They are part of the complex structure of ridicule, the
most external part of which consists in the frequent repetition of words
denoting scorn, scoffing, laughter, deriding, contempt, disdain, vanity,
and folly. The words reflect deeds, for besides the verbal abuse there is
great laughter and counter-laughter in heaven. The laughter is symbolic

action, but there is also real action that produces real laughter by the participants, besides the action that is intended to induce laughter in the reader.

If we think of the main events on their physical level alone (the other levels will make their significant comic additions), we shall see how consistent the line of ridicule is, and how close it approaches at times to what is almost a kind of epic farce. Satan's wound by the sword of Michael renders him physically ridiculous for the first time. His imbruting himself as a cormorant, as lion, as tiger; the more telling view of him, not *as* a toad, but without so much as the dignity of definition, merely the suggestive "Squat like a Toad"; the indirect view of his leaping into Paradise like a wolf or a thief—these views are less ridiculous through physical emphasis than they are through what is involved mentally and morally. (The fact that Satan later complains, as if for the first time, when he has to imbrute himself as a snake, helps bear this out.)

The wounding by Michael is parallel to Satan's first being exposed to complete ridicule by Gabriel, the Satan whom folly overthrew. Gabriel's ridicule is psychological, with physical overtones; Satan wounded is physically ridiculous, with psychological overtones (the difference between hitting any man, and a man proud of his bearing and composure, with a custard pie). The situation is physical, but we know Satan and his proclamation that the mind governs place—*is* place. Any physical discomfiture that he suffers will be most keenly felt in his mind. And though the material wound will heal without apparent scar, because of the vital nature of his "liquid texture," we are left to draw our own conclusions about the mental wound. We remember him "Gnashing for anguish and despite and shame." In physical terms alone this makes no sense, which is of course true of the whole war. But the physical is part of the metaphorical view (the narrator's, to begin with) that always has nonphysical as well as physical meanings. Even when the climax of defeat is reached and the physical metaphor becomes reality, it is a reality that surpasses the physical through the agency of the physical. But that is to look too far ahead.

In one important scene (which we must later return to, on another level) the good angels are also exposed to physical ridicule, "Angel on Arch-Angel rowl'd" by the shot from Satan's cannon. The situation, with all its details, is quite unsparing:

> Foule dissipation follow'd and forc't rout;
> Nor serv'd it to relax thir serried files.
> What should they do? if on they rusht, repulse
> Repeated, and indecent overthrow
> Doubl'd, would render them yet more despis'd,
> And to thir foes a laughter; for in view
> Stood rankt of Seraphim another row
> In posture to dispiode thir second tire

> Of Thunder: back defeated to return
> They worse abhorr'd. *Satan* beheld thir plight,
> And to his Mates thus in derision call'd.   (VI, 598 ff.)

The physical ridicule is capped by verbal derision as Satan and Belial vie with each other at word-play. Then the physical comes back, in what at the moment seems to be the climax of the war, the battle of the landscape.

It is epic comedy, even on its physical level—elevated to the epic by magnificent imaginative power, made comic by controlled excess.

> From thir foundations loosning to and fro
> They pluckt the seated Hills with all thir load,
> Rocks, Waters, Woods, and by the shaggie tops
> Up lifting bore them in thir hands: Amaze,
> Be sure, and terrour seis'd the rebel Host,
> When coming towards them so dread they saw
> The bottom of the Mountains upward turn'd,
> Till on those cursed Engins triple-row
> They saw them whelmd, and all thir confidence
> Under the weight of Mountains buried deep,
> Themselves invaded next, and on thir heads
> Main Promontories flung, which in the Air
> Came shadowing.   (VI, 643 ff.)

Part of the comic effect is in Milton's carefully interrupting the viewpoint at the crucial moment. We have the huge, comprehensive details of the rocks, waters, woods; and then the gigantic niceness of the detail that pictures the mountains, pulled up by the tops, coming bottom side up toward them (apparently in a slow arc, the way a shot is put). In between, we are forced to look away, to separate ourselves from the action, and see it as spectator, not as participator: "Amaze,/Be sure, and terrour . . ." (To introduce the custard pie again—we do not see it coming toward us and at the last moment hit the person behind us; instead, we are on the sideline watching the slow arc of the pie as it travels unerringly toward someone well off to our side; and then our eyes complete the arc before the pie does, so that we can watch the frozen amazement of the person who is the target as he watches the arc nearing completion.)

The scene reaches its height when the rebels reply in kind:

> So Hills amid the Air encountered Hills
> Hurl'd to and fro with jaculation dire,
> That under ground they fought in dismal shade;
> Infernal noise; Warr seem'd a civil Game
> To this uproar.   (VI, 664 ff.)

Surely it is naive to think Milton straining for grandeur in this passage. That is to read this as if it were the sort of humorless exaggeration that

Statius and Lucan can assault the reader with. The cumulative ridicule
will not permit our doing so. Besides, the effect that Milton achieves is
the effect of strain. Things have now been pushed to the utmost, beyond
which all heaven might have "gone to wrack." If we do not regard this as
humorless grandeur, we may suspect "jaculation" of being the kind of
exaggerated word that is calculated to embarrass the exaggeration, after
the manner more familiar in mock-epic. The fighting underground,
which Milton may have picked up from Statius, and improved upon, is
not presented as straight grandeur, but as both grand and grotesque. We
cannot ignore the controlling effect of "infernal," here suddenly introduced to echo Satan's threat of making a hell of heaven, and to anticipate
"Heav'n ruining from Heav'n." It is the approach to chaos, the result of
the violence that heaven cannot brook, the strain to the point of crack-
ing. But this is to move away from the physical level, which is our immediate concern. If we have been following the line of ridicule correctly
so far, we are probably right in suspecting that the excess in this passage
is laughing at an object: it is a materialistic concept of *might*. But to see
what this means we must go on.

In the grand finale of physical ridicule the rebels are again left exposed
to laughter by the interrupted point of view. The chariot of God rides
over the "Shields and Helmes, and helmed heads" of the prostrate pos-
sessors,

> That wish'd the Mountains now might be again
> Thrown on them as a shelter from his ire.   (VI, 842 f.)

The Son checks His strength, not wishing to destroy but only to "root"
them out of heaven. He raises up the overthrown (to heap new ridicule
upon them):

> and as a Heard
> Of Goats or timerous flock together throngd
> Drove them before him Thunder-struck, pursu'd
> With terrors and with furies to the bounds
> And Chrystall wall of Heav'n, which op'ning wide,
> Rowld inward, and a spacious Gap disclos'd
> Into the wastful Deep; the monstrous sight
> Strook them with horror backward, but far worse
> Urg'd them behind; headlong themselves they threw
> Down from the verge of Heav'n, Eternal wrauth
> Burnt after them to the bottomless pit.   (VI, 856 ff.)

Never do they appear so ridiculous, not even as a timorous flock, as when
they are caught isolated between the before and the behind.

The scene itself is magnificent and superhuman as an expression of
wrath and physical force. But the violence that the rebels naively set in
motion returns to deprive them of all superhuman grandeur, and then
of merely human dignity (if man had been then). They descend, as in a

series of explosions, the scale of creation. Though they have enough will
to throw themselves down, as a herd of animals, they have been *rooted*
out. It is "Heav'n ruining from Heav'n"—which seems to suggest the
descent of spirit to matter, and of matter to the unformed matter of
chaos, even to a kind of sub-chaos:

> confounded *Chaos* roard,
> And felt tenfold confusion in thir fall
> Through his wilde Anarchie, so huge a rout
> Incumberd him with ruin.   (VI, 871 ff.)

This is to be understood metaphorically, as the climax of their physical
humiliation. It does not last, any more than their later mass metamorphosis into serpents, with which this is parallel. But it is a punishment, on
the material level, for the material nature of their sin. If they regain
their form in hell, that is because they regain free will (which has been
interrupted by divine wrath). Spirits, we remember, "Cannot but by an-
nihilating die."

The Crisis of *Paradise Lost*

by E. M. W. Tillyard

It was Walter Raleigh who spoke of the crisis of *Paradise Lost* in the tone of greatest assurance. After setting forth the vast range of topics comprised in the poem he went on:

> All these are exhibited in the clearest and most inevitable relation with the main event, so that there is not an incident, hardly a line of the poem, but leads backwards or forwards to those central lines in the Ninth Book:
>
> > So saying, her rash hand in evil hour
> > Forth-reaching to the fruit, she plucked, she eat.
> > Earth felt the wound, and Nature from her seat,
> > Sighing through all her works, gave signs of woe
> > That all was lost.
>
> From this point radiates a plot so immense in scope, that the history of the world from the first preaching of the gospel to the Millennium occupies only some fifty lines of Milton's epilogue.

And Raleigh's assurance has been compelling. When studying *Paradise Lost* for my *Milton* I accepted his statement as axiomatic; and this seems to have been a common experience. . . .

But abstracted plot and actual poetry are different things, and we should not assume that they must each evolve with the same emphasis. And if we read *Paradise Lost* rightly, opening ourselves to the poetry, we shall find that Eve's eating the apple is by no means the one, exclusive, centre of the poem. There are reasons why in actual practice a poet would find it hard to make it so.

In the bare story Eve was sinless till the precise moment when she reached out her rash hand and plucked the fruit.[1] Milton may have intended to substantiate the story. He does indeed say that she was still

[1] With the argument that follows compare Waldock, *Paradise Lost and its Critics* (Cambridge, 1947), 61: 'Adam and Eve must already be fallen (technically) before they can begin to fall.'

sinless when she had so far yielded to the serpent's blandishments as to follow him to the tree whose fruit he had been advertising so skilfully. But intentions could be of no avail against the terms to which Milton submitted himself by offering to present in ample narrative the transition from a state of innocence to a state of sin. Under the terms of the story these two realms must be separated by a definite but dimensionless frontier: there cannot be a no-man's-land between; in the passage, time must not count. Such a lightning-quick change might be effective in a film; as mentioned above, it showed itself to be possible in the simple form of the Miracle Plays; but in a narrative poem it could only be ridiculous, and in his heart Milton knew that well enough.

In Book Four of *Paradise Lost* Milton pictured his state of innocence, and it is one of the most lovely and thrilling pictures in all poetry. But he could not possibly have conducted his account of the Fall with that picture for sole starting-point; the effect would have been sudden and violent and would have carried no conviction. And he makes no such attempt. Instead he resorts to some faking: perfectly legitimate in a poem, yet faking nevertheless. He anticipates the Fall by attributing to Eve and Adam feelings which though nominally felt in the state of innocence are actually not compatible with it.[2] The first stage is Eve's dream at the beginning of Book Five, an episode which, it is recognized, duplicates in its small way the greater temptation in Book Nine. Here Satan insinuates the insidious (and characteristically Cavalier) sentiment of 'suffer thyself to be admired', urging her to walk out in the night so that all heaven's eyes may admire her beauty. She is then made to imagine herself seeking Adam and finding herself suddenly by the 'Tree of interdicted Knowledge'. She sees to her horror an angelic shape eat the fruit, boast of its virtue, and make her eat too, on the plea that she will become a goddess. Having eaten, she seems to fly up to heaven and see the earth beneath her. In her wonder at her flight her dream ends. Adam does his best to comfort Eve, giving her a reassuringly academic account of the way dreams happen and ending with the general principle that *should* clear Eve of all offense:

> Evil into the mind of God or Man
> May come and go, so unapprov'd, and leave
> No spot or blame behind.

This means[3] that into the mind of angel or man evil may enter, and, if it is repudiated, fail to incriminate. In the abstract the doctrine may be

---

[2] Milton does the same with Mammon in i, 680-4. Even in Heaven, while yet unfallen, Mammon was more interested in the gold of Heaven's pavement than in the beatific vision. Such an interest in the heart of one of the principal angels shows him already fallen. But who minds in the reading or blames Milton for faking to the advantage of the poetry?

[3] See Maurice Kelley, *This Great Argument* (Princeton, 1941), 77.

tenable, but it cannot work in concrete literary presentation. No human
being can conceive or represent evil entering a mind quite alien to it.
Dramatically, the mere fact of entrance implies some pre-existing sympathy. And, in actual dramatic truth, Eve, though not approving the
implication of her dream, does by her symptoms imply that it has
touched her, that it is far from alien; for Adam, waking out of the light
sleep of perfect innocence, is surprised

> to find unwak'nd *Eve*
> With Tresses discompos'd, and glowing cheek,
> As through unquiet rest.

And if the dream has disturbed Eve so much, she has really passed from
a state of innocence to one of sin. This is not to blame Milton. He is
confronted with an impossibility; and to achieve dramatic poetry at all
he has to fake. And he has succeeded as well as a man, in the circumstances, can. We do accept, as we read, Milton's specious plea that Adam
and Eve satisfy the conditions of nominal innocence required by the
story; and with another part of our mind we know that Eve is really,
even if only a little way, on the far side of the line that divides innocence from experience.

Eve having made the transition, it was necessary for Adam to do the
same. And he does it at the end of Book Eight when he confides to
Raphael how Eve's beauty is apt to affect his mind in a way that is dangerous to the sovereignty there of the Reason. Not that Adam denies this
sovereignty, but by speaking of his transport of love for Eve as 'commo-
tion strange', he has admitted to feelings alien to the angelic and akin
to Eve's sleeping perturbation. Technically, he is still innocent, but in
our hearts we recognize him as just across the frontier. Nor is he straightforward in his dealings with Raphael. When rebuked by Raphael for
allowing Eve's physical charms to create in him the illusion of her wisdom, he neither answers nor admits the rebuke but merely shifts his
ground and says that it is rather her delightful manners that have this
effect. He then, with something near impudence, counterattacks and asks
if the angels love too.[4] Adam shows great charm and mental dexterity.
The irony was that Eve was to treat him, her superior, exactly as Adam
here treats his superior, Raphael, when they argue about separate or
joint garden-work in the next book. My main point is that both are virtually fallen before the official temptation has begun.

A further advance into the realm of experience is effected by means

---

[4] See the excellent analysis of these speeches by Paul Turner in *English Studies,* 1948,
1-5, where he disagrees with Waldock's contention that it is Raphael who misunder-
stands Adam (A. J. A. Waldock, *op. cit.* 43-4). But Turner underrates Adam's loverlike
fervour as Waldock overrates it. Surely the poetic virtue lies in the ambivalence: Raphael's rebuke was just, Adam's love (in a man virtually fallen) was also good up to a
point. Just so the loves of Paolo and Francesca were noble up to a point. Yet they mer-
ited their infernal punishment.

of the smoke-screen generated by the great prologue to Book Nine. Having there announced that he is changing his notes to tragic, Milton can risk presenting us with an Adam and Eve more human still than the two episodes just mentioned could dictate. Although ignorant as yet of the more violent human passions, Adam and Eve conduct their dispute about separate or joint gardening as evolved human beings such as we know.

The Fall, then, must be extended back in time; it has no plain and sensational beginning; and the actual eating of the apple becomes no more than an emphatic stage in a process already begun, the stage when the darker and stormier passions make their entry into the human heart.

The same is true of what happens after Eve has eaten the apple. The process of falling continues. It takes time for it to work itself utterly out. Indeed it could be maintained that the Fall is not accomplished, does not in deepest verity take place, till Adam's great despairing speech late in Book Ten (line 720), ending:

> O Conscience, into what Abyss of fears
> And horrors hast thou driv'n me; out of which
> I find no way, from deep to deeper plung'd.

By that time indeed Adam's education in the knowledge of good and evil is complete.

Raleigh's point of radiation, then, turns out in the poem itself not to be a point at all but an inseparable item in a substantial area of the whole poem. But once this is granted, it will be found that another theme has been added to, or intertwined with, the theme of the Fall; intertwined so firmly as to be inextricable: the theme of regeneration. Long before the effects of the Fall have made themselves fully felt, the process of regeneration has begun. It begins, although the characters in whom it operates are not conscious of it, when, early in Book Ten, the Son, having pronounced his judgment on the actors in the Fall, pities Adam and Eve and clothes their nakedness. And it reaches obvious fruition when, at the end of the book, Adam and Eve make peace with each other and confess their errors to God.

It comes then to this. Instead of a small spot in Book Nine for a watershed you have to take the whole great area of Books Nine and Ten. That Milton intended these to go together is evident from the way he concludes them: one end is the pendant of the other. Book Nine ends with the unresolved quarrelling of Adam and Eve:

> Thus they in mutual accusation spent
> The fruitless hours, but neither self-condemning,
> And of their vain contest appear'd no end.

Book Ten comes to rest with the contrasted picture of Adam and Eve reconciled in mutual amity and common humility, seeking the pardon of God:

> So spake our Father penitent, nor *Eve*
> Felt less remorse: they forthwith to the place
> Repairing where he judg'd them prostrate fell
> Before him reverent, and both confess'd
> Humbly their faults, and pardon begg'd, with tears
> Watering the ground, and with their sighs the Air
> Frequenting, sent from hearts contrite, in sign
> Of sorrow unfeign'd, and humiliation meek.

The habit, then, of subordinating Book Ten to Book Nine, is mistaken; and if you argue from such an assumption you may do violence to what the poetry should be telling you. And that is the fundamental question: to what does the poetry point? But only a fairly detailed account of the text can answer it. I turn therefore to an account of Books Nine and Ten of *Paradise Lost*, as I have come to read them.

In this account I shall attribute to Milton's treatment of Adam's and Eve's psychology a subtlety not usually allowed. At the same time I acknowledge the force of T. S. Eliot's recent pronouncement on them:

> They are the original *Man* and *Woman*, not types, but prototypes: if they were not set apart from ordinary humanity they would not be Adam and Eve. They have the general characteristics of men and women, such that we can recognize, in the temptation and the fall, the first motions of the faults and virtues, the abjection and nobility, of all their descendants. They have ordinary humanity to the right degree, and yet are not, and should not be, ordinary mortals. Were they more particularized they would be false, and if Milton had been more interested in humanity, he could not have created them.[5]

That is finely said, and it is mainly true. But at least Milton must be allowed to have been greatly interested in the human relation of man and wife. The triumph is that he can be so subtle and perceptive and yet not destroy the pair's essential generality. I turn to Milton's text.

The eighth book of *Paradise Lost* closes the long central episode of Raphael's visit to Paradise. It also shows night falling on the last happy day there; as he says:

> But I can now no more; the parting Sun
> Beyond the Earths green Cape and verdant Isles
> Hesperean sets, my signal to depart.

And his last words to Adam—

> And all temptation to transgress repel—

are a solemn warning that looks forward to the next book.

The great prologue to the ninth book both carries our minds back to the opening of the poem with its theme of disobedience and announces the entrance of the tragic. Milton has now to introduce his actors and

---

[5] *Milton*, British Academy Lecture for 1947, pp. 10-11.

he rightly begins with Satan. It was in Hell that the action began in Book
One; it is right that Satan should begin it in the culminating books. And
it is, for the time being, not the quite degraded Satan, the Satan who
took the form of a toad to spit evil dreams into Eve's ear, but the bad
creature still haunted by his remembrance of the good. His great soliloquy betrays an exquisite aesthetic sense, which now serves only to torture him. He is overcome by the beauty of the earth (line 103).

> Terrestrial Heav'n, danc't round by other Heav'ns
> That shine, yet bear their bright officious Lamps,
> Light above Light, for thee alone, as seems,
> In thee concentring all their precious beams
> Of sacred influence . . .
> With what delight could I have walkt thee round,
> If I could joy in aught, sweet interchange
> Of Hill, and Vallie, Rivers, Woods and Plaines;
> . . . but I in none of these
> Find place or refuge.

And Satan has still refinement enough to hate the degradation of having
to take the shape of a beast:

> O foul descent! that I who erst contended
> With Gods to sit the highest, am now constraind
> Into a Beast, and mixt with bestial slime,
> This essence to incarnate and imbrute.

And the very capaciousness of his mind makes him the more formidable
adversary. He arrives at Eden in the night, finds out the serpent, whom
he has already chosen among all animals as the fittest for his purpose,
takes possession of him, asleep, and awaits the dawn.

The dawn breaks; all creatures, plant, beast and man, send up their
praise to God; and the fateful conversation between Adam and Eve
about the strategy of their morning's gardening begins. Look at their
total conversation (lines 204-384), and several things emerge. From first
to last Eve takes and keeps the initiative, though she very nearly loses it
at the end. Her speeches are short, clear, and emphatic, and her mind is
working very fast. Adam, on the other hand, is unprepared, laborious,
and on the defensive, although he warms up and becomes really cogent
at the end. It is a state of affairs both entirely realistic and clean contrary to the ideal picture in Book Four where Adam's 'fair large front
and eye sublime declared absolute rule' and Eve's curls declared submission. The natural hierarchy has already been upset. The speeches
themselves are highly dramatic, and they come from two fully equipped
human beings like ourselves.

Eve begins with her proposal that since they waste so much time taking notice of each other they should garden separately and thus get more
done in the time. It comes out pat and has the air of having been

thought out beforehand. The proposal was relatively harmless but it was not sincere. The pair were still in the honeymoon stage, and the last thing Eve really wanted was to be separated even for a morning from her lover. So she lays a mild trap for Adam, hoping that he will not fall into it but will retort that she asks too much and that he cannot bear to lose sight of her. That she was not sincere is evident from the deliberately contrasted proposal Milton puts into her mouth after the Fall and when they have repented:

> But the Field
> To labour calls us now with sweat impos'd,
> Though after sleepless Night; for see the Morn,
> All unconcern'd with our unrest, begins
> Her rosie progress smiling; let us forth,
> I never from thy side henceforth to stray,
> Wherere our days work lies.   (xi, 171-7.)

Here Eve not only proposes to work with Adam, but is really anxious that they should do as much as possible. The exact reverse would be the case before.

Adam, after the manner of men when sleepy or not at their best, falls into the trap, taking Eve at her word, and proceeds to make two mistakes. Instead of being personal, he is vague and lectures her on the abstract principle of recreation, rather as if he were a seventeenth-century undergraduate upholding the thesis that work prospers best when interspersed with play. And then, not noticing her disappointment and her consequent deafness to argument, he chooses the wrong moment to advance his really important plea of danger and the folly of being separated when they know a foe may be at hand. And he ends earnestly but on the wrong note:

> Leave not the faithful side
> That gave thee being, still shades thee and protects,
> The Wife, where danger or dishonour lurks,
> Safest and seemliest by her Husband stands,
> Who guards her, or with her the worst endures.

Such apparent self-praise from Adam could hardly be soothing just then. Eve stands on her dignity and, her mind working very clearly and freely, makes a brilliant and telling retort. She replies with 'sweet austeer composure' that Adam plainly does not trust her and that this is an unfair slight on her character:

> But that thou shouldst my firmness therefore doubt
> To God or thee, because we have a foe
> May tempt it, I expected not to hear.

Of course Adam had not quite meant that, but how difficult to deal clearly and briefly with so dangerous a simplification! However, he sees he must do something to propitiate Eve and replies with 'healing words'. Even so, he begins badly, with the poor plea that he does not really fear that Eve will fall but that he fears the slur on her honour which any attempt on her firmness must imply; a very weak shift of ground and a shoddy piece of improvisation. However, it has given him time to collect his wits and he at last says something really effective: that he needs her help every bit as much as she needs his:

> I from the influence of thy looks receave
> Access in every Vertue, in thy sight
> More wise, more watchful, stronger, if need were
> Of outward strength.

There is still hope that Adam may save the situation, and Milton lets us know that Adam is now really doing his best, when he adds

> So spake domestick *Adam* in his care
> And Matrimonial Love.

Eve naturally is not to be appeased at once, and she goes on to score more points. She cannot agree that the mere attempt will scathe her honour; it is the foiled tempter who will be dishonoured. Heaven, the only criterion that matters, will approve. And she turns on Adam those doctrines of freedom reminiscent of *Areopagitica,* which she had doubtless learnt from his own lips:

> And what is Faith, Love, Vertue unassaid
> Alone, without exterior help sustaind?

Her speech is brief, decisive, masterly. But it is nevertheless wrong, for she confounds the sin of asking for trouble with the virtue of not avoiding the dust and heat when these are necessary. Adam is by now thoroughly roused, and his real intellectual superiority asserts itself. He grasps Eve's mistake, but forbears scoring off her. Instead he replies with fervour and humility. God supplied us, he argues, with the necessary armour against evil. But it should be used discreetly. You cannot be too careful: for the will may go wrong through the reason's acting on false data, through thinking false appearances to be the truth. And he really answers Eve when he says:

> Seek not temptation then, which to avoide
> Were better, and most likelie if from me
> Thou sever not: Trial will come unsought.

And he preaches the true contemporary and Miltonic doctrine when he says:

> Wouldst thou approve thy constancie, approve
> First thy obedience.

In other words, respect the natural leadership of the husband. Adam has been eloquent; we know that Eve must have been impressed. Indeed when she makes her next (and last) speech, she is 'submiss'. Adam really has the situation in hand. Eve has got not what she first wanted but something to take its place. She first wanted a small tribute to her charm; now she has had the satisfaction of rousing Adam and of obtaining a degree of attention she had never expected. And then comes the tragedy. Adam, who could now be firm with impunity, whom Eve expects to be firm, suddenly weakens. He goes on to find a specious argument why in this instance separation may be better, misapplies the doctrine of liberty, and almost recommends Eve to go against his true wishes. His argument is: it may now be that, having been warned so thoroughly, you will in isolation be better able to resist temptation than in the security and lack of vigilance that would follow on our being together. It is a false argument, because both of them are now thoroughly warned and there is no reason why the effect of the warning should wear off in each other's company.

Adam's misguided lenience makes things hard for Eve. She would now like to yield, but after all her protests it is hardly consonant with proper pride for her not to accept his offer. So she accepts it, and as a compromise says she does so in deference to Adam's final hypothesis. The whole situation is pervaded with tragic irony. Adam weakens just when he could so easily have been strong. Eve, having requested to garden alone, gains her request just as she has repented of it. With this important phase of the Fall Satan has had nothing to do: it has been conducted on the Meredithian principle:

> In tragic life, God wot,
> No villain need be! Passions spin the plot:
> We are betrayed by what is false within.

What, it may be asked, was Adam's motive in giving way? Perhaps mistaken chivalry. When he saw Eve yielding, he could not bear not to meet her half way. And the chivalry was stimulated by her surpassing charm. Like Bunyan's Christiana, Eve was a woman of quick apprehension. While baffling Adam's superior intelligence by her quickness she must have been highly attractive; and she has her temper in perfect control throughout. But her charm and the air of comedy that it creates do not prevent the essential tragedy or the hard fact that both Adam and Eve have sinned: Eve by assuming the leadership that Milton's age believed belonged in nature to the male, Adam in failing in the authority it was his duty to assert.

There follows one of the great moments of the poem, the description of Eve walking away from Adam with her gardening tools. It is in Milton's most delicate and enchanting vein and it gains in poignancy by being set between the tragic irony just described and the author's lament for Eve that her peace of mind is gone for ever:

> O much deceav'd, much failing, hapless *Eve*,
> Of thy presum'd return! event perverse!
> Thy never from that houre in Paradise
> Foundst either sweet repast, or sound repose.

Whether Milton meant it consciously or not, we should surely in reading these words think of what Iago said as he saw Othello approach, to be caught inevitably in his trap:

> Not Poppy, nor Mandragora,
> Nor all the drowsie Syrrups of the world,
> Shall ever medicine thee to that sweete sleep
> Which thou owd'st yesterday.

With the temptation itself, culminating in Adam and Eve eating the fruit, I shall deal more briefly. It has been handled over and over again, and the very attraction it holds out for unceasing reinterpretation proves how rich it is in content, how successful Milton was in making it interesting and inexhaustible. It would be going too far to say that all the interpretations are right, but it is true that more interpretations are simultaneously right than the single propounders of their own interpretations are prepared to admit, at least while in the act of writing up their pet notion. To such a failing I must plead guilty when putting the Fall mainly in terms of mental triviality in my *Milton*.[6] Not that I now think this motive to be absent. Milton does insist that Eve failed to grasp the issue through a kind of levity, and such an insistence accords perfectly with a train of thought running through many of his pamphlets: that what defeats human betterment is a kind of blindness to the issues. Nor is the sin of triviality a trivial sin. To quote from one of the most eminent modern novelists, the late L. H. Myers:

> If triviality takes an important place in the world, if it is the chief barrier between men and God, then triviality is important. . . . No corruption is more easily spread than that of trivial-mindedness. It is more wicked to be heedless of good and evil than to say: Evil be thou my good! The man who defies God thereby acknowledges Him, and for him salvation waits; but the man who ignores God, the man who is incapable of an emotional response to the universe in its august or divine aspect—that man is indeed beyond the pale.

Nevertheless, I may have appeared to narrow the motives overmuch to this single one. Certainly, I should now admit a number of other motives. A good deal has been said about the faculties of the understanding and the will in Milton's version of the Fall; and there is no doubt that, following St Paul and St Augustine, Milton showed Eve sinning through a defect of the understanding and Adam of the will. Indeed Milton probably turned the difficulty inherent in his myth of having two tragic

[6] I admit the force of Maurice Kelley's rebuke (*This Great Argument*, 150, note 31).

heroes into the profit of being able to express through this duality the traditional division of the human mind into wit and will. Anyhow Milton tells us that Adam did understand the issue (at least up to a point), that he was not deceived but was overcome by female charm. That Milton meant Eve to go wrong through a defective understanding is plain from the words Adam addresses to her in his last speech before they part (ix, 351):

> But God left free the Will, for what obeys
> Reason, is free, and Reason he made right
> But bid her well beware, and still erect,
> Least by some faire appearing good surpris'd
> She dictate false, and misinforme the Will
> To do what God expressly hath forbid.

These words do in the main foreshadow the process of Eve's temptation. Her reason is deceived by the Serpent's pretence that as he, a dumb beast, has by eating the fruit risen to the human faculty of speech, so she, if she eats, will attain a correspondingly superior state. And her will answers to the false premises submitted to it by the understanding. The species of temptation Eve undergoes comes out plainly if you contrast her with Spenser's Sir Guyon in Mammon's Cave. There, it was a pure question of will, of the will resisting the passions. Sir Guyon knew that it was the principle that mattered, that if he touched the tiniest piece of gold the fiend would get him as surely as if he trundled away a barrowload.

But in speaking of wit and will we must beware of simplifying, for Eve's will was swayed by her passions as well as by the misguidance of her intellect, and Adam allowed his intellect to sleep as well as submitting his will to his passion for Eve; for Eve's desire to be promoted in the natural scale was a passion, and Adam before eating the fruit, which he had already decided to do for love of Eve, half-fools his understanding with a piece of wishful thinking:

> Perhaps the Fact
> Is not so hainous now, foretasted Fruit
> Profan'd first by the Serpent, by him first
> Made common and unhallowed ere our taste;
> Nor yet on him found deadly, he yet lives,
> Lives, as thou saidst, and gaines to live as Man
> Higher degree of Life, inducement strong
> To us, as likely tasting to attaine
> Proportional ascent.

As we must avoid a narrow interpretation of motives, so must we of the crime itself. Milton himself, in the formidable list he gives in the *De Doctrina* of the crimes the eating of the apple implied, should keep us right here. But it is not simply a question of what crimes the prime sin of disobedience brought with it but one of how the sin itself is to be interpreted. I have to confess to making too little of the disobedience in my *Milton,* because I took it in the Addisonian sense and found that sense too impoverished to fit Milton's conceptions. That part of the crime involved in Milton's version of the Fall was simple disobedience to the ascertainable mandate of God is undoubted. But that does not mean that Milton considered the mandates of God so easily ascertainable as Addison and his age thought them. Nor does simple disobedience of a simple arbitrary command anywhere near cover the total meaning of disobedience to Milton. Its wider and more pervasive meaning is a breaking of the natural order as prescribed by God. Just as Satan had aspired, through pride, beyond his natural archangelic state to sheer godhead, so he tempted Eve to eat the forbidden fruit that she might transcend her natural human limitations. Adam also offends against the natural order by failing to maintain the hierarchical principle in his dealings with Eve. Whether or not Milton compels us to sympathize with Adam when he refuses to forsake Eve in her extremity, at least we can join with him in deploring Adam's crucial weakness, as described above, in allowing Eve to go away unprotected. And in the end Adam joins Eve in imagining that the forbidden fruit is bringing them nearer to godhead. Such disobedience is near to what is now popularly described as the acts of disregarding the facts of existence, going against the nature of things, or refusing to come to terms with the conditions of one's environment. And it is just because a large part of the Fall's meaning stands for something so simple and fundamental as this that the heart of *Paradise Lost* can never be superannuated.

Of course to Milton the 'nature of things' was other than to us: he inherited a belief in the grand, defined, diversified, and fantastic array of supposed facts that went to make up the Elizabethan world picture. But no change in the world picture can stale the notion that a large portion of wisdom is to understand the conditions of life and to submit ourselves freely to them. Thence comes true liberty. There is the initial liberty to revolt or not to revolt: common to all men. But revolt or disobedience is the loss of liberty, while acceptance of things as they are is the true fulfilment of it. Within that acceptance the greatest measure of legitimate choice will be attained.

But I have spent time enough on Milton's supposed notions as abstracted from his text; and I return to my main business, the text itself.

By rising so high in his description of Eve parting from Adam, Milton set himself an exalted standard, but he excels himself. He describes the garden with a beauty equal to that of the original description in Book Four, yet with greater intimacy as from within. Eve, working among the roses, is perfectly set in the natural beauty:

> Veild in a Cloud of Fragrance, where she stood,
> Half spi'd, so thick the Roses bushing round
> About her glowd.

And Satan's momentary relaxation, when he surveys the scene,

> Stupidly good, of enemitie disarm'd,

and his returning hate serve brilliantly to space Eve's fateful conversation with Adam from her culminating conversation with Satan.

This second conversation has been sufficiently described and admired. Its drift is clear. Satan relies on sheer flattery and on airing the temptation to aspire beyond one's lot. His grand argument is that *he* has done so and succeeded—

> And life more perfect have attaind than Fate
> Meant me, by ventring higher than my Lot.

It may not have been seen how much irony the conversation contains, mainly through its contrasts with Eve's other conversation that morning. The legitimate praise of which Adam unluckily had starved her is made good by the gross flattery of the Devil. If Eve temporarily upset Adam by the quickness of her thought, the Devil pays her back treble in her own coin in his final harangue. Waldock has shown excellently with what blinding effect Satan shifts from one premise to another to draw his specious conclusions. And finally there is an irony in the Devil's Pauline phraseology when he recommends the new life that the fruit will promote:

> So ye shall die perhaps, by putting off
> Human, to put on Gods, death to be wisht.

Satan as it were parodies by anticipation Paul's exhortations to die to sin, to put off the old man and put on the new.

The impetus that carries the action to Eve's eating the fruit is both worthy of the scenes that precede it and makes no pause at that point. On the contrary it presses right on, Milton spending no more than two and a half lines in describing Nature's lament at the Fall. There is no warrant in the actual poem for centring everything just here: on the contrary Eve's progress in sin is continued and intensified after she eats the fruit. She now proceeds to the sin of idolatry by praising the forbidden fruit as divine and then doing obeisance to it; and she identifies herself with Satan by repeating his most outrageous assertion: that the tree was not God's creation at all and hence not in the Gods' power to give or forbid,

> For had the gift bin theirs, it had not here
> Thus grown.

But as her speech proceeds and she thinks of Adam, the tone modulates and acquires a touch of that domestic comedy which had not been absent from her talk with Adam that same morning:

> But to *Adam* in what sort
> Shall I appear? shall I to him make known

> As yet my change, and give him to partake
> Full happiness with me, or rather not,
> But keep the odds of knowledge in my power
> Without Copartner? so to add what wants
> In Female Sex, the more to draw his Love,
> And render me more equal, and perhaps,
> A thing not undesirable, sometime
> Superior; for inferior who is free?
> This may be well: but what if God have seen,
> And Death ensue? then I shall be no more,
> And *Adam* wedded to another *Eve*,
> Shall live with her enjoying, I extinct;
> A death to think. Confirm'd then I resolve,
> *Adam* shall share with me in bliss or woe.

If you heed the sense alone and not the tone and feeling of these lines, you can turn them into a sheer exhibition of evil motives. C. S. Lewis has gone so far as to make them include the sin of murder. Of course they show Eve outrageously seeking to upset the natural order. But surely the lightened rhythm and the ironically delicate human observation forbid us to press them to the utmost solemnity. . . .

Whether we like it or not, *some* comedy has crept into Milton's treatment of the Fall. Why should this be? Perhaps he wishes, even thus early, to reassure us that all is not irretrievably lost, and that Eve's wicked thoughts must be viewed in proportion, that they do not really exclude all chance of better ones. After all Milton was not one of those Calvinists who believed that the Fall extinguished every spark of virtue in the human heart. But I fancy there is also a structural reason. Milton has by now been at a high pitch of intensity for a long time, and to continue so just here would be to make the eating of the fruit indeed the exclusive climax of the poem. It is just because he does not intend this that the pitch is now relaxed.

Nor does the intensity really grow in the scene when Adam also eats. Eve's speech to him is splendidly dramatic. We see her flushed face and hear her unnaturally fluent plausibility hiding the embarrassment and fear. There is little elaboration in Adam's yielding to her wishes and his resolve to stand by her. His horror, though nobly, is very briefly described and in a conventional, neo-classic manner:

> Adam, soon as he heard
> The fatal Trespass don by Eve, amaz'd.
> Astonied stood and Blank, while horror chill
> Ran through his veins, and all his joynts relax'd;
> From his slack hand the Garland wreath'd for Eve
> Down drop'd, and all the faded Roses shed.

Had Milton wanted emphasis and elaboration here, how easily could he have made Adam pause over his choice, wavering agonizingly this way and that. Instead, Adam seems to have made his choice beforehand, to have decided from the first that if Eve fell he would not forsake her. Certainly his decision is definite and unhesitating and has been taken without the least pressure from Eve:

> some cursed fraud
> Of Enemie hath beguiled thee, yet unknown,
> And me with thee hath ruind, for with thee
> Certain my resolution is to Die;
> How can I live without thee, how forgoe
> Thy sweet Converse and Love so dearly joyn'd,
> To live again in these wilde woods forlorn?
> Should God create another *Eve,* and I
> Another Rib afford, yet loss of thee
> Would never from my heart; no, no, I feel
> The Link of Nature chain me: Flesh of Flesh,
> Bone of my Bone thou art, and from thy State
> Mine never shall be parted, bliss or woe.   (ix, 904.)

No lines in Milton have been more discussed than these; and I should like particularly to mention Waldock's[7] remarks on them. I agree with him that as poetry and in their context these lines compel us to sympathize with Adam's love for Eve as manifested in them. It is equally clear that by the nominal requirements of the scheme we should be shocked and horrified; for what more shocking than the spectacle of a man, still innocent, choosing to flout God with his eyes open and to sacrifice eternal principles for an impulse to companionship? Yet in actual reading we are not profoundly shocked, and the reason is that Adam's innocence at this point is only nominal. As pointed out above, he has really crossed the frontier, and no abstention from eating the fruit can put him back the other side. The nature of Adam's action can best be seen by the analogy of a man who hates war and yet consents to fight. To fight is bad, yet not to fight is worse because it is a denial of the common human fate, of an incrimination it is as yet impossible for any human being to be free of. To keep clear on narrowly personal moral grounds would be to incur a self-righteousness worse than the taint of association in an evil which all humanity is doomed to share. That, I maintain, is a true analogy as dictated by the poetical effect. That it can easily be disproved by the doctrine of the poem in isolation from the poetry is a minor affair. Once again we have to do with a discrepancy with which Milton was powerless to deal except by faking. And if we follow the lead of the poetry, we can only admire him for doing as well as he does.

Having uttered to himself his memorable resolution to die with Eve, Adam turns his words to her 'in calm mood' and proceeds to put the best face on her action that he can. Thus Milton continues the less

---

[7] *Paradise Lost and its Critics* (Cambridge, 1947), 46.

intense strain that began with the intrusion of comedy, but at a price: there is something just a little starved about the account of Adam's fall. Animation rises when Eve blesses Adam for his resolution and weeps for gratitude and joy. And yet Milton does not allow the human feeling to go uncriticized. As he had previously tempered Eve's exhibition of criminal thoughts with comedy, so contrariwise he now corrects her effusion of understandable but all too fallibly human feelings with a stern reminder of the pair's fundamental incrimination.

> So saying, she embrac'd him, and for joy
> Tenderly wept, much won that he his Love
> Had so enobl'd, as of choice to incurr
> Divine displeasure for her sake, or Death.[8]

Nothing could be finer than the implied ironic comparison between his act as it appeared to her and as it appears *sub specie aeternitatis*. Nor does Milton's stern comment invalidate the sympathy he has made the reader feel with Adam's choice to stand by Eve; for that comment can apply by now to the whole process of the Fall as it began in Eve's dream and to fallen humanity in general and its pitiful deficiencies.

The ensuing description of how the fruit intoxicated the pair is admirable. Comedy re-enters but more grimly, in Adam's profane wish that God might have forbidden ten trees instead of one and in the description of their falling into lust. Then they sleep, and when they wake find their innocence lost and know themselves to be naked.

In describing how Adam and Eve waked to shame Milton was faced with difficulties. He had to recount their shame of nakedness, for it is so prominent in *Genesis,* being in fact the principal effect of eating the fruit. He meets his difficulty by making their shame go far beyond nakedness, and he reinforces the theme of the nakedness by introducing their act of lust. Even so, Milton's account is not very explicit; but it can be legitimately made so, if we set it in the total context of the poem. Adam and Eve had dropped off to sleep in the deceptive confidence that they were growing into gods; they woke into the rueful realization that they were less than their normal selves, suffering from a hangover. They had not experienced deceit previously (even if they were in some sense fallen, before they actually tasted the fruit) and that was part of their innocence: now they know the shame of having been tricked. Other motives of shame have to do with their appetites. Instead of eating their noontide dinner in a decent orderly way they had indulged in a pre-

---

[8] It is a few lines later that Milton describes Adam as not deceived but fondly overcome by female charm (lines 998-9). In my *Milton* I called the sentiment inconsistent with what went before because Adam had made up his mind before Eve exercised her charms on him (p. 263). I now agree with Paul Turner (*l.c.* 14) that 'female charm' refers not to Eve's caresses at this point but to the previous influence of her physical attractions. Adam, in fact, has put into action the state of mind Raphael reproved at the end of Book Eight.

mature, extemporary, and intoxicating picnic. Instead of waiting till evening and the ceremonious sequestration of their nuptial bower, where no
animal dared come, they had indulged in a hasty, unceremonious fit of
love: exactly what Milton in his great panegyric on married love had
called 'casual fruition' and had associated with harlots. When we think
of these contrasts we may understand how the sexual act has been soiled
for them and how they become conscious of their nakedness. It is to be
noted that Adam and Eve have forgotten God. Shame for disobedience
does not enter in. They are self-centred.

The book ends with the loosening of the full range of personal human
passions and the pair's mutual recrimination. It is a quite masterly ending, terribly true to ordinary human nature, and too sad to be called
comic. It brings no pause in the action; the effects of the Fall are only
beginning to make themselves felt.

Book Ten marks, not a new action, but the transfer of the existing
action from the bounds of Paradise to the whole universe. The full incidence of the Fall remains to be described. That incidence is double:
on the whole world outside, and back again on Adam and Eve through
the evocation of heavenly grace. This book is thus both cosmic and domestic, and for range and variety it excels all others in the poem.
Whether it is the finest of all the books need not be debated; at least it
is the worthy setting for what I now believe the culmination of the poem.

First the Fall is reported in heaven, and the Son descends to the garden
to pronounce judgment. Adam and Eve are tied up in their own shame
and barren passions:

> Love was not in their looks, either to God
> Or to each other, but apparent guilt,
> And shame, and perturbation, and despaire,
> Anger, and obstinacie, and hate, and guile.

And the Son's merciful bearing in pronouncing judgment, and his
active charity in giving them clothes, make no impression on their
conscious minds. To all appearances Hell has triumphed completely
in them; after which it is but fitting that the further triumphs of Hell
should be recounted.

There follows (line 229) one of the grandest of all episodes in the
poem: the building by Sin and Death of the causeway from Hell to the
universe. Since its richness of connotation may not have been fully
recognized, I will comment on it at some length. Milton describes how
Sin and Death, waiting at Hell's gate, sense the change that has been
brought about by the Fall and know that they may now range the earth
freely. To connect Hell and earth better they build a causeway from
hell-gate over chaos to the zenith of the universe, where there is the
entrance from space into the outermost bounding sphere of the whole
cosmic system. This is also the point whence the way to heaven ascends.

They construct the bridge through the deathlike operation of the qualities of cold and dry.

As well as grand the episode is grotesque. And it is so, partly because it is a parody: a parody of God's creating the world in Book Seven. Here are the lines describing the work on the causeway, Death having spoken:

> So saying, with delight he snuff'd the smell
> Of mortal change on Earth. As when a flock
> Of ravenous Fowl, though many a League remote,
> Against the day of Battel, to a Field,
> Where armies lie encampt, come flying, lur'd
> With sent of living Carcasses design'd
> For death, the following day, in bloodie fight.
> So sented the grim Feature, and upturn'd
> His Nostril wide into the murkie Air,
> Sagacious of his Quarry from so farr.
> Then Both from out Hell Gates into the waste
> Wide Anarchie of *Chaos* damp and dark
> Flew divers, and with Power (their Power was great)
> Hovering upon the Waters: what they met
> Solid or slimie, as in raging Sea
> Tost up and down, together crowded drove
> From each side shoaling towards the mouth of Hell.
> As when two Polar Winds blowing adverse
> Upon the Cronian Sea, together drive
> Mountains of Ice, that stop th'imagin'd way
> Beyond Petsora Eastward, to the rich
> Cathaian Coast. The aggregated Soyle
> Death with his Mace petrific, cold and dry,
> As with a Trident smote, and fix't as firm
> As Delos floating once; the rest his look
> Bound with Gorgonian rigor not to move,
> And with Asphaltic slime; broad as the Gate,
> Deep to the Roots of Hell the gathr'd beach
> They fasten'd, and the Mole immense wrought on
> Over the foaming deep high Archt a Bridge
> Of length prodigious joyning to the Wall
> Immoveable of this now fenceless world
> Forfeit to Death; from hence a passage broad,
> Smooth, easie, inoffensive down to Hell.

Though Sin and Death are not actually called vultures, yet, when you add the initial simile to the later adjective *hovering*, it is clear you are meant thus to picture them. Compare now the corresponding description lines 210-242, in Book Seven, of the Son and the Spirit going out from heaven to create.

> On heavn'ly ground they stood, and from the shore
> They view'd the vast immeasurable Abyss
> Outrageous as a Sea, dark, wasteful, wilde,

Up from the bottom turn'd by furious windes
And surging waves, as Mountains to assault
Heav'ns highth, and with the Center mix the Pole.
Silence, ye troubl'd waves, and thou Deep, peace,
Said then th' Omnific Word, your discord end:
Nor staid, but on the Wings of Cherubim
Uplifted, in Paternal Glorie rode
Farr into *Chaos,* and the World unborn;
For *Chaos* heard his voice: him all his Traine
Follow'd in bright procession to behold
Creation, and the wonders of his might.
Then staid the fervid Wheeles, and in his hand
He took the golden Compasses, prepar'd
In Gods Eternal store, to circumscribe
This Universe, and all created things:
One foot he center'd, and the other turn'd
Round through the vast profunditie obscure,
And said, thus farr extend, thus farr thy bounds,
This be thy just Circumference, O World.
Thus God the Heav'n created, thus the Earth,
Matter unform'd and void: Darkness profound
Cover'd th' Abyss: but on the watrie calme
His brooding wings the Spirit of God outspred,
And vital vertue infus'd, and vital warmth
Throughout the fluid Mass, but downward purg'd
The black tartareous cold Infernal dregs
Adverse to life: then founded, then conglob'd
Like things to like, the rest to several place
Disparted, and between spun out the Air,
And Earth self ballanc't on her Center hung.

There are many comparisons and contrasts between the two creative acts; and one account helps to make the other more precise. The divine Trinity is matched by the infernal trinity of Satan, Sin, and Death; and it is the second and third in each trinity who execute the creative work. God hushes chaos into peace before creation, Sin and Death prefer to create from discordant material. The Holy Spirit broods like a dove over the abyss, Sin and Death hover over it like birds of prey. The spirit creates through warmth and growth and purges away the intractable dregs. Death solidifies his causeway by chill and petrifaction, and the solid and slimy materials he uses are doubtless those very 'cold infernal dregs, adverse to life' which the Spirit had rejected. Generally, the second passage is violent and excessive where the first passage is easy, though vast, and serene. And this excess co-operates with the parody in creating the sense of the grotesque. Death, 'the grim Feature', is so vaguely cir-cumstantiated that we are all free to have our own picture of him, but, whatever the picture generally, it becomes grotesque when he 'upturns his Nostril wide into the murkie Air'. The mountains of ice piled up by polar winds cannot be pictured otherwise than as grotesquely huddled together.

I have dwelt on the nature of the passage describing how Sin and Death built their causeway because that nature is so important to the structure of the whole book. It is Milton's first stroke in creating an impression of threatening monstrosity.

When Sin and Death have done their work, they arrive at the upper end of the causeway: that fateful road-junction on the zenith of the universe, where there is access at choice to Heaven or Hell or Earth. There, very dramatically, they meet Satan, and in the conversations that follow the setting should be remembered. When Sin, addressing her parent Satan, tells him that God may

> henceforth Monarchie with thee divide
> Of all things parted by th'Empyreal bounds,
> His Quadrature, from thy Orbicular World,

we should picture the trio standing on the outer shell of the 'Orbicular World' with a clear view down into its recesses and with God's 'Quadrature', the 'Opal Towrs and Battlements adorn'd of living saphire' seen by Satan when emerging from chaos, in distant prospect. Further, when Satan begins his injunctions with 'You two this way . . .' he should be pictured as pointing the way he has just come from Paradise. Once more the vast, circumstantiated picture is organic to the total impression required.

The trio now part, Sin and Death earthwards and Satan back to Hell to announce his good news. He finds Hell a strange sight, with the gate wide and unguarded, the outskirts deserted, and only the citadel, Pandemonium, in use. With the dictator's flair for the theatrical he steps through the devils assembled in the great hall, in lowly disguise, and appears suddenly to the company, seated in full splendour on the throne. There is no need to stress the grotesqueness of the sequel—for it is well recognized—Satan's boastful speech followed by the elaborate symbolic *tour de force* of the devils turned to serpents and vainly seeking to slake their thirst on the ashen fruit.[9] It is doubtful whether Milton was wise to assert just then, even if in oblique, symbolic form, that Satan's apparent triumph was illusory. And assert he does because he contrasts man's single lapse with the serpents' repeatedly tasting their own illusive fruit:

> so oft they fell
> Into the same illusion, not as Man
> Whom they triumph'd once lapst.

But this assertion counts little compared with Milton's success in intensifying the grotesqueness, the monstrosity he has already created. By in-

---

[9] Waldock (*op. cit.*), 91, observes that Milton's technique in this scene is that of the comic cartoon. True, and in its setting it is none the worse for that.

serting the queer legend of Ophion and Eurynome, whom he equates with
the Serpent and Eve—a strained bit of academicism in keeping just because it is strained—Milton makes a transition from Hell to Earth and the
havoc now being worked there.

Sin and Death now arrive in Paradise and begin their work. They do
not know that God is watching them and using them for his own purposes. In fact God proceeds to co-operate with them by sending his angels
to shift the earth's angle so that the seasons may become less equable
and generally to make life on earth harder and more subject to mutabil-
ity. This is the third great account in Book Ten of evil or disorder gaining the mastery. The effects of the Fall are swelling to vast proportions.
And this time they visibly affect man. There is the same effect as before
of monstrous happenings. God does not just command, that things may
happen easily and directly: he works through his angels, and they work
laboriously, even doubtfully:

> Some say he bid his Angels turne ascanse
> The Poles of Earth twice ten degrees and more
> From the Suns Axle; they with labour push'd
> Oblique the Centric Globe;   (x, 668.)

and Milton piles up the astronomical detail. Finally the eating of the forbidden fruit is compared to the fatal and unnatural feast of Thyestes
with all its monstrous associations:

> At that tasted Fruit
> The Sun, as from Thyestean Banquet, turn'd
> His course intended.

Discord settles finally in Eden itself, where

> Beast now with Beast gan war, and Fowle with Fowle,
> And Fish with Fish; to graze the Herb all leaving,
> Devourd each other; nor stood much in awe
> Of Man.

The chaos caused by the Fall now fittingly culminates in the mind of
man. It had been shown in Hell, when the devils become serpents, and
in the natural world, and now at last it invades the human microcosm.
Adam, observing the growing miseries around him, falls into sheer
despair and utters a great tortured speech. He has changed greatly since
his dumb self-centredness before the judging God. Then his mind was
stupefied; now it works with terrifying speed and appears to take everything into account. The subject of the speech is justice self-applied. Adam
seeks one excuse for his conduct after another and finds that every one
fails. He then seeks one escape after another and finds each closed.
Worst of all, the effects of his crime are not confined to himself but will
be handed on to his posterity. He ends in unmitigated self-accusation:

> Him after all Disputes
> Forc't I absolve: all my evasion vain,
> And reasonings, though through Mazes lead me still
> But to my own conviction: first and last
> On mee, mee only, as the sourse and spring
> Of all corruption, all the blame lights due.

And he concludes that as his crime was simply that of Satan, so must his doom be likewise.[10]

To match Adam's despair we should go to *Samson Agonistes*; and for more than one reason. Adam and Samson both suffer so terribly because they can see no possible course of action; and they are both unaware that because they have searched their hearts to the bottom and really know themselves and admit every scruple of guilt they are even now saved men. And that is one of the many ironies into which the tenth book of *Paradise Lost* issues. You can put it another way by saying that in this place, where the processes of destruction and disorder appear to culminate, the process of regeneration has actually begun.

But it is only with a fraction of our mind that we apprehend the irony; with most of it we witness Adam's despair, and, in its vastness and complications, associate it with the vast grotesquenesses which have led up to it.

As Adam lies sleepless with these thoughts he makes a second and very different speech. It is short and though it is despairing in content it differs in tone from the storminess of the previous speech.

> Why comes not Death,
> Said hee, with one thrice acceptable stroke
> To end me? Shall Truth fail to keep her word,
> Justice Divine not hast'n to be just?
> But Death comes not at call, Justice Divine
> Mends not her slowest pace for prayers or cries.
> O Woods, O Fountains, Hillocks, Dales and Bowrs,
> With other echo late I taught your Shades
> To answer, and resound farr other Song.

It is not the terrible despair that here strikes us so much as the lyrical beauty. The Rev Dr Newton, whose sumptuous edition of *Paradise Lost* appeared in 1749 well in the middle of the age of reason, a man not given to excessive enthusiasm, in comment on the words,

> Justice Divine
> Mends not her slowest pace for prayers or cries,

(having duly noted an imitation of *Pede Poena claudo,* Hor. *Od.* III. ii. *32*), wrote

---

[10] As we read this speech we are meant to recall Satan's great speech on Mount Niphates at the beginning of Book Four. Both speakers are tortured, both admit God's justice. But Satan ends in a resolve to do evil, Adam in self-accusation.

The most beautiful passages commonly want the fewest notes: And, for the beauties of this passage, we are sure, the reader must not only perceive, but really feel, them, if he has any feeling at all. Nothing in all the ancient tragedies is more moving and pathetick.

And it is pleasant to be able to record independent agreement with this editor on this singular beauty. But the beauty has a function. It hints that Adam, without knowing it (as the Ancient Mariner blessed the watersnakes unawares), is beginning a little to relax his mind's tension; and it prepares for the approach of Eve, who now begins to make up to him. But even here, Hell has not yet quite done its worst, and Adam rejects her with bitter words to herself and bitter words about sex in general. Chaos has invaded not only the single mind but the bonds between man and wife. I have changed my opinion about Adam's famous words on the misfortunes of marriage. Speaking of the husband Milton says

> for either
> He never shall find out fit Mate, but such
> As some misfortune brings him, or mistake,
> Or whom he wishes most shall seldom gain
> Through her perverseness, but shall see her gain'd
> By a farr worse, or if she love, witheld
> By Parents, or his happierr choice too late
> Shall meet, alreadie linkt and Wedlock-bound
> To a fell Adversarie, his hate and shame:
> Which infinite calamitie shall cause
> To Human life, and household peace confound.

I now agree with Hanford,[11] and disagree with Walter Raleigh in thinking these lines appropriately dramatic and not a piece of extrinsic comment on Milton's experience of marriage. Adam has already been deeply concerned with his posterity and now lets his imagination dwell on what it will suffer in the matter of wedlock through his own disobedience. His bitterness towards Eve is ferocious. The worse cut of all is when he accuses her of 'longing to be seen though by the Devil himself'. But I fancy the bitterness is mixed: part sheer resentment, part fury in recognizing that he is, after all, still drawn towards her. Compare Hamlet's brutality to Ophelia.

And now at last, following on the significant word 'confound', which ended the last quotation, comes the resolution, the act to which all the accumulation of incident and description recorded in this essay leads up: the reconciliation of Adam and Eve. It begins with Eve's persistence:

> He added not, and from her turn'd, but *Eve*
> Not so repulst, with Tears that ceas'd not flowing,
> And tresses all disordered, at his feet

---

[11] *Studies in Philology*, (1917), 186, from an article on 'The Dramatic Element in *Paradise Lost*'.

> Fell humble, and imbracing them, besaught
> His peace.

The lines are few and simple and yet charged with meaning. There is the fitness, indeed the artistic necessity, that as Eve took the initiative in sin she should take the initiative in regeneration. And there is the exquisite irony that her noble action should follow close upon Adam's fierce denunciation of her sex. And her action, however simple and simply described ('not so repulst'), is a sublime display of courage, involving the terrible pain of making the first motion, of breaking free from the deadly sin of Sloth. And in the scheme of the whole poem it is crucial: the first motion of sincere, positive, good feeling after all the falseness and frustration that has followed the Fall.

Eve's conciliatory speech follows. She too has no hope, and death may come in a few hours. She has no pride and is utterly open about her own fault. Indeed she wants to take all the blame on herself. But death or no death, she knows that for Adam and herself to be at odds is intolerable, and her resolution is equal to her humility. The union of these two qualities is irresistible, and Adam's hardness both towards her and towards heaven is melted. Here, if anywhere, is the crisis of *Paradise Lost*.

> She ended weeping, and her lowlie plight,
> Immoveable till peace obtain'd from fault
> Acknowledg'd and deplor'd, in *Adam* wrought
> Commiseration; soon his heart relented
> Towards her, his life so late and sole delight,
> Now at his feet submissive in distress,
> Creature so faire his reconcilement seeking,
> His counsel whom she had displeas'd, his aide;
> As one disarm'd, his anger all he lost,
> And thus with peaceful words uprais'd her soon.
>   Unwarie, and too desirous, as before,
> So now of what thou knowst not, who desir'st
> The punishment all on thy self; alas,
> Beare thine own first, ill able to sustaine
> His full wrauth whose thou feels't as yet lest part,
> And my displeasure bearst so ill. If Prayers
> Could alter high Decrees, I to that place
> Would speed before thee, and be louder heard,
> That on my head all might be visited,
> Thy frailtie and infirmer sex forgiv'n,
> To me committed and by me expos'd.
> But rise, let us no more contend, nor blame
> Each other, blam'd enough elsewhere, but strive
> In offices of Love, how we may light'n
> Each others burden in our share of woe;
> Since this days Death denounc't, if ought I see,
> Will prove no sudden, but a slow-pac't evil,

> A long day's dying to augment our paine,
> And to our Seed (O hapless Seed) deriv'd.

In this speech Adam joins Eve in showing the first positive good feelings since the Fall. He pities Eve, he humbly admits his sin in allowing her to be exposed alone to temptation (an admission that was absent from his self-judgment in his tortured soliloquy), and he is courageous in facing the conditions of life and accepting the harsh fact that prayers cannot alter high decrees. And above all he has found the first outlet in action: they must 'strive in offices of Love' and seek to ease each other's burden.

But complete humility before God has not yet been reached. Eve still wants to deny the initiative to God. She, the practical one, has been thinking while Adam has been torturing himself with the metaphysics of justice. And she sees two ways out of their worst trouble, the incrimination of their posterity: namely, birth-control by abstinence, and suicide. Nowhere does Eve's quickness of apprehension come out better than in this speech. It is a model of lucid, practical reasoning. And she means what she says. But her mind is still in the grip of violent passion and—

> She ended here, or vehement despaire
> Broke off the rest; so much of Death her thoughts
> Had entertained, as di'd her cheeks with pale.
> But *Adam,* with such counsel nothing sway'd,
> To better hopes his more attentive minde
> Labouring had rais'd.

His more attentive minde: that is important, for in the speech that follows Adam recollects God's words and mien in giving judgment, hitherto lying dormant within him and quite overlaid by his own self-accusations. Adam also sees that Eve's proposals, though they argue the nobility of her nature, do imply acts of contumacy, aimed at defeating God's purposes. And God will not be cheated so easily. The Robinson Crusoe in Adam next begins to show itself, and he begins to have ideas about how life after the Fall can be lived. Hope has been born. But the only real cure is submission and penitence:

> What better can we do, then to the place
> Repairing where he judg'd us, prostrate fall
> Before him reverent, and there confess
> Humbly our faults, and pardon beg, with tears
> Watering the ground, and with our sighs the Air
> Frequenting, sent from hearts contrite, in sign
> Of sorrow unfeign'd, and humiliation meek,
> Undoubtedly he will relent and turn
> From his displeasure; in whose look serene,
> When angry most he seem'd and most severe
> What else but favour, grace, and mercie shone?

What had been latent in Adam's mind has now fully shown itself; and the rigorous justice by which he condemned his own acts is now consciously tempered by the mercy which he remembers God to have shown in the very act of pronouncing judgment.

Eve joins Adam in remorse, and the present phase of the action, so long sustained, at last comes to rest in Adam and Eve repairing to the place of judgment and imploring God's pardon.

Such are the details of the reconciliation and the penitence of Adam and Eve. It remains to say something of these things in the structure of the poem. For all the importance of the penitence, it is on the reconciliation that the fullest structural emphasis falls: in it Milton seems to have centred the most intimate significance of his poem. He has, in the actual poem, in his manipulation of his poetic material, carefully led everything up to this reconciliation. He had motivated the Fall with cunning skill, but not allowed us to dwell on it too long and too earnestly. Without pause he had widened the action from the bounds of Paradise. He had built up monstrous and grotesque pictures of chaos, while delicately insinuating the possibility of regeneration. And what issues out of it all? Something that initially looks like bathos: two ordinary human beings in despair, divided, and then coming together in ordinary human decency. The whole elaborate edifice has been staged to give all possible weight to a quite uncomplicated and commonplace trickle of pure human sympathy, the first touch of regeneration, a small beginning but stronger than all the pretensions of Satanic ingenuity, like some faint flow of pale, clear oil issuing from a huge and grotesquely carved oil-press: all this complication of apparatus just for *that*.

Looked at closer the human story of Adam and Eve's reconciliation is not bathos at all. First, it serves and crowns Milton's largest and most elaborate irony. According to Satan's plans the culmination of the story should have been the disobedient act and its dreadful consequences on earth and for its perpetrators. And these plans succeeded well enough in appearance to deceive Satan and Professor Raleigh. Now to the imagination of the Satan who stages so sensational a return to his fellows to report his success any retribution he feared for his daring would present itself in sensational terms. The war in heaven had been violent and noisy; and so had been the Son's entry to end the war in heaven:

> Forth rush'd with whirlwind sound
> The Chariot of Paternal Deitie.

Satan could recognize God in the whirlwind but not in the still small voice. And that God's retaliation could consist in evoking a simple effusion of decent human feeling out of the chaos he had created was beyond the grasp of his mind. And that all his strivings should have been the occasion of something so seemingly petty was a bitter piece of irony at his expense. So it is that the great and dreadful things that appear to be the most important subordinate themselves to what appears to be trivial and is yet surpassingly strong. And this is the essence of the way the nodal episode of *Paradise Lost* is plotted.

Secondly, Adam and Eve exemplify unconsciously in their acts the doctrine which Adam, instructed by the pageant of human history, pronounces in his last words to Michael near the end of the poem. Again it is ironical and perfectly true to life that the pair, while they are in the thick of action, do not know the full import of what they do, and that Adam has to be instructed from without before he can consciously formulate the principle on which he has already acted. Adam's comment on world-history and Michael's reply are poetry whose subdued tone is in inverse proportion to the passion of conviction that inspires it, and stand in the same relation to the great reverberant speeches of Satan in Book One as the episode of Adam's reconciliation with Eve stands to the monstrous events leading up to it. When Adam says,

> Henceforth I learne, that to obey is best,
> And love with fear the only God, to walk
> As in his presence, ever to observe
> His providence, and on him sole depend,
> Mercifull over all his works, with good
> Still overcoming evil, and by small
> Accomplishing great things, by things deemd weak
> Subverting worldly strong, and worldly wise
> By simply meek,

he might be describing his own and Eve's acts: their 'small' act of reconciliation 'accomplishing great things', their 'weak' prostration before God 'subverting' the 'worldly strong' of Satan, and their acceptance of the facts of their case constituting true obedience.

The Final Vision

by Joseph H. Summers

The last two books of *Paradise Lost* have caused difficulty if not actual pain to some of the most ardent admirers of Milton. Addison recognized that Book XI was "not generally reckoned among the most shining Books" of the poem, but he found some passages in it "which deserve our Admiration" (*The Spectator*, No. 363). He was greatly disturbed, however, by the shift from the visions to narration in Book XII, and it was there he felt "in some Places the Author has been so attentive to his Divinity, that he has neglected his Poetry" (No. 369). Mr Thyer, that librarian at Manchester who sent his notes on the poem to Thomas Newton when Newton was preparing his ambitious edition, approved of the devices in the final books which "give great ease to the languishing attention of the reader" (Newton [9th edn., 1790], II, 404). Newton concluded his own commentary with an interesting passage:

> The reader may have observed that these two last books fall short of the sublimity and majesty of the rest: and so likewise do the two last books of the Iliad, and for the same reason, because the subject is of a different kind from that of the foregoing ones. The subject of these two last books of the Paradise Lost is history rather than poetry. However we may still discover the same great genius, and there are intermix'd as many ornaments and graces of poetry, as the nature of the subject, and the author's fidelity and strict attachment to the truth of Scripture history, and the reduction of so many and such various events into so narrow a compass, would admit. It is the same ocean, but not at its highest tide; it is now ebbing and retreating. It is the same sun, but not in its full blaze of meridian glory; it now shines with a gentler ray as it is setting.
>
> (II. 446-447)

It was perhaps from Newton that the custom developed of considering the last two books as the work of an old and tired Milton. Without attempting to define the unknown causes, C. S. Lewis commented strin-

"The Final Vision." From *The Muse's Method: An Introduction to Paradise Lost* by Joseph H. Summers, Cambridge, Mass., London, 1962. Copyright © 1962 by Joseph Summers. Reprinted by permission of the author, Harvard University Press, and Chatto & Windus Ltd. Two portions of this chapter, as noted by ellipsis marks, have been omitted.

gently in *A Preface to Paradise Lost* on what he believed to be the failure of the final books—the major failure of the poem:

> It suffers from a grave structural flaw. Milton, like Virgil, though telling a short story about the remote past, wishes our minds to be carried to the later results of that story. But he does this less skilfully than Virgil. Not content with following his master in the use of occasional prophecies, allusions, and reflections, he makes his two last books into a brief outline of sacred history from the Fall to the Last Day. Such an untransmuted lump of futurity, coming in a position so momentous for the structural effect of the whole work, is inartistic. And what makes it worse is that the actual writing in this passage is curiously bad. There are fine moments, and a great recovery at the very end. But again and again, as we read his account of Abraham or of the Exodus or of the Passion, we find ourselves saying, as Johnson said of the ballad, "the story cannot possibly be told in a manner that shall make less impression on the mind."
>
> (p. 125)

These are the responses of careful readers from more than one century, readers, moreover, who considered *Paradise Lost* one of the few great poems. They are worthy of the most careful consideration.

Ultimately, of course, every reader has only his own reading of any poem—what the poem seems or has seemed to him—to go by. Other readers' criticisms are relevant only when he can feel them to be true while he reads the poem itself, not merely while he reads the criticism. If we are honest, though, we must admit that our reading over a number of years of any complex poem is neither so absolute nor so single as we often pretend. Our readings change as we change—in knowledge, or vitality, or sympathies—and they do not, alas, always change for the better. This does not mean that a poem is anything we think it; it only means that we are at some times more nearly able to recognize what it is than at others.

I present the pages which follow with a good deal of diffidence. In the past (and the fairly recent past, too), I have found myself in agreement at one time or another with each of the opinions I have quoted concerning the "sunset of genius" or the actual failure of the last two books of *Paradise Lost*. But I have been continually haunted by the numerous other occasions when, after concluding that Milton had failed or nodded in some passage or detail, major or minor, I have belatedly recognized that he had succeeded in achieving an aim which I had not perceived. (There is always the further question as to whether the aim was worth achieving. The answer to that is, I believe, irremediably personal: it depends upon what we ask of poetry and what we desire in life. But we confuse ourselves if we attempt to evaluate the deed without knowing what it is.) At the present time I believe that Milton knew what he intended in the last two books, and that he accomplished his intent.

From the beginning of the poem, one ending, traditional and to some tastes preferable, was ruled out. The "fruit" was double; the poem concerned rising as well as falling, providence as well as sin and death. Granted the personal and dramatic roles of Adam and Eve, it could not end with the two in despair, exiled from God, all paradise seemingly lost, as we have seen them in earlier paintings and reliefs. Milton did not believe it commensurate with God's grace that Adam and Eve should have been sent forth comfortless, the comfort reserved for the reader or viewer of a later age.

Fewer readers, however, have been disturbed by the comfort at the end of the poem than by their feeling that there is not enough comfort, that the final books are primary evidence of Milton's disillusion and pessimism. The eighteenth-century critics' concern with the very last lines of the poem is symptomatic of their uneasiness with the final two books. Addison wished to omit the last two lines ("They hand in hand with wand'ring steps and slow, / Through *Eden* took thir solitary way") because they were not happy enough: they "renew" "anguish" "in the mind of the reader." Bentley, always more daring, simply rewrote the lines in a manner which he believed more "agreeable" to the author's "scheme":

> *Then* hand in hand, with *social* steps their way
> Through Eden took, *with heav'nly comfort chear'd.*

It is too easy to laugh at the eigtheenth-century's desire for a happy ending; we have become suspiciously attached to our own visions of a catastrophic or meaningless one. After all, Addison and Bentley did recognize part of the "author's scheme." They knew that the major emphasis of the poem was on God's providence, and like many modern readers, they wished for an ending which would make that providence easier for the reader to understand and respond to. Milton had already indicated that the granting of death itself, after innocence was lost, was providential: Adam would not have to live through all history. Adam and Eve had already made their immediate peace with God and they had discovered, through a renewal of grace, how they might continue to live their personal lives, striving "In offices of Love, how we may light'n / Each other's burden in our share of woe" (X. 960-961). Surely the poet might have provided them a brief vision or narration of the promised Seed, the possibility of the inward paradise and the final paradise, and sent them forth rejoicing.

Such a conclusion would also have been easier—but Milton rarely took the easier way. The easier way, here as on so many other occasions, would also have meant the less significant way. In the final books as in the opening scenes in Hell or in the account of the War in Heaven, Milton preferred to risk losing his readers entirely than to provide them with an incomplete or merely literary simplicity or comfort. He was less concerned with his readers' acceptance of his poem, I believe, than with their acceptance of life; or, perhaps more accurately, he wished the least possible distance between those two acceptances. He would not allow the reader, any more than Adam, to accept ignorantly or with more than the minimum of mystery.

The dramatic and the rhetorical necessities of Milton's plan were at one here. If the visions of the final books emphasized the happiness and triumph apart from the horror, there would be the danger that Adam might too easily accept sin and death and, without ever knowing the full nature of evil, forget his own responsibility while rejoicing in God's goodness. He might, sweetly and innocently, as a child, make no connection between the acceptance of providence and the necessity of personal heroism. Such an Adam might be possible "in the motions," but he would be impossible in *Paradise Lost*. Milton would allow Adam neither to fall nor to be redeemed in ignorance. Nor would the readers whom Milton desired be satisfied with such an Adam or with such an ending for the poem. They might, through a "willing suspension of disbelief," find it charming and immediately enjoyable—a vision of delight, a holiday or retreat from the experience and the history which they had known. But they would soon discover that, in their own knowledge of evil, they were hopelessly superior to this Adam; there would still be an immeasurable distance between themselves and him, a distance which proved the source of the richest effects and insights when Adam was still innocent, but which must be finally eliminated if the poem was to fulfil its original promise that it concerned "all."

By the end of the poem Milton's Adam must be a man who could not be patronized, however affectionately, by any other man. He must know the worst that Satan, sin and death can provide in all of history, the worst and the most complex appearances which any one of his readers may have experienced. Knowing the worst, he must be willing to live, to conceive life as possible and as possibly blest. For Adam, with his knowledge of the future, to be willing to begin human history, as for the reader with his knowledge of the past to be willing knowingly to continue it, each must know of the Incarnation, the Redemption, and the Final Judgment which give that history meaning. Within the light of such knowledge, each must learn of the "paradise within."

The final books complete the education of Adam and the reader. The simple acquisition of information, the learning of what was to happen (or had already happened) in history, while essential, did not of itself constitute that education; it provided the occasion for it and the raw materials. Education, for Milton, implied that one was led forth from ignorance into a true vision, personally possessed, of the ways of man and the ways of God and the choice of one's own role. The method for it was imaginatively experiential if not experimental. In the visions, optical or intellectual, Adam is granted the opportunity to make the usual human mistakes. In his responses to those appearances he embraces the false consolations (and despairs) of philosophy, and the false or mistaken conclusions of religion; and then, through angelic guidance, he is led to recognize their falseness. Virtue as well as sin is developed by trial. The final books provide for both Adam and the reader the final temptations. If each sustains the vision of providence, he will have earned it.

The plan of the last two books is overwhelmingly Christian. It was hardly Milton's fault (although it has proved to be his misfortune) that the traditional Christian reading of the Old Testament soon declined and many subsequent readers have found it difficult to follow. The visions and narratives which Michael provides Adam by no means include all "sacred history." They are highly selective, and the omissions are notable and sometimes startling. There is no mention of Abraham's "sacrifice" of Isaac, of Jacob's dream, of Joseph's bondage and deliverance, of the birth and preservation of Moses, of the "murmurings" of the Children of Israel in the wilderness, of Moses' "lifting up the serpent," of Rahab, of Gideon, of Samson, of Samuel, of Daniel—the list could be extended at length. To discover why Milton selected the events he did, we must turn to the poem.

In his commission to Michael, God provides the outline and the rationale for what is to come:

> Haste thee, and from the Paradise of God
> Without remorse drive out the sinful Pair,
> From hallow'd ground th' unholy, and denounce
> To them and to thir Progeny from thence
> Perpetual banishment. Yet lest they faint
> At the sad Sentence rigorously urg'd,
> For I behold them soft'nd and with tears
> Bewailing thir excess, all terror hide.
> If patiently thy bidding they obey,
> Dismiss them not disconsolate; reveal
> To *Adam* what shall come in future days,
> As I shall thee enlighten, intermix
> My Cov'nant in the woman's seed renew'd;
> So send them forth, though sorrowing, yet in peace. . . .
>   (XI. 104-117)

The subsequent scene between Adam and Eve is given added poignancy by our knowledge of what is to follow. Adam is overjoyed at the discovery of the efficacy of prayer. He already anticipates the comfort of the Seed:

> For since I sought
> By Prayer th' offended Deity to appease,
> Kneel'd and before him humbl'd all my heart,
> Methought I saw him placable and mild,
> Bending his ear; persuasion in me grew
> That I was heard with favor; peace return'd
> Home to my Breast, and to my memory
> His promise, that thy Seed shall bruise our Foe;
> Which then not minded in dismay, yet now

> Assures me that the bitterness of death
> Is past, and we shall live. Whence Hail to thee,
> *Eve* rightly call'd, Mother of all Mankind,
> Mother of all things living, since by thee
> Man is to live, and all things live for Man.   (148-161)

The ironies are touching. Everything that Adam says is true, but none of it true in the sense which he imagines. The "bitterness of death" is truly past, but not the fact of death; they will live, but not as Adam thinks. Eve is all the things which Adam says, but she is also more and other. The "Hail" is startling; it embodies both Adam's "knowledge" and his ignorance of all the centuries which will ensue before the second Eve will be so addressed. Adam has assumed that the first and the second Eve are one. Eve, however, reminds Adam that she also "first brought Death on all" (168), and that nature and man are no longer at one:

> But the Field
> To labor calls us now with sweat impos'd,
> Though after sleepless Night; for see the Morn,
> All unconcern'd with our unrest, begins
> Her rosy progress smiling. . . .   (171-175)

But Eve can bear to live a fallen life in an alien nature so long as she is beside Adam—and so long as they are in Paradise:

> while here we dwell,
> What can be toilsome in these pleasant Walks?
> Here let us live, though in fall'n state, content.
>   (178-180)

The scene anticipates the characteristic pattern of man's responses to the visions and the narrations which follow. From a partial knowledge of a providential future, Adam and Eve too quickly and easily accept and are reconciled to *this* moment as the final end. Then with additional knowledge of the consequences of sin and death (in this scene, the omens and the announcement of their expulsion), they too quickly and easily despair of the possibilities of life, assuming that the moment of horror is the final end. Each vision extends the knowledge of human life in time; but it is primarily necessary in order to correct (or, later in Book XII, to substantiate) the partial conclusions which Adam has derived from the preceding one. We are immediately assured of the need for "further sight" by the fact that Adam, his eyes now dimmed, perceives the "glorious Apparition" (211) of the descending Michael and "his Powers" only as a portentous cloud. The ironies become heavy when, at last perceiving Michael but not his host, Adam says, "Eve, now expect great tidings" (226). These "great tidings" are of exile and the knowledge of sin and death; Adam will not hear fully the tidings of "great joy" until he has heard fully those of sorrow.

Although Michael "intermixes" comfort in his pronouncement of the "sentence," Adam's immediate response is close to that which he experienced when he first heard Eve had eaten of the Fruit:

> *Adam* at the news
> Heart-strook with chilling gripe of sorrow stood,
> That all his senses bound. . . .
>
> (263-265)

Anxiety extended to horror and despair is, in its "chilling," its binding of the senses, and its "blankness," a true anticipation of death. Eve discovers her hiding-place by her lament. Addison and other eighteenth-century critics remarked on the beauty of her speech; they were correct in seeing in it "something . . . particularly soft and womanish":

> O unexpected stroke, worse than of Death!
> Must I thus leave thee Paradise? thus leave
> Thee Native Soil, these happy Walks and Shades,
> Fit haunt of Gods? where I had hope to spend,
> Quiet though sad, the respite of that day
> That must be mortal to us both. O flow'rs,
> That never will in other Climate grow,
> My early visitation, and my last
> At Ev'n, which I bred up with tender hand
> From the first op'ning bud, and gave ye Names,
> Who now shall rear ye to the Sun, or rank
> Your Tribes, and water from th' ambrosial Fount?
> Thee lastly nuptial Bower, by mee adorn'd
> With what to sight or smell was sweet; from thee
> How shall I part, and whither wander down
> Into a lower World, to this obscure
> And wild, how shall we breathe in other Air
> Less pure, accustom'd to immortal Fruits?
>
> (268-285)

It is beautiful and moving as a lament for the native land and as a lament for the flowers and the bower of pastoral. But the context makes us recognize (and discover the future comfort in) the naïveté. With the "bred up" and the "rear ye," we recognize that this is the lament of a mother for her children—and that the children as yet are only flowers. In her lament for the "nuptial Bower," moreover, Eve has identified her human love with the place rather than with her lover. Michael's "mild" interruption helps us to recognize that Eve will achieve her maternal fulfilment and her maternal tragedy outside the Garden, and that she has not been asked to abandon love:

> Lament not *Eve*, but patiently resign
> What justly thou hast lost; nor set thy heart,
> Thus over-fond, on that which is not thine;
> Thy going is not lonely, with thee goes

> Thy Husband, him to follow thou art bound;
> Where he abides, think there thy native soil.
>
> (287-292)

Adam, too, has come to feel that the Garden is the only perfection left
to them. What "afflicts" him most is his belief that to leave it will also
be to leave God, "that departing hence, / As from his face I shall be hid,
depriv'd / His blessed count'nance" (315-317). He had imagined a future
in which he would tell his sons about the places of God's appearances,
visit them, and celebrate them with altars of turf and stone, "in memory,
/ Or monument to Ages, and thereon / Offer sweet smelling Gums and
Fruits and Flow'rs":

> In yonder nether World where shall I seek
> His bright appearances, or footstep trace?
> For though I fled him angry, yet recall'd
> To life prolong'd and promis'd Race, I now
> Gladly behold though but his utmost skirts
> Of glory, and far off his steps adore.
>
> (328-333)

Michael had already received his commission from God, but, as with
Raphael's earlier commission and narrations, Adam provides the occa-
sion. Michael comforts Adam with the knowledge of God's omnipresence.
He reminds Adam that his "kingdom" was never confined to the Garden:
"All th' Earth he gave thee to possess and rule, / No despicable gift" (339-
340). He assures Adam that he is not abandoned:

> Yet doubt not but in Valley and in Plain
> God is as here, and will be found alike
> Present, and of his presence many a sign
> Still following thee, still compassing thee round
> With goodness and paternal Love, his Face
> Express, and of his steps the track Divine.
>
> (349-354)

But for Adam to *know* this, to "believe, and be confirm'd" (355), he must
be granted the visions of the future. He must learn that the "footsteps"
will be found not in a direct path but in a "warfare," and that the "bright
appearances" will occur precisely when man's "appearances" seem most
hopeless. He must learn how man can live with the knowledge of death:

> Which that thou may'st believe, and be confirm'd,
> Ere thou from hence depart, know I am sent
> To show thee what shall come in future days
> To thee and to thy Offspring; good with bad
> Expect to hear, supernal Grace contending
> With sinfulness of Men; thereby to learn
> True patience, and to temper joy with fear
> And pious sorrow, equally inur'd
> By moderation either state to bear,

> Prosperous or adverse: so shalt thou lead
> Safest thy life, and best prepar'd endure
> Thy mortal passage when it comes. Ascend
> This Hill. . . .
>
> (355-367)

Eve had said "Lead then" to the Serpent when he invited her to an easy vision of godlike knowledge and power; Adam accepts another guide to a vision of knowledge which inevitably involves suffering:

> Ascend, I follow thee, safe Guide, the path
> Thou lead'st me, and to the hand of Heav'n submit,
> However chast'ning, to the evil turn
> My obvious breast, arming to overcome
> By suffering, and earn rest from labor won,
> If so I may attain. So both ascend
> In the Visions of God. . . .
>
> (371-377)

From the Mount they can see all the world—including America. The superhuman quality of the visions is dramatized by the purging of Adam's sight and by his trance.

The visions in Book XI are of "one world," extending from Adam's sons to the destruction of that world in Noah's Flood. There are six: Cain and Abel; the lazar house with its general vision of death; the technological advances of Jubal and Tubal-Cain; the new cities and war and Enoch; peace and corruption ending in the Flood; the survival of Noah and the promise of the rainbow. All of the first five visions but one seem, even to the purged sight of Adam, almost unbearably horrible; yet each proves to contain a secret consolation. The one vision of apparent good which Adam welcomes proves to contain the seeds of sin and death.

This duality of vision is central to the final books. From the Trinity MS. we can tell that Milton had conceived of the resolution of his drama on the Fall of Man in a different fashion. In one version, his fifth Act was neatly outlined:

> Adam and Eve, driven out of Paradice praesented by an angel with Labour greife hatred Envie warre famine Pestilence (*added in margin:* sicknesse discontent Ignorance Feare Death) mutes to whome he gives thire names likewise winter, heat Tempest &c enterd into yᵉ world
>
> Faith ⎫
> Hope ⎬ comfort him and instruct him
> Charity ⎭
>
> Chorus briefly concludes.

In the more detailed plan for "Adam Unparadiz'd," Milton attempted to make the masque of the future more integral to the dramatic structure: Adam is not "humbled," does not "relent," until he sees the visions. But the essential outline for the final Act is the same:

the Angel is sent to banish them out of paradise but before causes to passe
before his eyes in shapes a mask of all the evills of this life & world   he
is humbl'd relents, dispaires. at last appeares Mercy comforts him promises
the Messiah, then calls in faith, hope & charity, instructs him   he repents
gives god the glory, submitts to his penalty   the chorus breifly concludes.
compare this with the former draught.

In both versions, the horror and the comfort are separated: Adam is to
be reduced to despair by the facts and emotions of the future, and then
he is to be comforted and instructed by a Faith, Hope, and Charity seemingly detached from those events. The movement is mechanical, and
Milton may have concluded that it was as unsatisfactory poetically as it
was religiously.

For the consolation and the horror to be perceived together, for knowledge of both to be progressively unfolded, Milton placed the primary
emphasis of the visions of Book XI on the heroes of faith within their
historical and symbolic contexts. If we wish to discover a single "source"
for Book XI, ultimately more important for the poem than the shield of
Achilles or Aeneas' vision of Rome, we can find it in Hebrews xi. 1-7:

> Now faith is the substance of things hoped for, the evidence of things not
> seen. For by it the elders obtained a good report.
> Through faith we understand that the worlds were framed by the word
> of God, so that things which are seen were not made of things which do
> appear. By faith Abel offered unto God a more excellent sacrifice than Cain,
> by which he obtained witness that he was righteous, God testifying of his
> gifts: and by it he being dead yet speaketh. By faith Enoch was translated
> that he should not see death; and was not found, because God had trans-
> lated him: for before his translation he had this testimony, that he pleased
> God. But without faith it is impossible to please him; for he that cometh to
> God must believe that he is, and that he is a rewarder of them that diligently
> seek him. By faith Noah, being warned of God of things not seen as yet,
> moved with fear, prepared an ark to the saving of his house; by the which
> he condemned the world, and became heir of the righteousness which is by
> faith.

Abel, Enoch, and Noah are the heroes of faith in the visions of Book XI
who redeem the appearances and who provide the saving spiritual remnant. . . .

When, with the second edition, Milton divided the earlier Book X to
form the present Books XI and XII, he added the lines which mark the
break:

> As one who in his journey bates at Noon,
> Though bent on speed, so here the Arch-Angel paus'd
> Betwixt the world destroy'd and world restor'd,
> If *Adam* aught perhaps might interpose;
> Then with transition sweet new Speech resumes.

(XII. 1-5)

We have often seen before—and at the centre of the poem—this pattern of destruction followed by a new and greater creation. The division of the books emphasizes that basic pattern. It also emphasizes the change from scenic episodes to narrative in Michael's continued unfolding of the future to Adam.

Michael announces the change in method:

> Thus thou hast seen one World begin and end;
> And Man as from a second stock proceed.
> Much thou hast yet to see, but I perceive
> Thy mortal sight to fail; objects divine
> Must needs impair and weary human sense:
> Henceforth what is to come I will relate,
> Thou therefore give due audience, and attend.

(6-12)

These lines have caused a good many academic smiles: surely Milton is indicating that he knows the reader is weary of the visions; and perhaps he is weary of them himself? Addison thought he understood the reason for the change in method, but he also believed the change was a major flaw:

> *Milton*, after having represented in Vision the History of Mankind to the first great Period of Nature, dispatches the remaining Part of it in Narration. He has devised a very handsome Reason for the Angel's proceeding with *Adam* after this manner; though doubtless the true Reason was the Difficulty which the Poet would have found to have shadowed out so mix'd and complicated a Story in visible Objects. I could wish, however, that the Author had done it, whatever Pains it might have cost him. To give my Opinion freely, I think that the exhibiting part of the History of Mankind in Vision, and part in Narrative, is as if an History-Painter should put in Colours one Half of his Subject, and write down the remaining part of it.
>
> *(The Spectator, No. 369)*

Once again Milton has violated Addison's sense of epic propriety; and once again we may reasonably assume that Milton's sense of propriety and purpose in *Paradise Lost* was different from Addison's.

The reasons for the change are more complex than the eighteenth-century critics thought. Until the final vision of the rainbow, the immediate effect of all the visions of the "first world" in Book XI was to emphasize the horror of the temporary triumphs of sin and death. Adam responded to every one with alarm or tears except one—and he should have wept at that. From Michael's interpretations and from his own perception of the last vision, Adam has learned that, despite murder and war and corruption, man and nature will survive; God will not destroy man and he will not allow mankind to destroy itself. Abel, Enoch, and Noah have shown that goodness and the love of God, however rare, continue to be possible; and they will be sustained and rewarded, however mysteriously, despite violence and death. This is the world in which

Adam will live, and he foresees its images directly. But the nature of the divine plan, the final victory of "supernal grace" in its warfare with the "sinfulness of man," is still unknown. For Adam to understand fully the consequences of his deed, for him to know fully both the actions and the ends of sin and death and to rejoice, he must be granted a further revelation. He must know of God's redemption of the world. If his final experience is to be commensurate with the reader's, moreover, he must acquire that supernatural knowledge in the way that the reader has acquired it: through narration rather than spectacle, inward rather than physical vision. Adam is like us in that he does not see the day of the Lord directly. He learns of the future in the way that we learn of the past. He and we are among those "that have not seen, and yet have believed" (John xx. 29).

The visions of Book XI represent the state of fallen man in the "first world" and the necessity of redemption, alleviated by the assurance that redemption will occur. The narrative of Book XII relates the gradual unfolding in history of the nature and victory of the Seed. The heroes of faith and the wicked appear in both books, but in Book XII their chief significance is neither historical nor moral, but typological: they consistently point forward to the revelations of the Enemy and the Redeemer, their natures and warfare and the final victory with the new and eternal paradise. As in Book XI, Adam's responses in Book XII point the structure and make necessary the continuation of the revelations until the end of time. In Book XI, Adam usually responds to the visions with tears or horror; in Book XII, he responds to each episode of the narrative except the first with increasing joy. Although his joy is almost overwhelming, it is based upon partial knowledge; until the final narrative, each joyful response leads Adam to a further question.

Michael first describes the destruction of that order in which the descendants of Noah dwelled "Long time in peace by Families and Tribes / Under paternal rule" (XII. 23-24). Hebraic and Christian commentary had developed fully the suggestion of Genesis x. 8-10:

> And Cush begat Nimrod: he began to be a mighty one in the earth. He was a mighty hunter before the Lord: wherefore it is said, Even as Nimrod the mighty hunter before the Lord. And the beginning of his kingdom was Babel. . . .

The name "Nimrod" means "rebel," and Augustine had translated the phrase as "a mighty hunter *against* the Lord" (*City of God,* Bk. XVI, Chap. iii). Milton developed the traditional associations for a central significance. His Nimrod is not merely a "type of pride," as Augustine had called him; as ambitious rebel and tyrant, the desirer of "memory," "Regardless whether good or evil fame" (47), and ridiculous aspirant for godhead, he is the human type of Satan, the destroyer, the Antichrist. He is not one of the corrupted with whom it is possible to share human sympathy; he represents the Corrupter himself. The defeat of Babel with the "jangling noise of words unknown" (55) and the "great laughter" that "was in Heav'n" (59) look back to the absurdities of the War in Heaven and forward to the Comforter's reversal of Babel at Pentecost (485-502) and the Son's defeat of Satan.

Adam immediately recognizes the tyrant Nimrod as also the impious man who attempts to imitate God in relation to his fellow men:

> O execrable Son so to aspire
> Above his Brethren, to himself assuming
> Authority usurpt, from God not giv'n:
> He gave us only over Beast, Fish, Fowl
> Dominion absolute; that right we hold
> By his donation; but Man over men
> He made not Lord; such title to himself
> Reserving, human left from human free.
>
> (64-71)

In one of Milton's most famous passages on liberty and the problem of God's permission of evil tyrannies, Michael approves Adam's "abhorrence," but reminds him that man is no longer unfallen and that the Nimrod-Satan figure is inevitable in a world corrupted by sin and death:

> Justly thou abhorr'st
> That Son, who on the quiet state of men
> Such trouble brought, affecting to subdue
> Rational Liberty; yet known withal,
> Since thy original lapse, true Liberty
> Is lost, which always with right Reason dwells
> Twinn'd, and from her hath no dividual being:
> Reason in man obscur'd, or not obey'd,
> Immediately inordinate desires
> And upstart Passions catch the Government
> From Reason, and to servitude reduce
> Man till then free. Therefore since hee permits
> Within himself unworthy Powers to reign
> Over free Reason, God in Judgment just
> Subjects him from without to violent Lords;
> Who oft as undeservedly enthral
> His outward freedom: Tyranny must be,
> Though to the Tyrant thereby no excuse.
> Yet sometimes Nations will decline so low
> From virtue, which is reason, that no wrong,
> But Justice, and some fatal curse annext
> Deprives them of thir outward liberty,
> Thir inward lost. . . .
>
> (79-101)

Virtue, not cleverness or intellectual agility, is identified with reason. (As the portrait of Satan shows, Milton believed the Machiavellian possessed

only the corruption of reason, anti-reason.) Tyranny is usually the evil
punishment of evil; only rarely, in a situation of immense corruption
under a precise curse of God, can the loss of liberty be associated with
justice. Tyranny characterizes the history of man under Satan—or Nimrod. This is the history and world from which God will "withdraw / His
presence" and "avert / His holy Eyes" when he selects "one peculiar Nation" "From all the rest, of whom to be invok'd, / A Nation from one
faithful man to spring. . . ." (107-113)

The following narrative moves from the calling of Abraham "from his
Father's house" to the warfare for the land of Canaan. Michael sees the
events as in a vision and relates the narrative to the landscape which
Adam sees. God calls Abraham

> into a Land
> Which he will show him, and from him will raise
> A mighty Nation, and upon him show'r
> His benediction so, that in his Seed
> All Nations shall be blest. . . .
>
> (122-126)

It is the prophetic nature of the events that is of first importance. Michael points out to Adam the geographical boundaries of the Promised
Land, but Adam is to "ponder" something else:

> This ponder, that all Nations of the Earth
> Shall in his Seed be blessed; by that Seed
> Is meant thy great deliverer, who shall bruise
> The Serpent's head; whereof to thee anon
> Plainlier shall be reveal'd.   (147-151)

Michael tells quickly of Isaac, Jacob and the twelve sons (without naming them), the reception of Jacob into Egypt by Joseph, and the new
Pharaoh:

> Till by two brethren (those two brethren call
> *Moses* and *Aaron*) sent from God to claim
> His people from enthralment, they return
> With glory and spoil back to thir promis'd Land.
>
> (169-172)

The plagues of Egypt symbolize the judgment and ultimate destruction
of Satan's "perverted world." (More than the "crocodile" which Addison
noted is involved in "Thus with ten wounds / The River-dragon tam'd
at length submits" [190-191].) The passing of the Children of Israel
through the Red Sea is a promise of the final deliverance. Milton presents the wandering in the wilderness not as punishment for "murmuring" and rebellion but as the necessary preparation for the task ahead.
In describing the granting of the Law to Moses, Michael does not mention
the moral law (which Adam, and supposedly the reader, have already en-

graven in their hearts) but the civil and ritual laws, those that concern the earthly government of men and those that typify the future revelation of the Redeemer:

> part such as appertain
> To civil Justice, part religious Rites
> Of sacrifice, informing them, by types
> And shadows, of that destin'd Seed to bruise
> The Serpent, by what means he shall achieve
> Mankind's deliverance. (230-235)

Moses' role indicates that the Deliverer must be a mediator between God and man:

> But the voice of God
> To mortal ear is dreadful; they beseech
> That *Moses* might report to them his will,
> And terror cease; he grants what they besought,
> Instructed that to God is no access
> Without Mediator, whose high Office now
> *Moses* in figure bears, to introduce
> One greater, of whose day he shall foretell,
> And all the Prophets in thir Age the times
> Of great *Messiah* shall sing.
>
> (235-244)

The Tabernacle is a promise of the Incarnation:

> such delight hath God in Men
> Obedient to his will, that he voutsafes
> Among them to set up his Tabernacle,
> The holy One with mortal Men to dwell. . . .
>
> (245-248)

The promise of future providence is embodied in the "Mercy-seat of Gold" over the Ark with its "Records of his Cov'nant" (251-253). The pillars of cloud and fire promise the immediate presence of divine guidance in the long journey. "The rest / Were long to tell, how many Battles fought, / How many Kings destroy'd, and Kingdoms won" (260-262), but Michael does describe the prophetic power of Joshua (later described [311] as bearing the "Name and Office" of Jesus) when the sun and the moon obey him.

At this moment Adam "interposes." Like his descendant Abraham (cf. John viii. 56), he rejoices that he has begun to "see" the day of the Lord:

> O sent from Heav'n,
> Enlight'ner of my darkness, gracious things
> Thou hast reveal'd, those chiefly which concern
> Just *Abraham* and his Seed: now first I find
> Mine eyes true op'ning, and my heart much eas'd,
> Erewhile perplext with thoughts what would become

Of mee and all Mankind; but now I see
His day, in whom all Nations shall be blest,
Favor unmerited by me, who sought
Forbidd'n knowledge by forbidd'n means.

(270-279)

Despite his joy, Adam recognizes in the very existence of the Law the
problem which necessitates continued revelation:

This yet I apprehend not, why to those
Among whom God will deign to dwell on Earth
So many and so various Laws are giv'n;
So many Laws argue so many sins
Among them; how can God with such reside?

(280-284)

In answer, Michael explains the nature of the Law and gives a brief
account of sacred history from Joshua until the birth of Christ. The purpose of the Law is to "evince" sin and to show the necessity for the larger
sacrifice:

that when they see
Law can discover sin, but not remove,
Save by those shadowy expiations weak,
The blood of Bulls and Goats, they may conclude
Some blood more precious must be paid for Man,
Just for unjust, that in such righteousness
To them by Faith imputed, they may find
Justification towards God, and peace
Of Conscience, which the Law by Ceremonies
Cannot appease, nor Man the moral part
Perform, and not performing cannot live.
So Law appears imperfet, and but giv'n
With purpose to resign them in full time
Up to a better Cov'nant, disciplin'd
From shadowy Types to Truth, from Flesh to Spirit,
From imposition of strict Laws, to free
Acceptance of large Grace, from servile fear
To filial, works of Law to works of Faith.
And therefore shall not *Moses,* though of God
Highly belov'd, being but the Minister
Of Law, his people into *Canaan* lead;
But *Joshua* whom the Gentiles *Jesus* call,
His Name and Office bearing, who shall quell
The adversary Serpent, and bring back
Through the world's wilderness long wander'd man
Safe to eternal Paradise of rest.

(289-314)

Meanwhile the Children of Israel are in "thir earthly *Canaan*" (315), and
Michael turns quickly to the renewal of the promise of the Seed in the
eternal throne of David:

> the like shall sing
> All Prophecy, That of the Royal Stock
> Of *David* (so I name this King) shall rise
> A Son, the Woman's Seed to thee foretold,
> Foretold to *Abraham,* as in whom shall trust
> All Nations, and to Kings foretold, of Kings
> The last, for of his Reign shall be no end.
>
> (324-330)

Solomon is mentioned not by name but by symbolic deed:

> And his next Son for Wealth and Wisdom fam'd,
> The clouded Ark of God till then in Tents
> Wand'ring, shall in a glorious Temple enshrine.
>
> (332-334)

(Milton assumed his readers would recognize the most "glorious Temple" of which Solomon's was a type.) None of the succeeding kings, "Part good, part bad, of bad the longer scroll" (336), is mentioned. The corruptions lead to the Babylonian captivity, the return, the dissensions among the priests, and the birth of the Messiah:

> at last they seize
> The Sceptre, and regard not *David's* Sons,
> Then lose it to a stranger, that the true
> Anointed King *Messiah* might be born
> Barr'd of his right; yet at his Birth a Star
> Unseen before in Heav'n proclaims him come,
> And guides the Eastern Sages, who enquire
> His place, to offer Incense, Myrrh, and Gold;
> His place of birth a Solemn Angel tells
> To simple Shepherds, keeping watch by night;
> They gladly thither haste, and by a Choir
> Of squadron'd Angels hear his Carol sung.
> A Virgin is his Mother, but his Sire
> The Power of the most High; he shall ascend
> The Throne hereditary, and bound his Reign
> With earth's wide bounds, his glory with the Heav'ns.
>
> (356-371)

Adam's joy is so intense that, without words, it would be indistinguishable from grief. He has at last heard the "glad tidings," and he thinks that he has seen all:

> O Prophet of glad tidings, finisher
> Of utmost hope! now clear I understand
> What oft my steadiest thoughts have searcht in vain,
> Why our great expectation should be call'd
> The seed of Woman: Virgin Mother, Hail,
> High in the love of Heav'n, yet from my Loins

> Thou shalt proceed, and from thy Womb the Son
> Of God most High; So God with man unites.

(375-382)

Like the early disciples, Adam expects an earthly kingdom and an immediate and final victory over Satan. He is eager to hear of it. He must still
learn the nature of the Messiah's warfare. The true warfare is inward,
and man himself is the battleground:

> Dream not of thir fight,
> As of a Duel, or the local wounds
> Of head or heel: not therefore joins the Son
> Manhood to Godhead, with more strength to foil
> Thy enemy; nor so is overcome
> Satan, whose fall from Heav'n, a deadlier bruise,
> Disabled not to give thee thy death's wound:
> Which hee, who comes thy Saviour, shall recure,
> Not by destroying *Satan*, but his works
> In thee and in thy Seed: nor can this be,
> But by fulfilling that which thou didst want,
> Obedience to the Law of God, impos'd
> On penalty of death, and suffering death,
> The penalty to thy transgression due,
> And due to theirs which out of thine will grow:
> So only can high Justice rest appaid.
> The Law of God exact he shall fulfil
> Both by obedience and by love, though love
> Alone fulfil the Law. . . .

(386-404)

Suffering and joy, which Adam has experienced before successively or,
when together, mysteriously, their relationship only partially understood
in the promise of the future, are here evoked together in Michael's description of Christ's experience of life and death and its significance for
man:

> thy punishment
> He shall endure by coming in the Flesh
> To a reproachful life and cursed death,
> Proclaiming Life to all who shall believe
> In his redemption, and that his obedience
> Imputed becomes theirs by Faith, his merits
> To save them, not thir own, though legal works.
> For this he shall live hated, be blasphem'd,
> Seiz'd on by force, judg'd, and to death condemn'd
> A shameful and accurst, nail'd to the Cross
> By his own Nation, slain for bringing Life;
> But to the Cross he nails thy Enemies,
> The Law that is against thee, and the sins
> Of all mankind, with him there crucifi'd,

> Never to hurt them more who rightly trust
> In this his satisfaction. . . .
>
> (404-419)

Those emotions are related to the falling and the rising, the descents and the ascents which we experience and which Milton has continually recreated for us in the poem. The death and the resurrection of the Messiah provide the ultimate source of our ability to see all that "vicissitude" as "grateful," to rejoice in the midst of the Fall:

> so he dies,
> But soon revives, Death over him no power
> Shall long usurp; ere the third dawning light
> Return, the Stars of Morn shall see him rise
> Out of his grave, fresh as the dawning light,
> Thy ransom paid, which Man from death redeems,
> His death for Man, as many as offer'd Life
> Neglect not, and the benefit embrace
> By Faith not void of works: this God-like act
> Annuls thy doom, the death thou shouldst have di'd,
> In sin for ever lost from life; this act
> Shall bruise the head of *Satan*, crush his strength
> Defeating Sin and Death, his two main arms,
> And fix far deeper in his head thir stings
> Than temporal death shall bruise the Victor's heel,
> Or theirs whom he redeems, a death like sleep,
> A gentle wafting to immortal Life.
>
> (419-435)

The institution of baptism is the sign, not merely of the "washing" of believers "from guilt of sin to Life / Pure" (443-444), but of their "mind prepar'd, if so befall, / For death, like that which the redeemer di'd" (444-445). The new faith and the new revelation are to make possible the possession of beatitude within the very act of martyrdom. The gospel will be preached to all the world and the prophecy fulfilled:

> for from that day
> Not only to the Sons of *Abraham's* Loins
> Salvation shall be Preacht, but to the Sons
> Of *Abraham's* Faith wherever through the world;
> So in his seed all Nations shall be blest.
>
> (446-450)

The Ascension and the promise of the Last Judgment complete the establishment, and the possession through faith, of the new paradise:

> Then to the Heav'n of Heav'ns he shall ascend
> With victory, triúmphing through the air
> Over his foes and thine; there shall surprise
> The Serpent, Prince of air, and drag in Chains
> Through all his Realm, and there confounded leave;

Then enter into glory, and resume
His Seat at God's right hand, exalted high
Above all names in Heav'n; and thence shall come,
When this world's dissolution shall be ripe,
With glory and power to judge both quick and dead,
To judge th' unfaithful dead, but to reward
His faithful, and receive them into bliss,
Whether in Heav'n or Earth, for then the Earth
Shall all be Paradise, far happier place
Than this of *Eden,* and far happier days.

(451-465)

Michael pauses, "As at the World's great period" (467). Before this vision Adam no longer knows whether he should repent or rejoice more;
he must do both, and, although he is incapable of resolving the rival
"duties," we recognize in the lines that joy predominates. His speech
should put at ease those readers who have been perplexed as to whether
the action of the poem is happy or unhappy, comic or tragic. It is and it
must be both. But God's providence is infinitely larger than the sinfulness of man:

O goodness infinite, goodness immense!
That all this good of evil shall produce,
And evil turn to good; more wonderful
Than that which by creation first brought forth
Light out of darkness! full of doubt I stand,
Whether I should repent me now of sin
By mee done and occasion'd, or rejoice
Much more, that much more good thereof shall spring,
To God more glory, more good will to Men
From God, and over wrath grace shall abound.

(469-478)

This is the climax. Another poet would have ended the narrative here.
But Adam has not yet been brought to know the time between the Ascension and the Judgment, the time which we know. He has not yet been
made the reader's equal. Moreover, for neither Adam nor for most of his
descendants is the "final vision" the end of life. The vision provides an
image of the end, of purpose and meaning, and it can be (Milton would
say, I believe, must be) possessed at moments with "joy and wonder." But
time and life continue and actions must be performed when the vision is
not immediately present, but possessed in memory and faith. This is the
field of our testing, the place of heroism.

Adam has seen enough of the history of mankind to guess at what will
follow:

But say, if our deliverer up to Heav'n
Must reascend, what will betide the few
His faithful, left among th' unfaithful herd,

The enemies of truth; who then shall guide
His people, who defend? will they not deal
Worse with his followers than with him they dealt?

(479-484)

Michael assures Adam that he is right; he also tells of the "Comforter" "who shall dwell / His Spirit within them" (487-488), guide and arm them in the spiritual struggle, and recompense them with "inward consolations" through torments and death.

The bleakness of Michael's account of post-Apostolic history has disturbed readers from the eighteenth to the twentieth centuries. (The eighteenth-century readers were more disturbed than their successors by the fact that Michael makes no mention of the Reformation.) If Milton had written a poem on the subject of *Paradise Lost* twenty years earlier, he might have emphasized the Reformation and the continuing possibilities of "renewals" in religion and in civil government. Yet, whatever his personal convictions about such possibilities (and I know of no evidence that Milton ever abandoned his opinion that heroic individuals in an heroic society could mould society and the church nearer to both the divine will and the heart's desire), such opinions were largely irrelevant to the establishment of Adam's faith. For those triumphs had always been temporary, and Milton believed they would be temporary until the Day "of respiration to the just" (540). They were to be worked for and to be welcomed; they represented those moments when men followed the guidance of that Spirit which had triumphantly reversed the confusion of Babel. But they were sustained only so long as men followed that Spirit; and they were always followed in this world by the renewed triumphs of sin and death. The apocalyptic vision of St John had established the supposition that in the last days Satan's power over the kingdoms of this world would seem absolute.

Michael's last narrative provides the final trial of faith in the poem for Adam and the reader. It emphasizes Milton's conviction that the Christian faith could not be dependent on any dream of man's continued moral or spiritual progress; on the establishment of any particular secular government at any one time; on the incorruptibility of any tradition or institution; or on the external happiness, prosperity, or longevity of the faithful. It depended only on the providence and power of God. It was available to individuals, "His living Temples" (527), and it was manifested in their freedom to follow God in the midst of almost universal corruption. Its essence was the conviction that the Spirit of God, gracious and forgiving, would make possible such freedom and, inevitably, the achievement of the inward and eternal paradise. . . .

In his final speech, Adam expresses his recognition of the fullness and the limitation of his knowledge and his perception of the paradoxical nature, the foolishness to this world, of God's methods. His predominant emotion here is neither "surprised joy" nor sorrow (at this moment he perceives his sin as "folly"), but peaceful acceptance. His revelation is complete and he understands at last:

> How soon hath thy prediction, Seer blest,
> Measur'd this transient World, the Race of time,
> Till time stand fixt: beyond is all abyss,
> Eternity, whose end no eye can reach.
> Greatly instructed I shall hence depart,
> Greatly in peace of thought, and have my fill
> Of knowledge, what this Vessel can contain;
> Beyond which was my folly to aspire.
> Henceforth I learn, that to obey is best,
> And love with fear the only God, to walk
> As in his presence, ever to observe
> His providence, and on him sole depend,
> Merciful over all his works, with good
> Still overcoming evil, and by small
> Accomplishing great things, by things deem'd weak
> Subverting worldly strong, and worldly wise
> By simply meek; that suffering for Truth's sake
> Is fortitude to highest victory,
> And to the faithful Death the Gate of Life;
> Taught this by example whom I now
> Acknowledge my Redeemer ever blest.

> (553-573)

This, as Michael assures Adam, is "the sum / Of wisdom"; he cannot hope for higher. The scientific knowledge of his descendants, the riches of Croesus, the power of Alexander or Augustus, would provide merely lower, instrumental knowledges, perhaps congruent with but not essential to the highest. He has learned of God's power and providence, his methods, and the ultimate good of man.

But before we descend from "this top / Of Speculation," we are reminded that this is the "sum" of the wisdom of vision, of intellectual and imaginative insight; Adam has not yet begun the experience about which he has learned: the life of man outside the earthly paradise. The recovery of the inward paradise will depend not merely on the wisdom and insight of man as contemplator, but on the qualities of man as actor:

> only add
> Deeds to thy knowledge answerable, add Faith,
> Add Virtue, Patience, Temperance, add Love,
> By name to come call'd Charity, the soul
> Of all the rest: then wilt thou not be loath
> To leave this Paradise, but shalt possess
> A paradise within thee, happier far.

> (581-587)

The lines are adapted from a passage from the epistles of Peter (writings never far in the background in this book), those counsels of action and the possibilities of joy in the midst of trials and temptations, oppressions and persecutions, as the early Christians awaited what seemed the long-delayed return of the Christ:

> And beside this, giving all diligence, add to your faith virtue; and to virtue knowledge; and to knowledge temperance; and to temperance patience; and to patience godliness; and to godliness brotherly kindness; and to brotherly kindness charity. For if these things be in you and abound, they make you that ye shall neither be barren nor unfruitful in the knowledge of our Lord Jesus Christ.
>
> (II Peter i. 5-8)

Michael tells Adam to awaken Eve, comforted by "gentle Dreams," and to tell her "at season fit" what he has heard. Her knowledge, too, is essential for human kind to live with the double emotions of the godly life:

> That ye may live, which will be many days,
> Both in one Faith unanimous though sad,
> With cause for evils past, yet much more cheer'd
> With meditation on the happy end.
>
> (602-605)

Eve's final speech indicates that she has already recovered the inward paradise.

Everyone knows the final lines of the poem—and almost everyone has commented on them. Their power is recognized even by readers who misunderstand them or are disturbed by them. The lines stand up beautifully to almost any amount of "close analysis," but, for those who have read carefully what precedes them, one can doubt whether such analysis is necessary. With the expulsion from Paradise, Adam and Eve begin human life as we know it. The double motions and emotions which the entire poem has created and interpreted for us, are here present quietly, indissolubly, and without comment. We, like the Labourer, are "Homeward returning"; and Adam and Eve, although they have never been there before, are turning to the only home which they can now know. For with all our dreams and memories of the earthly Paradise, we see that it is no longer what it was, that we could not now live within it. If we are now physically expelled, we have been long absent from the unalloyed perfection with which it was once experienced. And at this moment we are released from the unremitting contemplation of the mass of human history and cosmic purpose—larger than man's mind—which the final hours in Paradise have involved. With the essence of those visions possessed by memory and faith, we are left with that portion for which we are, by grace, responsible, with which we can and must come to terms: our own lives with our own loved ones, with the place and the way still to be chosen and found.

We must weep and we must dry our tears. We have all that Alexander desired—the world—and we have, moreover, the assurance that Prov-

idence will guide. But with the memory of the past immediate presence of
God, our steps must be at our first entrance into this new world "wand'r-
ing" and "slow." After what has past, the way seems "solitary"; we have
discovered our alienation and our loneliness. But we also discover that
our way is shared; with the possibility of human love, we can begin the
journey. In the final lines we see human life in its simplest terms. The
emotions we share are those defined at their most triumphant by St Paul:
"as sorrowful, yet alway rejoicing" (II Cor. vi. 10).

> High in Front advanc't,
> The brandisht Sword of God before them blaz'd
> Fierce as a Comet; which with torrid heat,
> And vapor as the *Libyan* Air adust,
> Began to parch that temperate Clime; whereat
> In either hand the hast'ning Angel caught
> Our ling'ring Parents, and to th' Eastern Gate
> Led them direct, and down the Cliff as fast
> To the subjected Plain; then disappear'd.
> They looking back, all th' Eastern side beheld
> Of Paradise, so late thir happy seat,
> Wav'd over by that flaming Brand, the Gate
> With dreadful Faces throng'd and fiery Arms:
> Some natural tears they dropp'd, but wip'd them soon;
> The World was all before them, where to choose
> Thir place of rest, and Providence thir guide:
> They hand in hand with wand'ring steps and slow,
> Through *Eden* took thir solitary way.

(632-649)

Chronology of Important Dates

1608	John Milton born in London, December 9.
1617?	Begins studies at St. Paul's School, London.
1625	Enters Christ's College, Cambridge.
1629	B.A., Cambridge.
1632	M.A., Cambridge.
1632-38	Private studies at Hammersmith (London) and Horton (Buckinghamshire).
1634	Performance of Milton's *Mask* ("Comus") at Ludlow Castle.
1638-39	Journey to Italy.
1639	Begins teaching as private schoolmaster in London.
1641	First treatises dealing with ecclesiastical controversy: *Of Reformation in England, Of Prelatical Episcopacy,* and *Animadversions.*
1642	*The Reason of Church-Government.* Marriage to Mary Powell. Return of Milton's wife to her father's house in Buckinghamshire.
1643	*The Doctrine and Discipline of Divorce.*
1644	*Areopagitica.*
1645	Return of Mary Powell Milton to her husband's house in London. *Poems of Mr. John Milton, Both English and Latin* (collected minor poems).
1649	*The Tenure of Kings and Magistrates.* Appointed Secretary of Foreign Tongues to the Council of State for the Parliamentary government.
1651	*A Defense of the English People* (in Latin).
1652	Milton becomes blind. Death of Mary Powell Milton and of their son, John.
1654	*A Second Defense of the English People* (in Latin).
1655	*Defense of Himself* (in Latin).
1656	Marries Katherine Woodcock.
1658	Death of Katherine Woodcock Milton.
1659	*A Treatise of Civil Power.*

1660   *The Ready and Easy Way to Establish a Free Commonwealth.*

1663   Marries Elizabeth Minshull.

1667   *Paradise Lost. A Poem Written in Ten Books.*

1670   *The History of Britain.*

1671   *Paradise Regained. A Poem. In IV Books. To which is added Samson Agonistes.*

1673   *Of True Religion, Heresy, Schism, and Toleration.* Enlarged edition of Milton's minor poems.

1674   Second edition of *Paradise Lost,* divided into twelve books. Death of Milton, Nov. 8.

Notes on the Editor and Authors

LOUIS L. MARTZ, the editor of this volume, is Douglas Tracy Smith Professor of English and American Literature at Yale University. He has published two books on English religious literature of the seventeenth century: *The Poetry of Meditation* (1954, 1962) and *The Paradise Within: Studies in Vaughan, Traherne, and Milton* (1964); and he has edited *The Meditative Poem: An Anthology of Seventeenth Century Verse* (1963). His latest book, *The Poem of the Mind* (1966), is a collection of his critical essays dealing with poetry of the seventeenth and the twentieth centuries.

T. S. ELIOT's death in 1965 marked the end of an era that may well be known to future generations as "The Age of Eliot."

WILLIAM EMPSON is Professor of English Literature at Sheffield University. His early book, *Seven Types of Ambiguity* (1930, 1947), is one of the germinal works in modern criticism. He is also the author of *The Structure of Complex Words* (1951) and *Milton's God* (1961); and he has published three volumes of poetry.

C. S. LEWIS, after teaching at Oxford, became Professor of Medieval and Renaissance English at Cambridge University. He died in 1963. His numerous writings include novels, poetry, children's books, religious treatises, critical essays, and two major studies in English literature: *The Allegory of Love* (1936) and a volume on non-dramatic literature of the sixteenth century for the *Oxford History of English Literature* (1954).

BALACHANDRA RAJAN is Professor of English at the University of Windsor, Canada. He has taught at Cambridge University and the University of Delhi; and he held for over ten years a post in the diplomatic service of India. His latest book is a study of the poetry of William Butler Yeats (1965).

F. T. PRINCE is Professor of English at the University of Southampton. He has published three volumes of poetry.

A. J. A. WALDOCK was Professor of English Literature at the University of Sydney, Australia. He died in 1950, shortly after completing his book *Sophocles the Dramatist* (1951).

GEOFFREY HARTMAN is Professor of English and Comparative Literature at Cornell University. He is the author of *The Unmediated Vision: An Interpretation of Wordsworth, Hopkins, Rilke, and Valéry* (1954) and *Wordsworth's Poetry, 1787-1814* (1964).

DOUGLAS BUSH is Gurney Professor of English at Harvard University. His many books include *Mythology and the Renaissance Tradition in English Poetry* (1932) and a volume on non-dramatic literature of the seventeenth century for the *Oxford History of English Literature* (1945, 1962).

W. B. C. WATKINS taught at Princeton University and at Louisiana State University. He died in 1957. He is the author of *Perilous Balance: The Tragic Genius of Swift, Johnson, and Sterne* (1939) and *Shakespeare and Spenser* (1950).

ARNOLD STEIN is Professor of English at the University of Washington, Seattle. He is the author of *Heroic Knowledge: An Interpretation of Paradise Regained and Samson Agonistes* (1957) and *John Donne's Lyrics: The Eloquence of Action* (1962).

E. M. W. TILLYARD was Master of Jesus College, Cambridge. He died in 1962. His many books include: *Shakespeare's Last Plays* (1938), *The Elizabethan World Picture* (1944), *Shakespeare's History Plays* (1951), and *The English Epic and its Background* (1954).

JOSEPH H. SUMMERS is Professor of English at Washington University, St. Louis. He is the author of *George Herbert: His Religion and Art* (1954).

Selected Bibliography

The following list does not include works mentioned in the *Introduction,* nor works from which selections have been given. For additional bibliographical materials, see the editions of Merritt Hughes listed below.

Editions

John Milton: Complete Poems and Major Prose, edited by Merritt Hughes. New York, Odyssey Press, 1957. With helpful introductions, full annotation, and extensive bibliographical references.

John Milton: Paradise Lost, edited by Merritt Hughes. New York, Odyssey Press, 1962. With revised annotation and additional bibliographical materials.

The Complete Poetical Works of John Milton, edited by Douglas Bush. Boston, Houghton Mifflin Co., 1965. With excellent introductions and brief annotation.

Complete Prose Works of John Milton, Don M. Wolfe, General Editor. 7 vols., New Haven, Yale University Press, 1953—. A new standard edition in progress, with many editors and translators; four volumes have thus far appeared, with extensive introductions and annotation.

The Works of John Milton, Frank Allen Patterson, General Editor. 18 vols., New York, Columbia University Press, 1931-38. Important for the establishment of Milton's texts, and especially for making available Milton's prose, both English and Latin.

Studies

Allen, Don Cameron. *The Harmonious Vision: Studies in Milton's Poetry.* Baltimore, Johns Hopkins Press, 1954. Interesting essays on all of Milton's more significant poems.

Barker, Arthur E. *Milton and the Puritan Dilemma, 1641-1660.* Toronto, University of Toronto Press, 1942. An excellent commentary on Milton's prose treatises.

Broadbent, J. B. *Some Graver Subject: An Essay on Paradise Lost.* London, Chatto and Windus, 1960. Actually a series of essays dealing fruitfully with many aspects of the poem.

Daiches, David. *Milton.* London, Hutchinson, 1957. A concise introduction to the poet's career.

Daniells, Roy. *Milton, Mannerism and Baroque.* Toronto, University of Toronto Press, 1963. An interesting effort to interpret Milton by analogy with works of visual art.

Diekhoff, John S. *Milton's Paradise Lost: A Commentary on the Argument.* New York, Columbia University Press, 1946. A concise study of Milton's thought.

Ferry, Anne Davidson. *Milton's Epic Voice: The Narrator in Paradise Lost.* Cambridge, Mass., Harvard University Press, 1963. An acute and original interpretation.

Gardner, Helen. *A Reading of Paradise Lost.* Oxford, Clarendon Press, 1965. Excellent lectures on central issues.

Greene, Thomas. *The Descent from Heaven: A Study in Epic Continuity.* New Haven, Yale University Press, 1963. Contains an important essay placing Milton in the context of epic poetry, from Homer down to Milton's day.

Hanford, James Holly. *John Milton, Englishman.* New York, Crown Publishers, 1949. A reliable survey of Milton's whole career.

Harding, Davis P. *The Club of Hercules: Studies in the Classical Background of Paradise Lost.* Urbana, University of Illinois Press, 1962. Particularly helpful with regard to Milton's use of Vergil.

Kelley, Maurice. *This Great Argument: A Study of Milton's De Doctrina Christiana as a Gloss upon Paradise Lost.* Princeton, Princeton University Press, 1941. The classic study of Milton's theology.

Kermode, Frank, editor. *The Living Milton: Essays by Various Hands.* London, Routledge and Kegan Paul, 1960; New York, Macmillan, 1961. An excellent collection, notable for Mr. Kermode's long essay, "Adam Unparadised."

Le Comte, Edward S. *A Milton Dictionary.* New York, Philosophical Library, 1961. A handy reference book.

MacCaffrey, Isabel Gamble. *Paradise Lost as "Myth".* Cambridge, Mass., Harvard University Press, 1959. A sensitive, imaginative interpretation, illuminating the poem's structure and style.

Madsen, William G. "The Idea of Nature in Milton's Poetry," in *Three Studies in the Renaissance.* New Haven, Yale University Press, 1958. A hundred-page monograph dealing with essential issues in Milton's poetry.

Parker, William Riley. The Life of John Milton, forthcoming from the Oxford University Press. The work of many years of fine scholarship, this should become the new standard biography.

Peter, John. *A Critique of Paradise Lost.* New York, Columbia University Press; London, Longmans, 1960. A stimulating and controversial approach, strongly influenced by Waldock.

Rajan, B. *Paradise Lost and the Seventeenth Century Reader.* London, Chatto and Windus, 1947. An important study of the background of Milton's thought, with good comments on the poetry.

Ricks, Christopher. *Milton's Grand Style.* Oxford, Clarendon Press, 1963. A fine piece of verbal analysis, in the Empsonian mode, showing the subtlety of Milton's poetic effects.

Tillyard, E. M. W. *Milton.* London, Chatto and Windus, 1930. An indispensable commentary on the whole range of Milton's writings.

The Miltonic Setting. Cambridge, Cambridge University Press, 1938. A good collection of essays on various aspects of Milton.

British Authors in the Twentieth Century Views Series

European Authors in the Twentieth Century Views Series